Linger By My Side

JoAnn DuCote Smith
Linger By My Side

EAGLES RISE BOOKS
East Palatka, Florida - Springdale, Arkansas

To My Husband Bobby Ross Smith -
who will remember

To our daughters for whom we waited -
Deidre Lynn
Jena Jeree
Melissa Gaye
Bali Bea

And for our grandchildren who knew where
to find us -
Justin Arliss
Jennifer Morgan
Samantha Meagan
Emily Grace
Kendal Marie
Savannah Jane

JoAnn DuCote Smith

Linger By My Side
AN EAGLES RISE BOOK / November 1998

Cover Photography by S. Dale DuCote

Book Design By
Judy Miller

Library of Congress Catalog-in-Publication Data
Smith, JoAnn DuCote, 1931-

First Printing

Published in the United States of America by EAGLES RISE Books
It's trademark consists of the words "EAGLES RISE Books"
and the portrayal of an eagle

PRINTED IN THE UNITED STATES OF AMERICA

I would like to thank
my tireless and exacting editors

Deidre Lynn Strong
B.R.Smith

Research thanks to

Gladys Sands, Curator
Eureka Springs Historical Museum

Max Churchill, Muscatine Area Heritage
Association, Muscatine, Iowa

Marsha Tate, Reference Librarian, Muscatine,
Iowa

Manon Wilson, Shiloh Museum of Ozark History,
Springdale, Arkansas

Mark Christ
Arkansas Historic Preservation Program

Ken Story
National Register Coordinator, Arkansas Historic
Preservation Program

JoAnn DuCote Smith

*Lest men suspect your
tale untrue
Keep probability
in view*

John Gay

JoAnn DuCote Smith

Author's Note

Haunted places are a rare phenomenon. "Ghost" stories however, abound and are still a favorite pastime around late night campfires. Yet, regardless of how chilling the tale, or possibly because of it, few relate it to any real life circumstance. Few give serious thought to its authenticity, its verifiability however complexly sweetened or embittered by the perceiving mind. And still fewer are brave enough to risk name and reputation; curious and adventurous enough to launch their own investigation.

During the Victorian Age curiosity reached an all time high with the birth of Spiritualism and the scientific study of spirit communication began in 1882, when the Society of Psychical Research (SPR) was founded in London, England.

Spiritualism is the belief in communication between the living and the so-called dead through psychic mediumship. The word psychic, is used as an adjective to describe the process by which mind brings forth information from outside the physical realm. A medium is anyone who exhibits the ability to act as a passive conduit through which spirit communicates, a relater of messages from one dimension of reality to another. That some of these messages consistently contain verifiable information regarding some past, present or future event is reason enough for some to assign proof.

Psychic phenomena is the term used to describe an occurrence that cannot be explained by orthodox, scientific means and includes ESP (extra sensory perception) clairaudience (clear hearing), clairvoyance (clear seeing), telekinesis (the ability to move an object without touching it), and telepathy (mind

I

reading). The study and investigation of this and other related esoteric phenomena became known as parapsychology.

Today, Dr. Elizabeth Kubler-Ross' work and subsequently that of Dr. Raymond Moody Jr.'s work with dying patients has revolutionized our thinking about death. Anyone who is interested or has seriously tried to understand the phenomenon we call death will find worthwhile an in depth study of the newly evolving field of thanalogy. Perhaps it may lead the unaware skeptic to a better understanding, reevaluation of their position concerning the process of physical death.

Humanity has always carried a constant hope and fear concerning immortality. However, these are times of great change. Steadfast researchers, inner space pioneers have gone before us into this once unknown realm and have left us maps and memoranda, recorded innumerable cases of life continuing after so-called death which in some cases resulted in hauntings.

While apparitions are visual, hauntings are sometimes visual and auditory such as a baby crying, footsteps, laughter, knocking, heavy objects being moved. It can involve the sense of smell, foul odors and fair, even to the identity of specific fragrances which may have been worn or associated in some way with the deceased. It can include tactile experiences such as pockets of warm or cold air, feelings of being touched, punched or pushed, caressed.

High energy emotions, such as love, compassion, hate, fear, an affinity for whatever took place with the deceased, most often assures successful sending and receiving. A keen expectation marks the true medium. While the low energy of the nay-sayer who is uninterested and non-concerned has the opposite effect.

In the words of Paracelsus: He who knows nothing, loves nothing. He who can do nothing understands nothing. He who understands nothing is worthless. But he who understands also loves, notices, sees... The more knowledge is inherent in a thing, the greater the love... Anyone who imagines that all fruits ripen at the same time as the strawberries knows nothing about grapes.

When an apparition is habitually witnessed by various disparate people over a long period of time and in one particular place, this constitutes a haunting. Hauntings are specific acts or sounds constantly repeated sometimes emanating from an apparition.

Perhaps no existing hotel in Arkansas preserves more of it's original quality, specific acts and sounds of ghost sightings than does the old Crescent Hotel in Eureka Springs. Possibly because it has been less tampered with; and because too, time has not been unkind.

The Crescent's greatest glory, it might be ventured, is it's spectre of tragedy.

And in the moonlight, when it comes in silver softness whispers to us of things ---- evoking evanescent phantoms. We listen, and for an interval we might recite and try to measure...

III

Foreword

Shall Be In Water Writ

In Northwest Arkansas, high in the enchanting Ozark Mountains between Missouri and the rest of Arkansas, lies a hamlet called Eureka Springs which has the look of a child's toy-town of little wooden houses painted shades of pink, lavender, green, yellow; muted, Victorian colors. Each, with it's petite lawn spread out around it like a dainty, flower bordered tea napkin laced and punctuated with light, is nestled against and atop tiered limestone terraces of varying width and height. These magnificent symbols of turn-of-the-century architecture can be seen along steep, narrow streets and sidewalks where ladies in bustled dresses used to stroll beneath fringed parasols, escorted by gentleman at their leisure.

This in itself, while charming and pure, does not make Eureka Springs unique for today there are many such approximations around the country. It is, instead, as though someone has materialized out of a Victorian post-card found in our grandmother's attic, taken our hand and walked us back to simpler times, the appeal for which has spread across America like a fever in the form of old house and building restoration. As if, in so doing, to heal and restore a world-weary spirit. New housing projects like stage sets are made to look old, complete villages and theme parks with all the attending business of dress, auto-mobile, furniture, art, craft and the like, are seen, owned and enjoyed in the most surprising places around the country.

The appeal of present day Eureka Springs lies instead, in it's origin and continuity of purpose. The fact that Eureka Springs' houses and buildings were erected and cared for since 1879, is still reason enough to gain international attention.

The visitor knows and feels an immediate affinity for the genuine article. As Archimedes had shouted 'Eureka!' on discovering a method for determining the purity of gold, so too some more recent pioneer here must have exclaimed on discovering the purity of it's springs. However, as in most cases of "discovery" in this country, these opportune explorers came into knowledge of the water's purity from our native Americans. The Cherokee, Sioux and Osage Indians some seventy years prior had found and dug out the Basin Spring and proclaimed the water possessed magical powers to heal.

Stories of the healthful, restorative quality of the waters in this remote valley circulated around the world. The very inaccessibility of the rugged terrain seemed only to entice people all the more to invade it's isolated remoteness. Undaunted by tangled foliage, vicious bears, water moccasin and copperhead snakes they came; stalked the clear, sweet water springs as vigorously as mountain lions stalked the deer and wild turkey. Down between the mountains they came. Into the deep shadowed foreignness of it they advanced like latter-day Poncé deLeons and it might as well have been a wild Amazon jungle they went into, for all their opportune daring. Like the rush to gold in California where each might have supposed their lives to be at stake, Eureka Springs was no exception. They expected and knew their reward to be the much touted fountain of youth, the illusive immortality without which they would not be favored, and in life could not be told apart from their neighbors.

By horseback and wagon they came, until the Frisco Railroad System saw the necessity of extending the line down from Seligmon, Missouri in 1882 and Eureka Springs had grown to 8,500 enterprising people. Some rushed into the dark green chasm between the mountains with hopes of rescuing themselves from the brink of some catastrophic illness. Others came imbued with a sense of cavalier adventure and a devil-may-care attitude as though to halt or infuse a previously dull existence. Perhaps even solving the mystery of life into the bargain.

VI

Still others saw it as a golden money making opportunity and the town that water built was born.

Above the valley the Crescent Hotel, built in 1886, crowns West Mountain like the diadem of some late dowager queen caught between her youth's desire and it's fixed adamantine fate. From a youth filled with noble expectations, she was inexorably guided toward an alternate fate. A fate so sure and determined it can still be seen atop the mountain as a precisely cleaved diamond, albeit viewed behind a reticulated glass.

Built expressly to house the droves of health and pleasure seeking millionaires at the height of the Victorian era, the massive, 100 room, five story hotel stands today a Victorian-Gothic mountain of grand self confidence.

 Gone, however, are the carriages filled with revelers in holiday finery arriving under the hotel's entrance portico from the railroad station. Tea dances in the afternoon are things of the past; waiters in white jackets hover no more; music and dancing feet are stilled; the orchestra long departed.

Where are the cool gazebos, the shaded boardwalk, and hiking trails now? The Tally-ho with it's large open coach drawn by teams of matching horses? What has become of the ladies riding side-saddle in long skirts, hats and veils? When did gentlemen, astride haughty broad shouldered mounts, quit their escort. Where, on the many miles of mountain trails, do they appear now?

The years of the 'Gay Nineties' Victorian grandeur are gone. Around the country many grand old hotels, such as the Crescent with their enormous operating costs, had been gradually abandoned for the "tourist court". A more convenient place for the highway traveler to rest for a night or two as increasing numbers of automobiles took to the road. These, in turn, were all but forgotten in favor of today's modern motels.

Now, with the fascination of all things "traditional", and the ever increasing need for tourist accommodations in Eureka Springs, everything which can house has been refurbished, including the once maligned and all but forgotten native stone 'tourist court' as indicative of bygone days as they are charming and serviceable. As well, large numbers of beautiful old mansions have been converted to the Bed and Breakfast trade providing a homey cushion, however brief, from the onrushing outside corporate world.

In this rebirth stage of everything "charming" and "quaint" Eureka Springs is very much in tune with those nostalgic yearnings.

Linger By My Side

One

Hour's Bright Promise

Alicia had, as a child, discovered that by holding tightly to the edge of the counter at the Yesteryear Antique Shop she could, by pulling herself up and standing on the tips of her toes, see through the glass to what enchanting object lay inside the jewelry case.

"Ooo," her eyes widened and her mouth made a small sucking sound of surprise and wonder.

To her three year old mind, the world held nothing so fine, nothing so deeply fascinating as the elusive treasure she envisioned would be hidden inside some storybook pirate's locked and chained watery chest. In her young life and circumstance she could only dream of how it would feel to find such a treasure trove. Limited only by precocious imagination she would scoop double handsful of jewels up into the light. Necklaces, bracelets and rings she could touch and trace with tiny fingers the fine intaglio carving on brooches and cameos. Each diamond, ruby and emerald of perfect clarity and cut dressed in their intricate settings of gold, silver and platinum would trail, rings intertwined, from her fingers in thick strands and loops. Chalices of pure silver she would find encrusted with black pearls and blue sapphires set around elaborately swirled arabesque engravings. Though she knew these marvelous treasures existed somewhere, little Alicia could only dream through cheap imitations.

To search, find and adore had become a ritualized pattern with her. When taken to visit anyone's home Alicia would slip away from the adults, find her way to the owner's bedroom, climb onto a dressing stool or bench, until the inescapable jewelry case was found on the table, or if not there, would unabashedly open drawers or pull up chairs to reach the higher cabinet or bureau top. If anyone had asked for what she searched she would not have known how to answer. 'Just lookin,' seemed as appropriate as anything. Always mindful of leaving everything exactly as she found it, she would explore the usually meager offerings she found there to her hearts content.

She would hear her mother's voice, "Now 'Licia, don't touch anything." Or call from the next room, "Member 'Licia, no touching." But she longed to touch. Touching with her fingertips was part of the delicious way she "saw" things. So with the most delicate, mesmerized care she lifted lids, moved pieces aside to peer underneath, searching. That she searched for something in particular was never verbalized or scarcely recognized within herself.

As she followed her mother into the antique shop late one Saturday evening to sell some of her grand-mother's fine crochet pieces she had worked before she died, it was as if a hand had reached out and ushered her straight to a treasure of such wondrous mystery that to merely catch sight of the vibrant thing lying on it's cushion of white cotton was to be suddenly transported into another world. Her eyes fixed on their target; consciousness accepted the offering.

"Ooo," she drew an arrow of air into her small heart. The crowded walls of the shop began to recede as she gazed upon an old and discolored celluloid brooch in the form of an eastern looking Punjabi-type man sitting cross-legged on a horizontal scimitar holding a tiny crystal ball in which she could see her own curved reflection. Around his head he wore a white satin turban. On it, above the black arch of his eyebrows, was pinned a sapphire studded crescent moon. The strange man's face was dark and his eyes full of secrets. He wore an ornate bolero top which had a pattern of little silver stars and crescent moons scattered on a ruby red background, the whole of which was fringed and spangled with small gold and silver coins and worn open to reveal a muscular chest above gold colored pantaloons tied with thin gold braid at the ankles. Additional bangles of silver and gold ringed his brown upper arms and pierced his tiny brown ears.

With her face pressed against the glass case her child's mind fell still in contemplation of the absolute separateness and queerness of the thing from any else she had ever known when the frightening experience of largeness and smallness first came upon Alicia. As she stared down at the Pun-jabi man the world in which her smallness dwelt suddenly ceased. The world as she knew it instantly disappeared and it's familiar sounds quit her ears; stopped as effectively as if a switch had been thrown. Gone, as if the shop and all it's fixtures had vanished into thin air. To an adult it would have seemed that a heretofore insuperable hurdle had been cleanly vaulted. Alicia thus transported, saw in an instant with the larger part of herself and a far away truth was recognized.

In place of the dark colored walls of the antique shop, she beheld, on a sun drenched lawn of purest green, the white columned palace of some grand Kafir. In place of the aroma mix of floor oil and furniture polish of the shop she caught the quick fragrance of patchouli, and sandlewood as from an exotic garden.

All this was clearly visible and vivid to her in every detail: it was colors, white and blue veined marble, cool to the touch. It was sky, billowed white and streaked

21

with lapis lazuli. It was shimmering sea under full sun, swirled azure and teal beyond her ability to imagine. It was fragrance and swatches of pink, lavender and white from orchids, diandria, fragrant frangipani, and all of these flowed slightly luminous before her like crystalline adornments landscaped in perfect symmetry along the arched colonnade walks, finishing at pool's edge where her Pun-jabi man had seated himself in silent meditation.

With the smaller portion of herself she could hear someone say to come away now, she must go; tugging her mind back toward the shop and as from afar she recalled her mother's voice. Yet, no amount of her mother's cajoling or whispered reciting of shortages of money for groceries, clothes or gasoline could persuade Alicia from the sudden flood of tears and gulps of anguish at the thought of leaving until she felt herself unable to breathe. And it was clear, if she was to be brought back to endure the smallness, the life of limitation, she could not be brought back to live without this singular treasure, this invaluable discovery or rediscovery of something of such vital importance and magnitude. Alicia stood resolute, as if rooted to the floor until this truth could be recognized by her mother and a bargain had been struck.

The smaller portion of herself rode home with her Pun-jabi man clutched to her heart and watched the sudden light of a rising moon out the window and would not in her present state of lightness have been surprised if the car had lifted, taking them rocket-like, straight into it.

That she had found a mysterious portion of herself, there was no doubt, but she could not have answered the worth of that moment any more than she could have explained to her mother how, as a six month old baby, she had managed to get out of her crib. Her mother had left her asleep one day after lunch and gone out to hang wash on the line in the side yard. When she returned Alicia was standing on the floor holding onto the corner of the crib, laughing up at her with eyes that sparkled like fresh falling rain in bright sunlight.

She had left Alicia sound asleep just moments before yet saw that the side of the crib was still up in it's locked position. She checked the narrowly spaced slats for damage, knew Alicia could not have squeezed through and about the only thing the frightened, uncomprehending mother could think to say was, "Why, Alicia Ann Townsend, how in the world did you do that?"

"Pig!" Alicia held onto the crib with one hand and jiggled herself up and down with delight. Her mother thought she had actually heard Alicia say "pig". As far as she knew, all Alicia had learned to say was, "Mama, Daddy," and sometimes "Hi, there," which was certainly remarkable enough for a six month old.

"'Licia, did you say "pig" sweetheart?"

Alicia laughed, and nodded her head up and down holding onto the crib with her left hand and gesturing out the window with her right. "Pig!" She repeated.

Her mother picked her up, smoothed back her damp hair from her forehead and laid Alicia's head on her shoulder. "Yes, darlin'. We can see the pigs later. Right now you have to take a nap." She gently patted Alicia on the back, "shush now, shhh," she crooned and swayed back and forth as much to quell her own shaking body as it was to calm the excited baby. "Later, sweetie. Later." She buried her face in Alicia's hair and kissed her neck. Noticed it too was damp and smelled of all outdoors, like ozone after a rainstorm.

As she left the room after putting Alicia down for the second time she heard Alicia say sleepily, "Pig..." She looked at the clock and wondered how it had gotten so late. Wondered where the afternoon had gone.

Alicia was unable to explain her dream of a giant metal pig that had landed in the back yard and taken her for a ride.

From the first time Alicia felt the peculiar sensation of largeness and smallness she tried to explain it to others in terms she hoped they would understand. Hoped someone could tell her what it was all about. She felt herself suddenly compressed into a 'tiny, little bitty round speck,' she would say, holding her index finger as close to her thumb as possible, she'd squint up her eyes to be sure her fingers were close together as possible without touching. 'Then bang! Huge ball!' She'd shout, and throw her arms out to the side like a shot as far as she could reach as if trying to encompass the universe. "Just like that!" She'd say, eyes sparkling. "Did you ever do that?"

There was no light in the atom sized ball she tried to describe so she called it a tiny black speck. Conversely, the gigantic ball was all light; blinding white light. SHE was the dark speck and SHE was the flash of blinding light. No one could give her a satisfactory answer. They just looked at her and shook their heads. And, as those who are confounded by incongruous information usually do, tried to make light of the situation or change the subject.

It was after this she first felt a warm tingling in her hands as her mother lay moaning with a searing headache on the couch in the small living room. Alicia had felt an instant rush of compassion and in a quiet, loving manner, laid her warm little hands against the sides of her mother's head and wished for her to feel better. Simply that.

"Mama." She said softly into the pain clouded eyes. "Mama?"

As she watched, her mother's eyes began to clear and focus as if seeing her child in a new light. Her hands flew to her temples, examining, exploring. The steady drumming in her ears had stopped, the constant pressure inside her head had quit between heart beats.

Her mother sat straight up. "Why 'Licia, what have you done?" Free of pain for the first time in hours her voice took on such an incredulous sound of excitement that the small child in front of her at first mistook it for one of alarm.

"Nothin' Mama..." She started, and slid her hands quickly behind her as if to hide the offending members. "I just wanted to help," she said. She had felt her way into healing with the quiet delicateness of a sibyl touching a handrail.

Her mother swung both legs down and fixed both feet flat on the floor as if to ground herself. Around them in the small, tidy room no sound was heard no movement detected. She reached slowly out and drew the small hands from behind Alicia's back. For some minutes she sat staring into their palms as if the answer to her deliverance was written there; could be read in the few pale pink lines and somehow defined.

"Licia, hon," she said, trembling with something like fear in her voice, "how'd you do that ...? What'd you do?"

"Well," said Alicia, made newly aware of something momentous having taken place. "I just did what the angel told me to Mama," herself not a little shaken.

"Angel?" Her mother said. "What angel, 'Licia ..., where?"

She held onto her daughter's small hands, scanned

the room with her eyes while a mixture of fright and reverence trembled up her spine and made goose flesh skitter across her arms.

"She came from the light, Mama. All a sudden light was *all* over everywhere. "Alicia took back her hands and made a wide sweeping motion. "She was a bright angel with light all around."

"But, how…" her mother's voice broke off.

Alicia seemed transported. Her eyes gave off little luminous shoots of attention and her voice was like a pledge.

"I saw her in the doorway, Mama. Light streaming all around her. When she came over here the light came with her and she stood right beside me and she said my name. 'A l i c i a,' she said it like that, real soft, sweet as a kitten purring. You know, like that?" Alicia looked unwavering into her eyes. "And Mama? It seemed like I knew her from somewhere before, you know? And I looked at her and listened real close and she said, 'Your mother is in great pain A.. l.. i.. c.. i.. a.' Like that. ' You must h..e..l..p her, she said.' And then the angel held her head like this and then made a pushing motion toward you Mama, like this with her hands?" Alicia held her own head between her hands and then made a scooping gesture with both hands.

"And then I knew just what I was to do." She drew back and examined her mother's eyes. "Mama, are you better now? I can do it again if you still feel bad…"

"Licia, sweetheart, you took the terrible pain clean away. It's completely gone…," her hand fluttered like a small butterfly to her temple. "Where…," she started. 'Oh boy', she whispered to herself, 'what do you do now, Rachael?' Aloud she said, "Is the angel, uh…here now…?" Her voice trailed off as she looked around the room, straining as hard into the dim recesses as she sometimes did in the middle of the night when waked by some inexplicable noise or vague disturbance. It was not so much a question as it was a diligent reckoning with her eyes.

There was a small, tender sound, like a sigh... only that... from the child standing before her with a sudden adult assurance.

"Oh, Mamma." Alicia held her by the shoulders and crooned to her as if her mother was the infant emerging from a high fever and she the adult; comforting, sure.

"She is here, Mama. She told me if I needed her, she is still here." She stood for a long time with her cheek pressed against her mother's face and with tears mingling down both their faces Alicia whispered, "She loves me, Mama." Alicia said, again and again. "Oh, Mamma, I can just feel she loves me..." Her eyes sparkled with the love and light of a vivid and seeking intelligence.

Two

Sometimes From Her Eyes....

Alicia was the only child of Rachael and Hank Townsend who farmed a small piece of rocky Ozark Mountain land willed to them by his elderly parents on Beaver Lake outside Springdale, Arkansas. To live within their means, as these hard working people must, did not necessarily mean they lived in abject poverty. There were vegetables and fruit aplenty, a few pigs and usually a chicken house full of new chicks. That, and a few head of cattle kept them from harm's way.

That they were luckier than most people at this particular juncture in their lives, did not mean they had a dime to spare for some strange looking, frivolous doodad such as had caught Alicia's fancy in the antique store, Hank had said to himself as much as to Rachel. He had to admit however, Alicia was usually a happy, bubbly child, content with an occasional bag of chocolate kisses she called 'silver bells' and a doll at Christmas time.

This thing about Alicia curing Rachael's sick headache for instance and last month there had been the crisis with the deep well. Her sudden ability to dowse for water had him going in circles of confusion. It was deeply puzzling to him.

Farming is a tremendous hard work even with enough water. To farm without water is hopeless. The precious little water being pumped out of the well was coming up foul and muddy. Even that must be boiled for at least three minutes before it could be used. For all intents and purposes there had been no rain to speak of in five months.

At first people joked good naturedly. "Unless you count the four incher we had the other day." Others would look quizzically.

"Yep," they'd say. "The drops were four inches apart!"

While farming communities for miles around depended on the White River for their water, which in part formed Beaver Laker, townspeople were mostly concerned if they had enough water to wash their cars and it seemed that about all the Chambers of Commerce in several counties worried about was how it would effect fall color and tourism in the Ozarks. A group of lake property owners were concerned about their boats being stranded 100 or more feet from waters edge. Even with this inconvenience there was a scramble for more dock permits and being allowed to mow the grass down to the shoreline. One newspaper article gave vent to the rights of everyone to enjoy the lake no matter whether they owned shoreline property, commuted a few miles, or visited from Astoria, Oregon. It was times like these that the farmer did not appreciate hearing that the U.S. Corps of Engineers had drawn down the water on the south side of the dam up at Eureka Springs so that the rich and famous on the upper end out of Branson, Missouri could run their jet skis and fish and generally lollygag on it's shores while farmers below the dam were just looking to survive.

Several of the neighbor men had come by to talk to Hank. Alvin Roberts and Pernel Frey had pastures across the county road, knew Hank for his level headed coolness. They had brought an older man by the name of Ike Perry, whose cattle were dying on his ranch in the valley.

They were standing out by the almost dry well

under a scorching August sun, talking over the draught and what help they could expect from the Corps in general and their own critical situation in particular. But, for the most part, they stood silent. The omnipresent cicada sound sawed the air while they watched the far off pattern of heat ripple above the parched ground. Into the stillness Alvin Roberts absentmindedly turned over a couple of rocks with the sharp tip of his boot, kicked them aside in a little puff of red dust, said his cattle pond had about a foot of water left and he'd have to do something quick. The usually kind face of Ike Perry looked deeply lined and tough as rawhide in the almost blinding sun as he reached down and scooped up a handful of dust and scattered it to the side. "I don't know but what it's already too late for my herd, boys." He turned his head and spit on the ground as though to install a period at the end of a despicable sentence instead of it being a social habit among friends; a seeming comfort, however fleeting.

Pernel Frey took off his hat and was in the process of mopping his forehead with a colorless sodden handkerchief when he said with alarm, "Hank! Look at Alicia!"

They had been too absorbed in their own concerns to notice that Alicia had come out of the house. Standing a few yards away, she appeared like a willow rooted to the spot, shaking in a high wind. Holding her little arms tight around her middle as if to keep herself from flying apart, her eyes stared blankly ahead while her light cotton skirt and tiny stem legs shook so hard it appeared she might come uprooted despite her best effort.

"Alicia!" Hank shouted, running towards her, his first thought was of high fever. 'Oh no, not on top of everything else.' He thought, 'all we need now is a

31

round of summer flu!' His voice seemed to alert some unseen bond within the earth as his knees dug into the dust at her feet and he grabbed her up into his arms.

"Licia, honey, what's wrong?" Her body felt like rubber and he was almost too frightened to speak, "What's the matter, 'Licia girl?" She didn't seem to have a fever but she shook so hard his own arms vibrated like an electric shock. The shaking had stopped the instant she came off the ground and she appeared her normal self again.

Alicia drew back her head and looked at her father as if to say, 'Weren't you talking about needing more water? Hadn't he asked what should be done about the lack of water?' She wriggled out a little space for herself in the tight circle of his arms. Standing firm and solid now on her own, she lifted a hand to shade her eyes from the sun's white hot glare and looked from her father to the men as if measuring the distance between them and their understanding of the situation. She examined the face of her father as though she could not believe the reason for his question while buzzards made idle circles in the sky and cicada's lapsed into another parched silence in the dust colored weeds along the fence line. Alicia looked at a space between her father and Ike Perry and squinted her eyes almost shut. She sensed by their silence that they were waiting for some sort of clue from her and somehow seemed to know she was in charge of something. Almost willing her certain answer, they waited.

"Daddy," she said finally. "The angel said, 'Stand here Alicia.' She turned and pointed back at the spot where she had stopped. "'Stand here for water.' She told me, 'you will not have to worry about water anymore if you dig right here'."

So saying, Alicia took two steps and bent her short

little body and, as if for emphasis, twice poked with one dimpled index finger, the hot, dry ground where she had stood. "Right here, Daddy!"

Hank gave her a long, studied look. "Licia..., Hon." He said finally. "Uh..., could you go back in the house and get your mother? Tell her we need a kerchief out here, and when you come back, will you show us again where the angel said to dig the new well?"

As Alicia, short legs pumping, disappeared into the house, Hank could scarcely believe this new development and the everyday naturalness with which his daughter had accepted the bidding of this 'angel'. And, he was afraid. He was afraid and he couldn't decide of which he was more afraid, this apparent ability to divine water, or face the fact and the shame if she was proved wrong, for as everyone knew, they desperately needed water and lots of it. Besides, listening to and cajoling a small child clearly was one thing, while spending time and serious money digging a new well in the wrong place was another matter entirely. Still, something was going on. She had, after all, miraculously cured Rachael of her headaches. And the chronic pain had not returned.

The men waited. The rounds of cicada sawing was taken up in mid-song as if they had suddenly remembered their places, and in seconds the stereophonic volume increased as they were joined by a well rehearsed new group from over the hill and the sun seemed to turn the heat up to match.

A cow bellowed plaintively from across the gully in the far pasture and Ike thought surely she was not calving this time of year. They all thought it. No one spoke it. They scarcely looked at each other. Afraid of what they might read there. A red-tail hawk cast a gray shadow on the stubble of dull grass as it flew across the yard and the men by long habit turned up their faces to scan the sky for any sign of change.

Rachael's left arm made an arch for Alicia to walk under as she pushed open the screen door from inside the hot narrow kitchen. They joined hands and came down the steps one at a time and crossed the baked ground to where the men stood.

The back yard was divided in half. The garden on one side and a barbed wire fence on the other served as a border between the house and the pasture with the almost dry well as a central feature in the middle of the back fence close to the barn. Next to the fence three old scrub oaks lent the only shade around and there the men had retreated to wait in spotted reflection. A lacey swarm of gnats dipped and waved between the tired looking branches as if to rouse an unlikely energy.

"What's going on Hank?" Rachael said, shading her eyes with the front of a forearm. With the other hand she extended a red patterned bandana to her husband while looking from one to another of the men who met her restless gaze, each searching for a sign of order and sureness in the other.

Hank raised the palm of his hand in a wait and see attitude to Rachael. He took the handkerchief and stooped one worn jean clad knee on the ground in front of Alicia. "Licia, honey," he said.

"How about if we play a little game of blindman's bluff?"

"O.K. daddy," she said trustingly, as she accepted as a matter of course the unfamiliar suggestion from her father.

"It works this way," he explained as he began to fold the cloth into a narrow strip over his knee. "First, we have to make a shield for your eyes with Mama's kerchief." He placed the blindfold over her eyes and began to tie it behind her small dark head. Sweat dripped, stung his eyes with salt, while a lone buzzard made wide circles between them and the broiling sun. With both hands holding the ends of the blindfold his forehead dipped to make a quick swipe against an already wet sleeve. "You can't see anything can you honey?"

Alicia shook her head. "No, Daddy." The others stood quietly watching.

"Good," he said. "So, now I turn you around, and around, slowly, like this." He gently turned her a few times, holding both her arms straight down at her sides to steady her.

"Now then, you walk around and try to find the place again where the angel said to dig for water." He smoothed back a few strands of baby fine hair above the blindfold and kissed her damp forehead. "O.K., honey?"

"O.K. daddy." She said and started off, at first feeling her way gingerly with the toe of her right shoe.

"I'm right here honey. It's O.K." Hank said patiently behind her, moping his face with a wet handkerchief. He did not intend exposing his family to much more of this murderous heat.

Alicia took one small uneasy step at a time until she was fairly skipping across the sparse brittle grass. Back and forth she went in this fashion while the others stood apart and watched. Still, while they earnestly believed in the validity of dousing, they had only seen it done with metal rods or willow twigs, knew in their hearts the impossible odds of three year old Alicia, ever finding water.

They watched, waited, as round after round the cicada maintained the same mesmerizing, metallic see-sawing sound in the dust covered thicket of every other scalding yellow summer.

Hank seemed by proxy to feel the vibration begin to crawl up his legs before Alicia stopped. She took one more step and began to tremble as if she stood at the epicenter of an earthquake.

Rachael, not having witnessed the previous episode, made an animal sound in her throat and started on instinct toward her daughter who, for all she knew was having some kind of seizure. Hank, remembering his own first reaction, held out an arm to hold Rachael back and lifted his daughter aside. He was shaken to the core while Alicia appeared no worse for wear. Rachael rushed at them in a flurry of skirts, and dust, caught Alicia up into her arms, lifted her up out of the vortex of perceived harm.

Hank and the men stared unblinking down at the spot where Alicia had stopped. Her small shoes were unmistakably imprinted there before them in the dust. One set of prints exactly on top of the other.

Three

Constant As The Northern Star

It was with a kind of catechism Rachael and Hank viewed their days as they watched Alicia develop into a beautiful young lady. At first she helped relatives and friends and then, as her reputation for compassion and knowledge of how the unseen forces worked, her circle of influence widened.

People came from everywhere, sometimes driving themselves but often-times too sick and feeble they were driven to the little house at the end of the flower fringed lane. Limp and fevered children, as well, were driven there and all these simply came to sit, listen to her consul, await her healing touch. Benches were placed on the small front porch where men, women and children alike waited. Sometimes men sat with an uncommon patience, hat in hand, staring squinty eyed off into the distance as if trying to see over the mountains or into another life to what lay on the other side. Women often brought count-and-cross stitch or knitting to work, talked softly among themselves and waited their turn.

It was as if, in Alicia, they had for a leader, instead of a slender, vivid, young girl, some sort of wondrous super anodyne, something apart from them. In them, Alicia found an unassailable trust, devoid of duplicity.

Once a husky sixteen year old boy waited his turn on the porch. Alicia could hear him before she saw him: hiccoughs so strong that it rocked him back on his heels. It took about twenty seconds to cure him. She looked steadily into his eyes as he sat in a chair across from her.

Alicia asked his name.

"Randall Motes," he said timidly.

"How long have you had these hiccoughs, Randall."

He reddened. "Bout two weeks solid....(hiccup)."

"Do you like having hiccoughs?" She asked with concern.

"Well, no, sir! er... I mean miss!" "Er, no, of course not (hiccup)." He frankly did not know how to address this beautiful girl whom he could be dating for god's sake. It was embarrassing. But his mother had insisted that she would surely take him to a doctor if he did not go to see Alicia.

"I can't eat!" (hiccup). "It hurts, ya know?" He held three fingers up to his throat and pressed hard as if to squeeze shut his windpipe. "Can't sleep." (hiccup). "I've tried everything anybody's told me from holding my breath, blowing into paper bags and eating sugar and sour apples; all like that. People have tried sneaking up on me, trying to scare me out of 'em. You name it, I've done it; and it's two weeks of no good." (hiccup)

Alicia, stared unwaveringly into his eyes. "I want you to breathe deeply Randall, look me in the eyes but think right here," she put her forefinger and middle finger on the soft hollow at her own throat to indicate where, "and b..r..e..a..t..h..e.. deep.

"That's it Randall, think right here and b..r..e..a..t..h..e deep". She said, her fingers still on the pulse spot; "again..., again." The two sat in locked harmony staring into the others eyes, breathing deep regular breaths. Seconds passed without the spot jerking at Randall's throat. "Breathe... thats it... breathe... breathe." Alicia's voice soothing, insistent.

"They're gone!" Alicia pronounced him cured. His face could not stop smiling as he walked out the door and jumped off the porch instead of using the steps.

She had fascinating eyes, he thought.

People brought gifts to her in appreciation. Small things at first: toys, dolls, and clothes. Usually respectable hand-me-downs from their own children, starched and pressed and these usually made of simple calico or denim. Frequently there would be a sweater or scarf knit by loving hands and occasionally they gave articles made from scarce and precious fabric. Once, when she was nine she dreamed of a new coat of such rare lightness it was like touching a fluff of pink cloud. The very next day a fine cashmere and velveteen coat with matching muff was brought wrapped in white tissue paper printed all over with pink bunnies and presented to her by a lady who came smelling of JOY perfume with tears in her eyes because Alicia had told her of a dead son's affirmation of love and continued happiness. When Alicia spoke additionally to her of a desk drawer behind which some very important insurance papers had fallen, the lady was that grateful.

When she first began to help powerful people, people of great wealth and influence, for they came in greater and greater numbers, standing respectfully with the poor and downtrodden on the porch as well, Alicia was surprised yet flattered that they would consider her talent so important.

It was not uncommon to see an airport limousine pull up to the small farm house and hear that a famous movie star or wealthy couple had brought a sick child to see Alicia. Many times she would be saddened to say she could not cure, could not interfere with the soul's chosen course. At which times an unexpected calm would descend on the group as if a basic correctness had been finally recognized and accepted.

Showing sick people that they could be healthy was not the only thing they got in their minds that Alicia could do. Once a man in black scuffed cowboy boots and faded blue-jeans came from a farm over in Oklahoma on a Sunday morning and spread colored pictures in front of her on the kitchen table. "Little Miss," he began slowly. "I want you to think real hard about this land for me, if you will, please," he said as he took off his sweat stained hat and pointed to several pictures of the pasture land where black and white cattle grazed.

"Mr. Metcalf, can I tell you something?" She said immediately.

"Why lands, I wish you would Miss Alicia."

"Mr. Metcalf, I hope you don't get mad at me for saying this but you need to sell those cows or put them somewhere else real quick because they are not going to like swimming in all that yucky black stuff." She pinched her nose. "Phew! It stinks! Like oil or something."

"Well, I swany." Mr. Metcalf said quiet like, a grin beginning to twitch at the corners and finally to widen his mouth. "Miss Alicia, can you tell me just where this oil is?"

"Oh, all over there," she took her hand from her nose and pointed with one small finger, "around here, and back up in here too." Her hand moved to indicate the vastness beyond the last picture represented by the scarred but spotless wood table. "Pretty much all over the place. I hope you have a pasture somewhere nice for those poor cows to go because they sure can't stay there!" Without guile, she added. "And Mr. Metcalf? I hope you are not too disappointed but you will have to move your house too or else get a new one someplace else!" In leaving, before his boots had hit the bottom step, Mr. Metcalf had already made up his mind what to tell the oil companies. Before he came to himself, he had given out such a larruping loud whoop that he couldn't take it back and for all he knew it might have been heard all the way to his ranch outside of Bartlesville. He headed the truck back over the hills in that direction.

Once word got around about the further talents of Alicia Townsend people brought maps of every kind; treasure maps, diamond, gold and silver mines. She saved many from needless expense on worthless ventures and made many rich on speculation.

These things she did gladly and as easily as a little bird flitting from one branch to another. It was the heavy hearted task of locating children or missing loved ones who had been stolen away from terrified parents, injured or killed by their assailants, whose struggle Alicia found fiercely daunting and monumentally crushing. At such times her eyes would darken, recede into their sockets and she spoke in quick sharp jabs as if she agonized over each deplorable word, each syllable spilled from the tongue like acid.

If asked, Mrs. Steven Slocum would say it was certainly worth the dozen jars of wild strawberry preserves, even though it took her the better part of a week to pick enough they were so tiny, to have Alicia pin-point the location of her 13 year old son Alex, dazed and wandering a Colorado Springs outlet mall after being abducted from the men's restroom in the Siloam Springs, Arkansas city park by a man in a green Volvo.

Sandra Lockwood's husband, a multi-millionaire from Bentonville said on live television that no amount of money could have found her when she accidentally fell into a deep narrow hidden crevice one day when she was hiking while her husband was at work and the children were at school. To him she had vanished from the face of the earth without a trace. The police were alerted but after three days had no leads whatsoever and began to suspect Gary Lockwood himself of having done something to his wife. They went to Alicia as police often did for help. While holding Sandra's hair brush next to her heart Alicia was able to tell them that she was lying at the bottom of a deep chasm, bruised, dehydrated and hoarse from yelling for help, but, alive. She recovered rapidly and Gary had been overwhelmingly generous to Alicia.

It was a daily thing. Sometimes when Alicia came home from school the porch would be lined with people where Rachael had asked them to wait. Alicia would duck her head in unassuming deference to their suffering as she went into the house where they one by one filed in after her.

Loving things they did for her in return. As her talent grew, she grew. As she gave, they gave.

"Mama," she had said." What am I going to do with all this money?" Alicia never charged a fee, never asked for anything. Money, however, was one of the ways they chose to repay her many acts of kindness. She always said a simple thank you in return. She would no more have thought to refuse their gifts than she would have thought to refuse them succor. If they gave flowers, a bright bird's feather or a smooth river stone, as many children did, offering these to her with open yielding hands, love and gratitude in their eyes, they were received as graciously by her as if it was so much solid gold. And, as precious.

"Leave it in the bank, Alicia honey, until you can decide what to do with your future," her mother had said. Rachael and Hank had for many years now regarded her as her own best council and knew that she asked her questions largely out of respect and politeness for their place as parents. Alicia, on the other hand, while helping others with decisions of far reaching proportion, needed and wanted in her young life the special guidance only her parents could give.

Four

Earth's Shadows Fly

Almost from the first moment Alicia Townsend sat in the old Cord automobile she felt a definite male presence in the car. She was not surprised at the sudden awareness. In fact with an automobile of that vintage she would have been surprised had she not felt something of a lingering personality there.

"Zee?" She spoke from the back seat. "When the auto-body shop repainted the car, did they strip it down to the original paint?"

"Yeah, they did." Sam Cravens, Zee to his friends, said as he steered through the heavy after school traffic. He remembered Chuck Barnes' laughing about the color they had found under two coats of paint.

"It was kind of strange." Zee turned his head, "Why do you ask?" He spoke over his shoulder in the direction of the back seat as he drove north on Highway 71 through Springdale, Arkansas. Although they were best of friends all through school he was now in her employ as driver and could not be happier about the arrangement. He had driven her in her cousin Beth's car a few times but this was only the second time he had driven her in her own automobile, if you counted his delivering her to the high school's auditorium for graduation three days before. On that glad occasion she had been so preoccupied with her Valedictory address that she hardly noticed the stunning antique car. Alongside the 1997 cars, the newly renovated 1936 Cord had caused quit a stir with it's wide chrome bumpers and grillwork, the unusual taupe color and fat white sidewall tires, had been a befitting graduation and 16th birthday present to herself.

When Alicia did not immediately respond he glanced at her in the rearview mirror. He saw a young girl with straight dark hair and fine features who looked about twelve years old as she sat low in the corner. The palm of her left hand moved slowly over the new chocolate colored leather. "Hmmmm...," she intoned, oblivious to his voice. Cars whizzed by on the highway unnoticed as she absently traced the lines of burnished walnut around the window frame. "Ummmm...," her eyes closed.

Zee knew that sound. Alicia made it when she sensed something. She called it picking up vibrations. It was remarkable to him how she could tell about a person just by touching an object which belonged to them or had been in their presence for any length of time. Psychometry she called it. Almost anyone could do this but most people lacked the curiosity and learned sensitivity, she said.

Presently Zee said, "Charles Barnes Restoration out on Highway 412 did the work, Alicia." He could not tell from her reflected image what she was thinking." You know. Out by the old Jones place?" He continued, knowing that she heard him from wherever she had temporarily gone.

"He's the best in the Springdale, Rogers, Fayetteville area, you know?" He paused glanced in the mirror again as if trying to decide if he should be silent or continue.

"Chuck's all right," Zee said mostly to himself settling into easy routine, cruised slowly in the right hand lane. He knew when Alicia got this way she might, in the middle of traffic, change her mind about what she needed to do, where she wanted to go. He had been headed home to the lake but who knew? Maybe she'd want him to turn the car around and head back toward Springdale to talk to Chuck. With Alicia he could never tell what was going to happen next. The certainty of the unpredictable. It was one of the things he liked about this job, he told himself with satisfaction. Doing his job well was what mattered.

"Chuck knows everything about vintage cars." Zee continued, as he waved to friends who drove by, honked the horn. The Cord's large white wall tires made slick, skimming sounds on the pavement as they passed.

"You should see his office, ...Chucks, I mean. Pictures of himself with all the special old cars he's restored hanging on the walls of his office and garage. He's got books and manuals piled everywhere. His mechanics all say he talks to the cars like they were people. They say it's spooky how much attention he gives each one. Almost more than people, you know? People just naturally trust Chuck with their automobiles when they see how much attention to detail he gives every one of 'em."

Alicia continued to look, non-seeing, out the window. Her left hand pressed hard into the seat as if searching out the imprint of the old springs underneath.

"The thing is," Zee said talking to her reflection in the rear view mirror, "with Chuck, he likes to gossip, you know? He likes to joke and carry on with his customers. For instance, while he was working on this one he told everybody who came in that he was working on a sweet old Cord. He used the word sweet a lot. He'd say something like, 'Sweet old thing, this Cord.' He'd stop and shake his head back and forth to make them think he was confused about something or other but they didn't dare interrupt.

You just have to be patient with Chuck. Sometimes he'd even stop to pick his teeth, he keeps a toothpick behind his ear at all times. 'But, you shoulda seen the original color of it.' He'd continue after a bit. ' Wow, beat anything I ever saw!' Chuck'ed start out real slow…, work up the story to people and watch their reaction, you know, like he was enjoying every minute of the attention he got out of telling about it. 'Yes sir,' he'd say, 'yes sir, now you take most Auburn Cords, they'd nine times outa ten be black. As a matter of fact, back then, most cars were black as a rats ass!' Chuck'ed stop there for effect, you know? Like everybody else naturally wouldn't know that!

"'Well,' Chuck'ed say finally. 'Well, you know, judging by the color, this Cord was originally owned by a sweet ole' thing.' He'd take his own sweet time inspecting his fingernails and wiping his hands on an old blue rag he keeps in his back pocket. He'd be waiting to see if people were listening real close, then all a sudden he'd spring it on 'em. 'Either a sweet old rich gal or a very sweet young man, if you get my drift!' He'd wink and slap the side of his leg with the rag, like everybody would appreciate his brand of humor or else they'd be bad sports. His kind of sport anyway."

As Zee drove north they passed the A.Q. Chicken House and he thought for the hundredth time how he would like to have the old truck sitting out front in the grass strip to work on in his spare time. It had been moved a time or two but for many years it had just been a part of the famous restaurant's parking lot decoration. To look at it's peeling two tone yellow and mustard colored paint, it's rotted wood running-boards and collapsed white wall tires made him feel sad. He viewed it like a trainer might take on a down and out prize fighter, to rebuild and polish; he'd like to make it his own private rescue mission.

"I get a sense of purple or lavender with this car." Alicia, non-hearing, spoke softly, stroked the window frame.

"Chuck sure knows his cars though…" Zee began to add as if in apology for Chuck's bigoted attitude.

"And I smell English Lavender after shave. But definitely the color lavender and purple, with this car."

"Bingo!" Zee shook his head at her mirrored reflection. "Alicia, you sure don't miss much." One eye on the road he glanced over his shoulder at her. "The original color of this Cord," he poked the steering wheel with one finger, "was lavender!" He had long ago ceased to be amazed when she picked up obscure pieces of information like that.

"Oh, that reminds me," he leaned over and pulled a scrunched, yellowed paper from the glove box and handed it over the back of the seat to Alicia. "Chuck said he found this inside one of the door panels."

As with any antique, authenticity is crucial to establishing price. The Cord's almost pristine condition: no parts from other makes or models, had not yielded a clue as to it's original owner. Zee, as Alicia's agent, had found and purchased the car at DO♪RE♪ME HERREN CLASSIC CARS in Fayetteville and they had been unable to trace it's ownership past an estate sale in Neosho, Missouri, a few years ago.

As Alicia unfolded and smoothed what appeared to be a brochure of some kind, a small lavender business card fell into her lap.

Alicia read aloud the purple embossed lettering:

Norman Baker Hospital
and
Health Resort, Eureka Springs, Arkansas
Atop The Ozarks A Castle In The Air

The brochure's 1937 copyright depicted the Crescent Hotel on it's cover. Inside, it proclaimed: "Where sick folks get well...Baker Hospital.""We treat all ailments." "We cure cancer tumors without operation, Radium or X-Ray."

The brochure referred many times to organized medicine as, "The Medical Octopus." Additionally it stated, "Baker Hospital does not cut out any organ."

Mr. Baker and the hospital presumably wanted a chance to "Save thousands from the grave," as was it's stalwart proclamation. Lastly, this impassioned plea: "Help us!" fairly shouted to the world and anyone who'd listen. "Help us battle for medical freedom!"

As Alicia fingered the brochure, handled the venerable business card of Norman Baker, something resembling kaleidoscopic flashes began to play against the back of her closed eyelids like colored images projected on a docudrama screen with full accompanying sound.

As she watched, a tall man dressed in a white suit rushed through what appeared to be a narrow underground tunnel. Alicia took a deep breath and relaxed against the seat, giving in to the fullness of her perceptions.

The strong odor of dampness and bare earth, acrid and musty, was instantly there to sting her sinuses and provoke her senses.

The sound of pounding feet, beat through her head; sharp, rhythmic intakes of breath, keys jangling, watch fob beating up and down, slapping his thigh in time to the pounding, beating, pumping heart. Pumping blood, pounding feet throbbed in her ears.

Overhead, naked orbs rushed intervals of light towards him, casting oncoming shadows onto his face; erratic, sudden shapes rushed frantically to meet retreating others of himself on the narrow tunnel path and close rock walls.

As he ran forward he swiped in the general direction of the offending dark smudges he knew must be on his white pants and cursed the men who had burst like gangbusters through the front door of the hospital. He had known it was just a matter of time before they acted on their threat to arrest him. They had threatened to arrest him and close the hospital down because he refused to comply with their idea of what cancer treatment should be and, in fact, only that morning he had said as much to his secretary Margaret.

What a political football. Cancer is curable! And they know I have the proof if only they will investigate. I've urged, "Talk to my patients." I've begged them, "let them tell you how desparetely sick they were after the so called real doctors got through cutting them up. There are hundreds of thousands! The A.M.A. would hear or investigate none of our cured cases." The instant he heard their brusque voices in the lobby he had bolted from his desk and without thought plunged himself downward into the dark passageway before switching on the tunnel lights and in the darkness had hit the dirt wall.

It had come into his mind to stand them off with the German Luger pistol he always kept in his desk drawer but at the moment of decision something seemed to stay his hand and he had jumped to open the hidden panel in the wall behind his desk instead and dived into the tunnel before the door closed behind him.

"Must not panic." Alicia heard him recite as if in time with the beat of his heart. "Must not fall," as he groped for the light switch in the black darkness. "Not get dirty. Wreck suit." The tunnel opened with sporadic light. Pant. Beat. "Everyone will know. It's so embarrassing." He wanted to look down at himself as he ran, check the front of his lavender shirt and white pants. One gold ringed hand brushed instinctively toward the offensive tell-tale smudges he knew must be there.

"'Oh! This can't happen now! Can't close us down, mustn't..., mustn't..., mustn't...,' Thought beat in time with his heart. "What will happen to Dr. Bailey now? His brain tumor treatment only half done. What will he do, he was coming along so well! Damn those fools to hell anyway!" The heart stopping inconsistence, the absolute unfairness of the "medical octopus." "Damn them!"

Pant, beat, pant. He felt the cold moisture spread in ever widening circles under his armpits. "Look at me, Norman Baker, running like a coward. How can they do this? Why can't they understand!" Feet pounded, heart beat. "After all I've done for them? A respected member of this community. I thought they were impressed with our cure rate." Pant, beat, pant. "Oh," sweat shivers over his arms, "what will happen to our poor patients! Unjust, not fair at all." And his may well have been the beating heart of the planet.

His mouth set in a wide toothed grimace as pain shot up both legs, toes slammed into shoe's pointed tips. Pain stitched his side. "No time for pain!" Momentum propelled him down inside the mountain. Down, ever downward he plunged past jagged, protruding rocks down into who knew what inevitable fate, as if casting himself like a sacrificial lamb down the throat of some unjust god or wicked king.

"Zee." Alicia's small voice from the back seat. "How far is Eureka Springs from here?"

Zee glanced at her reflection in the mirror. She was staring non-seeing out the window. He waited for what he knew was coming.

"I need you to take me to the Crescent Hotel in Eureka Springs," she said.

"All right, Alicia!" Zee said. 'Music to my ears,' he thought, rearranging himself in the seat. 'The first chance to do some real driving. Steep mountains, switchback roads. We'll see what this baby can do.' Then he checked the play in the wheel, automatically testing the steering. People frequently drove over the sides of those mountain roads. Guardrails or no, in good weather or bad but especially at night when visibility was poor. Brakes could fail. Either steering went out or some speed freak idiot would try to pass another car around curves despite dire warnings and double yellow lines. How many accidents had been caused on those treacherous hairpin turns, he wondered. Albeit dangerous, if the brochure was correct and the Cord had belonged to this Mr. Baker, it would have been driven over those same challenging mountains many times and the roads would have been in much poorer condition. And not so incidentally he wondered exactly what kind of wear and service those old gum tires would have had in those bygone days. Even now the better tires don't cannot last long when they are regularly driven over the razor-sharp rocks which some of the back roads consist of in Northwest Arkansas.

"No problem!" Zee set his cap on tighter and sat taller in the seat. Like an overgrown kid he gripped the big black wheel and almost stomped the gas before he remembered his place. A shining example of one of the finest automobiles ever made, driving the Cord was a glad pleasure. On the other hand he was conflicted as a purist, silently wished for automatic windows and signal lights. And don't forget the air conditioning, lord-a-mercy, he thought, we could sure do with some air conditioning about now. Must be 90 out there today. The lowered windows and little gasps of air from the side vents told him that. It was stifling in the car, like the heater was on. He automatically glanced at the heater's knobs to make sure it was not. He was still getting used to the Cord's idiosyncrasies. He would have had Chuck Barnes install more modern features had it not impugned the car's antique status. Instead, he stuck his arm out the window and signaled manually for the left lane and headed north toward Rogers and Highway 62 east to Eureka Springs.

It was to the Crescent Hotel Alicia followed the spirit voice of Norman Baker, it's one time owner, and fell a willing hostage to both.

Five

Sleep to Wake

It was Monday morning, about 10:30. A large, caramel and cream colored cat sat quietly on the hearth before an enormous freestanding fireplace in the lobby of the old Crescent Hotel and watched the glass paneled entrance doors.

Morris had awakened suddenly in the night to discover that the hall and his pallet were full of moonlight and felt rather than knew that today she would come and, at last, it would begin. How or by what means he did not know, but that she would, he was certain.

He had risen with a feeling of interest he did not understand but began without hesitation to move as if he did. The round moon rolling from window to window, had alternately turned his coat silver and dark as he, alert as if notified by some keen common sense, padded softly across the lobby, past tall straight chairs as colorless and vacant as the surface of the moon. Today she will come.

Morris had, as a kitten, first presented himself one sultry afternoon following a heavy rainstorm on the other side of these same panes a half drowned, soggy, disarranged ball of fur and bones in unfeigned need of charity. If he blinked his eyes he could, just at the fringe of memory, recall that newly born pain, that aching need.

Blue lightning streaked from one to the other turret peaks at the top of the hotel and a mighty thunder slammed against it's century old windowpanes. Sheets of rain began to pelt the storage shed below where he cowered to the side and felt himself to be in danger of losing the poised and tenuous life he'd scarcely had time to know.

The next bolt hit the tin roof and exposed his meager, premature body to every whim and wile of nature. An unrehearsed bloodcurdling scream shot from his mouth like something almost human as he was slammed stiff legged into the opposite corner. All the fur on his scrawny arched back flew straight up while the temporarily appeased blue air crackled and rolled with electricity. Stunned out of his natural growth he no doubt was, still he managed to get all four legs back under him at once. Resisting the almost uncontrollable urge to stop and groom himself, he drew his dazed little self fully up and with something like unscathed dignity, began to rethink strategy. His legs took a wider stance and despite the harrowing ordeal, his eyes became more, not less, focused. This was not the mere kitten that he had been just moments before. As he moved forward he did not go as his former self might have timidly gone. No. This cat, regardless of shape and size, moved resolutely forward, instinctively lowered his head to the elements and counted cadence across the water rushed parking lot. He had only just arrived on the hotel's steps in this outwardly miserable condition when without fan-fare the entrance door opened and a warm voice said, Oh, you poor little thing!" As if his doppelganger had foretold his coming. There he was. Scooped up against an ample bosom, dried and fed from a gold lined saucer until even he, born of such recently impoverished conditions, and in spite of such a strong and restless resolve, even he had to renounce a certain natural inclination toward independence. He now thought he possibly could, probably would, spare a few moments of his valuable time.

"He just showed up one day. Dripping wet and pitiful looking," the hotel staff commented." A scrawny, puny little ole thing. And scared, he was shaking all over." As his self appointed guardians, they had cared for him and his title had swelled in direct proportion to his girth until he was often respectfully referred to as The General Manager. As he began to look and act more the part of a pampered stockholder, he was given the purloined name of Morris, a famous television commercial look alike. And like all cats, Morris preferred to be kept, without complication, rather than be owned.

For a long time there had been a weary fustiness of decline in the old hotel. A grey water color-like wash, as if applied by some broad and melancholy brush, had affixed itself on windowpane and counterpane alike, until the previously proclaimed "most elegant hostelry west of the Mississippi" had by insipid degrees of ennui, been turned into a faded and worn, sepia picture of itself. It would not be long now, for today she would come.

Behind the front desk someone coughed and a chair scraped across the bare floor causing a staccato burst of sound to shoot into the room like a barrage of gunfire. Morris' head thrust back as if he was hit point blank and his eyes jerked toward the sound as if it were an alive, tangible thing to be caught and reckoned with. The loud report struck the floor, ricocheted like bullets against the ceiling, set the crystals in the chandelier to dancing and cracked like reachable thunder over the spectre of a man dressed from head to toe in black who stood anxiously watching out the front windows; skittered past the ghost of a young man dressed in a slouch hat and workman's clothes waiting at the head of the stairs; rode a current of stale air along an upstairs passageway where a nurse clad in starch whites repetitiously rolled an empty hospital guerney as if through endless corridor's of time, until by degrees, the sound's diminished portions vanished over the side of a balcony high overhead as the ghost of a young school girl's spent vanity might fall into a looking glass.

Alicia walked about the hotel that first day, the green parade of Zee and Morris followed at a gentle distance. She went, hand holding banister and rail, fingertips trailing along doorframes and walls, literally feeling her way down dim corridors like a blind person seeking light. In this heedful way she went, sought to avoid bluff intrusion, rather to reverently seeking a public as well as private knowledge of the old hotel. Sought and found each spirit presence there. Wanting. Needing. She vowed to be as the ever flowing waters had been, constant, reliable. Do what it had done; cleanse, heal the body and the human spirit with creative energy. Her own energy suddenly rose as a flood and built like mother's milk; coursed along arteries like heat lightning; washed over organs, flooded glands and shot into her brain like a thrill floods the heart. That these high emotions were connected with the build up of healing energy there is no doubt. For if a human being is the product of a creative force, then being human is totally an emotional expression of such energy.

Alone, from a window seat in a closed upstairs bedroom, Alicia parted the flower bordered chintz curtains and drank in the sight of Eureka Springs nestled amongst the trees and mountains under the star shot sky.

After walking undisturbed through the hotel that first summers afternoon, Alicia met with the new owners. They talked of the old hotel's magnificent beginnings, and of it's several, sad, inglorious closings.

Through it all, they said, the Crescent Hotel had never lacked character. Additionally, it had gained the well deserved reputation of being authentically haunted from the first sighting of Michael, the young Irish stonecutter who fell to his death before the hotel was completed. They said many people came with more than curiosity. Wanting proof to substantiate the stories, they go about actively seeking their own experiences with the ghosts; cameras, camcorders and recorders at the ready. Others, less sensitive than skeptical, simply question the management as to what the fuss is all about but, in spite of, or perhaps because of, the rich tradition of the hotel's hauntings still brings more visitors than it drives away.

"Like the time a picture appeared and floated around the hotel in the air. No one knew the source of it but it seemed to have been photographed in one of the honeymoon suites, like room 202. It looked like a bony old man standing in a closet at the right side of the bed. The desk clerk sometimes showed the picture to couples when they checked out of the room, especially if they asked if the hotel was really "haunted."

Having endured many a gala opening and quiet closing enjoyed by workers and patrons alike, it is no wonder that the Crescent's varied career is shared by those who have died within her walls, leaving a famed legacy of their own.

Alicia spoke to the owners of business possibilities and together they formulated a plan whereby she would co-op two of the rooms and her dream of a consulting studio could become a reality. They would arrange for renovation work to begin immediately, adhering closely to accepted architectural design.

Alicia knew, from the outset, the real essence of the old hotel. Thousands had come to visit the Crescent, some had even called it home. She knew it's image, it's dramatic presence soaring atop West Mountain, to be extremely compelling and grand but more than that she recognized it's energy. There was an alive flowing energy from the mountain on which it stood, up through it's foundation, within the dolomitic veins of it's limestone walls, to the top of it's highest turret. From the outset, like any well planned Feng Shui site, a balance of energy had been struck, as alive and natural as the outpouring waters from the springs below. Energy flowed for the benefit of all.

Before leaving she paused in the expansive lobby and felt profound respect for the prophetic words carved into the stone of the immense fireplace:

> Although, upon a summer's day
> You'll likely turn from me away;
> When Autumn leaves are scattered wide,
> You'll often linger by my side;
> But when the snow the earth doth cover,
> Then you'll be my ardent lover.

The one man most responsible for the building of the Crescent Hotel, the man who founded the Arkansas Industrial University, a land-grant college in 1872 which became the University Of Arkansas in 1899, Governor Powell C. Clayton wrote these few simple lines and probably thought no more about it. However, since it's beginning the ones who died there seemed to have taken these carved words quite literally; there to linger until life's network of cause and effect could be disentangled. There to linger until gaining an understanding and acceptance of death as simply a temporary prelude to spirit's ultimate restoration. Michael's may have been the first in a long line of deaths associated with the Crescent Hotel but conversely, it's profound history and tradition has been as charged with variegated light and gladness as it ever has been with darkness and intrigue. To everything there is a season of experience and awakening.

It appeared to Alicia, thus informed, she was there in answer to a summons so persuasive from those who lingered, it might as well have reached her through direct, common means for all the clarity and sureness of their purpose now. To those who had died there Alicia appeared to move as a bright light in front of a curtain; they, on the darkened stage behind, waiting. To them, her young bright form moved onto the stage of their perception, beckoned them towards the light until, by degrees, they became conscious of vague sounds into which they listened with all their will. An unnamed quickening had begun as if they would soon understand and recognize in themselves some long forgotten covenant. Perhaps they could recover their senses and seize from this place of their confusion and constant unrest the chance to end what they, in life, had put into motion in death. To them, Alicia seemed a kind of beacon to shine their way home from a missed track of opportunity, as if on life's journey they had gotten off at the wrong station or had too soon arrived.

Six

In A Light Fantastic Round

It seemed to Morris he had always sat on the hearth and waited. He knew now for whom he waited. She was no longer a stranger to him. Many times he had regarded Alicia who, like he, had simply presented herself in the lobby one day. He had shamelessly traced her steps as she wandered the hotel; in the dining room, on the stairway, even in the elevator. She spoke quietly with the old time folks he sensed more than saw were there. Folks who had lived in the hotel long before he came. In himself he identified them as the busy ones that never seemed to extend themselves or accomplish anything. They were just there; replaying the very same actions over and over in what seemed to him like endless circles of monotony as if fixed like a phonograph needle in non-gaining grooves of a tedious record. Their thoughts and actions so protracted and heavy he wished he could figure out, if this was the real world, how it was put together; what it was meant to show. But, Oh! He. He in her presence, felt light and fine!

In himself, Morris at times felt a lightness which could best be described as a type of sequestered happiness in an existence thus far without accounts, one completely devoid of responsibility to any but himself. The only assets and liabilities of which he must keep track, by some tacit agreement with whomever was in charge of things, are hardly worth the mention: fur balls and mice and, when the night clerk remembered, the occasional bowl of cream.

But today, the account of this day when totaled, would bring something like a sigh to his heart, an instinctive relief as perhaps by some evolutionary whim now he would be allowed to distinguish good luck from bad. A settling of terms and of contract inactivity.

From early morning, Morris, as though informed by secret code or messenger, had fixed himself in that indomitable and time honored pose in front of the fireplace.

The entrance doors, which framed the steps and portico, reflected in his amber colored eyes like cross hairs on a target. Above the reception desk the minute hand of an outsized wall clock climbed painfully, and in the dead pause of each notch, the sound of the clock ticking it's certainty filled the lobby.

Abruptly, as the sound of a car crunched up the drive, his front legs struck a pose. One stout paw readjusted itself on the hearth while the other seemed to take a calculated measure against the other as if an even distribution of weight was crucial and allowed a look of attention and recognition to play across his usually expressionless face. Still, he sat; watched the light and dark blurs move on the other side of the glass. His ears twitched, pitched forward as if to catch and caress the slightest sound of her approach. The polished brass doorknob turned and the reflected room righted itself.

As the heavy door was pushed inward by a white gloved hand Morris' head shot forward like an electronic telescope automatically adjusting it's site; a movement, not one of cunning, as might be predicted for such a sturdy and lion surfaced fellow, but freeing instead, an action at once involuntary and naturally calculating; more of an anticipatory response to events outside himself.

His eyes widened and a fever-like tremor coursed along his body as the door opened and admitted a vision dressed from head to toe in white.

The length of white, diaphanous gauze fabric framed her face and long dark hair, loosely fell past rain colored eyes, brushing the side of her flushed cheeks and laid itself in soft puddles along narrow shoulders before cascading in sari-like folds over every portion of her small body until the whole of it ended in a narrow opening at the bottom just large enough for her feet to walk through in small, white kid shoes.

To Morris it seemed Alicia's bright gaze locked onto his as a beacon of satisfaction and it was for him like the last day of dimness and the first day of light coming together.

The tall, uniformed man she called Zee let himself in behind her and in one fluid motion gently shut the door, lifted his taupe colored cap by the black bill, removed both gloves and wedged them inside the band and shoved the whole affair under his arm; ending the routine by running a practiced hand through his wavy, taffy-colored hair.

Alicia spoke something soft and short to the clerk behind the desk which Morris could not understand no matter how far he leaned toward it. The eager clerk seemed to be expecting her and quickly placed a key into her upturned hand which she accepted with a smile and passed on to Zee.

So great was his fascination, Morris looked to be an artist's rendition of himself as he watched the shiny brass key pass from hand to hand. It could have been, for all he knew, his passport to eternity, and would have followed her into the fires of hell if that was where she intended going. She turned instead toward the doors she had just entered and his breath caught at the thought of her going so soon.

Zee reopened the front door and spoke to someone on the other side, motioning inward while Alicia stood patiently aside with both feet perfectly still.

The double entrance doors were swung wide. Morris watched while men marched through the opening bearing all manner of large and small cartons. A wondrous assortment of furniture they carried through the doors to follow Zee up the flight of stairs. Alicia moved behind them and Morris, who, finally stirred into action, turned and followed the jaunty entourage to the second floor as naturally as if he went by engraved invitation.

He had watched for weeks while workers removed to the bare walls everything in rooms 216 and 218. Watched as they knocked a large opening in the common wall, essentially making one large room. Morris sat away to the side. He had learned the hard way that corners were not a safe place to hide. Corners were the first place workers headed to stack things. At first they almost ran him down with ladders and paint buckets. Then they ignored him until he felt himself to be invisible.

Invisible like Michael. Michael, of the old time people, who came on silent feet to watch by the windows. Morris knew that Michael, as well as others, had been there a long time roaming the hotel as if they owned the place, disappearing into walls and floors or even tenuous air. As a kitten he had tried following them once or twice but that action only made his head ache. He made a game of running up and down the halls, skidding around corners trying to anticipate where they might reappear. But that was like chasing his tail and he soon tired of the game. As he got older and arthritis set in he just wished he could take such an easy shortcut as that.

What kind of life must they own? Morris had often wondered. Or was it just that they had not laid claim to it? He, like them.

Sun filtered through the tall, unadorned windows and mingled a sparkling benefaction of light in the center of the room. New solid walnut cornices cast golden shadows of artificial light around the sand colored walls and onto the polished oak floor. Morris felt he had gone suddenly deaf as a deeply sculpted white carpet, effectively muffling all sound, was rolled across the floor leaving a three foot wood border all around.

Rich walnut book cases made instant wall dividers. Filled from the contents of brown boxes they created an attractive entrance from the hallway as well as an effective baffle for her office space behind.

A music center and speakers, together with all the attending wire and compact discs were brought and placed according to some unnamed law Morris could not read. The movers began to uncoil and connect wires which he, suddenly tempted by an unreasonable urge to chase and pounce upon, resisted in the name of accountability and something resembling mock decorum.

Furniture of classic make and design was maneuvered into perfect position. Likewise, lamps with lustrous gold bands and tall, light diffusing shades were placed on free formed end tables created from slabs of solid walnut. Softly cushioned occasional chairs and an over-sized sofa upholstered in a coarse eggshell colored fabric reminiscent of Mediterranean richness were set out from the wall on the carpet.

A large walnut desk was brought across the room and placed out from the windows. It's top caught the natural light and the tightly burled patterns shimmered like pulled and knotted taffy. A matching high backed arm chair sat straight and stately behind the desk with its back to the windows.

Black lacquered Chinese screens ornately inlaid with jade, mother-of-pearl and ivory were placed behind the sofa and chairs. Ivory colored pedestals supported Chinoiserie pottery and cachepots of luxuriant green ferns.

All were directed into their assigned places like musical notes; Alicia stood, the conductor, as before a well rehearsed orchestra. A glorious blend of taste and utility, the beautiful room appeared now a complete monochromatic symphony of cream and white. The occasional smattering of color expressed in paintings and screens, silk pillows and fern, was scattered like extravagant jewels around the room.

As the last of the furniture was placed, the movers, having worked throughout the day departed and the young girl and the marmalade cat turned to close themselves into room 218.

Seven

Visit The Soul In Sleep

As the door clicked behind him, Morris, anticipating Alicia's every move, stepped aside and raised his yellow, almond shaped eyes to her face. She had, during the course of the day, pushed the veil-like swaddle from her head. It lay in diffused white folds around her shoulders. From the windows a late afternoon sun divided fine wisps of her hair into two dusky wings around her face.

At her throat a star shaped spark of light pierced Morris' open stare and for the first time he caught sight of the unusual brooch she wore. It was a likeness of a dark, foreign looking little man holding a small crystal ball in the hollow of his crossed legs. Morris' head realigned and he stared into the crystal as if to fathom a future in his own reflection.

Morris and Alicia surveyed with satisfaction the finished room. Alicia gave a little Zen-like bow of respect for the room she had so often seen in her minds eye. A bow for the discovery of the task; the task at hand; the task yet to come.

She had always had it. Respect had been there for the dream of it; had been there in the search for it, and deep respect was there for the reality of it. To this room she had come in her dreams. Many times called there at first by an otherness, a personality in need of experience and clarification; a need to explore its dimensionality. She had behaved towards each task as if it existed before the materialization.

Alicia crossed to the stereo and selected a compact disk from its white and red jacket, gently fitted it into the round receptacle in the machine and punched the play button.

Strains of Jan Van der Roost's *Flashing Winds* gathered and formed around her like a glad friend. 'Oh.' She felt rather than thought. 'Oh, the music we made.' Her hands automatically arranged themselves around a vanquished flute and her fingers flew as if they trilled along the real instrument instead of air and her breath stopped in her throat as she raised her eyes as if for direction and met the eyes of Ms. Ellie Patterson who caught the notes in the very air around her.

During her senior year in high school when she was fifteen, and the band was competing in the Mid-West International Band and Orchestra Concert in Chicago, she had looked up from the composed notes of *Where Never Lark or Even Eagle Flew* to read of some manifest calamity betrayed in Ms. Patterson's sorrow filled eyes.

Afterward, when she had managed to play through the mist, she was told that her parents had been killed in an automobile-train accident.

They had crossed the same tracks, in the same manner, many times. She saw them in her minds eye. Her mother reading the newspaper as her father drove them home. She, sitting beside him, had opened the newspaper and held it up to shield her face from the setting sun as she read. He was preoccupied with something on the radio as they approached the hazardous crossing. There was neither automatic arm to block the traffic nor alarm to sound at this country road crossing. It had been a matter of split second timing as the crossing lights began to flash right to left, right to left. Lights as hidden behind her newspaper as the blare from the oncoming train was cloaked by the radio.

Alicia had not known. Had for a time blamed herself for not knowing. Had not foreseen and accused herself for being too busy to see. Could not readily know or see the overview from her parent's perspective. Could not bring herself to think it was their soul's choice to leave her alone in the world. But, she knew without question that Rachael and Hank had in life been inseparable, could not by death, be parted. This was the way of it, this was the why of it. The closer the bond between people, she knew, the closer they followed each other into the other dimensions of life.

Alicia's had been a very busy senior year. Among many other academic activities the Springdale High School Symphonic Winds, of which she was an important member, had been chosen as one of four bands out of 150 international applicants to perform in Chicago.

Ms. Patterson had chosen, whether by chance or fate, for this concert, the intricate, life validating piece of John Curnow's *Where Never Lark or Even Eagle Flew* based upon a poem by John Gillespie Magee, JR.

Written by the 19 year old American volunteer with the Royal Canadian Air Force who was killed in action December 11, 1941, the noble elegance of the poem began for her with the first lines as read in Ms. Patterson's resonant southern voice.

"Oh, I have slipped the surly bonds of earth." These words seemed to intertwine with those of her mother and father until it seemed a chorus swell of joy could be heard even by those earth-bound entities which were the essence of the old Crescent Hotel. Though these lyric's were meant to convey John Magee's glorious feelings of flight, they seemed prophetic, appropriate and calming in retrospect. *"And danced the skies on laughter-silvered wings."*

The retelling washed over her still bright loss and

71

the words rang and the music swelled after the bittersweet memory: *"Up the long delirious blue I've topped the wind-swept heights with easy grace, where never lark or even eagle, flew; and while with silent, lifting wind I've trod the high untrespassed sanctity of space, put out my hand, and touched the face of God."*

"Oh, the music. I remember the music." She said aloud to Morris. "To be again in it's sweet ebb and flow, for are we not as Shelly imagined us to be; formed as notes of music are, for one another, though dissimilar?" Morris squared his listening eyes and basked in her attention.

Alicia imagined the pride in their music as if she had been the parent; felt a foster pride beyond parental ownership. We may have been young, she thought, some of us may even have been unwise but when we made music all were conducted forward into a stream of consciousness beyond any dazzling independence, transcending individual talent. Each became a vibratory unit of sound; resonating, leveling in distended waves of sound apart from our knowledge or even consent. Sound, we glorified in that far away place; notes we brought as trophy's home.

Alicia used music as a life force; felt it on a different level. Music seemed to insert itself directly into her veins, hastening a seeming preternatural psychic ability out of the realm of customary onto another level of being as genuine and viable as that of any life around her. And so it seemed to her, in that person-alized dusk, it could not be imagined that children thus tethered by adolescence were so freed by their music, this precocious enmity of sound, free to fly, to explore every nuance of sound yet be fully controlled. Controlled as if the conductor held by the feet a gentle lark one minute and the next had everything she could do to stay the flight of a powerful, rising eagle bound for glory. Control, however sought, however gained could not equal that contribution given by each individual, that which was offered up for its own sake.

A prescience of sound now as crashing water everywhere beat upon rocks a multiple crescendo of heart beating percussion..., clearly designed..., clearly arriving, entwined with haunting melody, climbed toward a known end..., ever arriving, so near childlike, tender and innocent one moment, like bells on bicycles frolicking on a summers day. Next, an entire knowledge, transported now by their own will to rise and fly and if a song was any sweeter, it has never been heard.

Does music, she wondered, could music in and of itself, so mount and build in places as to compel itself forward no matter the instrument, no matter the players, can then be caught..., as if in loosely woven baskets..., the conductor..., the weaver?

Alicia did not have the kind of close relationship with friends which is the bellwether of youth. While they respected the general use of her talent, of it they had no real understanding. She was confident for what she was in herself; for the way she held still.

Because Alicia sometimes answered questions before they were asked, it was supposed and feared she could always read minds. Therefore she did not enjoy the easy camaraderie on which her peers seemed to flourish. As well, she had only observed their combat and struggles, the exaggerated fits and starts of emotion in which the young seemed to embroil themselves daily.

In truth, they had little in common. For instance, Alicia did not particularly enjoy watching television with it's two dimensional subjects when the full drama of real life recreated itself daily in her own living room. She did not understand the fixed fascination some had with video games and did not own a personal computer. For another, unlike most teen age girls, clothes and makeup and boys were not her obsession. She did not realize that for most girls her age hanging out at the shopping mall was as important to them as breathing.

They explained when asked about their classmate Alicia's attitude about such things, it was "no big deal." Alicia's live and let live attitude went a long way toward promoting respect and caring between them. From her they sensed a deeper level of understanding; a non-judgmental, unconditional empathy.

Alicia held the respect and compassion of many. Like some prearranged code between them, Zee had understood from the beginning. As had Ms. Patterson, who, not only listened, she had a way of listening as though your's was the only voice.

For the rest of her senior year of high school an adult cousin of her mother's from Spring Creek, Beth Anne Sharp had come to live with Alicia and her life, if not the bright, weightless waltz her parents had envisioned for her future, had achieved a sureness of purpose, a deep sense of knowing, and a need to assist others with their life's struggles.

Eight

The Pale Cast Of Thought

In this way Alicia Townsend, at age sixteen, already one of Arkansas' most famous psychic, healer and trance mediums, arrived and installed herself at the Crescent Hotel. It was in her mind to create a beautiful and peaceful, yet accessible setting for her work.

She had not wanted a storefront in which to display her talent. Heaven only knew how many neglected windows and dilapidated signs she had seen along streets; in run down sections of disturbed and intractable cities where once even complete billboards had announced a bright hope; offered solutions to life's complexities on an hourly basis, and perhaps, for all anyone knew, it's advertiser might have given more than was taken. Many such had been seen along country highways in garishly painted houses set tenuously behind hand painted signs which, however optimistically, read:

Tea Leaf

Card and Palm Reading

OPEN, COME IN

Signs which invited the troubled and curious passersby to ask personal questions of "Madame" whomever; who knows all, tells all; presumably day or night. These signs, whether painted on plate glass or wood shingle, implied a singular advice or dauntless intercession could be gained between the client and some unseen, all knowing agency, in exchange for coin. This impersonal activity had never appealed to her, neither had it seemed exceptionally life affirming.

The management and staff of the Crescent Hotel

would later recall and mark the day Alicia Townsend chose the Crescent Hotel as her headquarters as having been itself a fortuitous event bordering on the supernatural, while the owners would regard her medical intuitiveness as a natural progression for all concerned.

From the hotel's window Alicia saw, in the gathering dusk, past the garden to the parking lot below where Zee made slow, deliberate, dust annihilating strokes with a soft chamois on the restored Cord. She smiled to herself as she remembered the excitement in his voice and the total gladness on his face when he first told her he'd found the perfect car for her. Her only instruction to him: it must be old and it must be fine.

While others were driving their parent's cars in carefree social assembly Alicia had found it a risky business for herself. After her parent's accident she tried a few times to drive her cousin Beth's car. Almost from the start she discovered she could not keep the larger part of herself from being pulled wherever she was needed. Once while driving she had felt her 'self' tugged away, as if it were at the end a piece of stretched elastic, leaving her body to run the car into a ditch. That little episode had forced her back to a sudden, irrevocable truth and she learned the hard way that you can not really drive safely and do anything else at the same time. No matter how hard you try. After that Beth had said, "It's easy Alicia, but you have to keep your mind on the road." Easier said then done, she figured, and asked Zee to help.

Sam Cravens had lived with his hard working mother and younger brother in a small house at the edge of the Springdale High School campus just off Highway 71B on Emma Avenue. Sam was intelligent with a ready smile; liked by all who knew him as long as he didn't try to sing. Friends would howl and stop their ears when he began his out-of-tune crooning. "M..a..n!" they said. "You couldn't carry a tune in a bucket!" Singing was definitely not his forte. Fortunately he was a respectable Bulldog running back and knew how to carry a football. No singing required.

The nickname Zee began when, as a lanky sophomore, with a little helpful blocking from his friends, he, even with thick eyeglasses, consistently ran the football up the field in a zigzag pattern and the cheerleaders took to yelling "CRA Z!, CRA Z!" every time the ball was snapped. Tall and arrow straight with sun streaked blond hair and blue agate eyes he was thought to be quite a catch by the girls but due to his absent father and limited funds was not necessarily viewed by their mothers as marriage material. They somehow found it in their hearts, however, to let their daughters date Zee if only for the prestige it lent the fathers at lunch every Monday morning at Rotary Club.

Zee did not have a car and held no hopes of ever owning one. The family barely scrapped by on his mother's small salary at a clothing store downtown. Of course he had done the usual boy things for spending money. Paper routes on a second-hand bicycle, mowing lawns with an outmoded push machine, and when he got old enough moved up to counter clerk at a McDonald's around the corner. In short, he did anything which did not require transportation. Virtually everywhere he went he either walked, was driven or hitch-hiked. He depended mostly on caring friends, football buddies, Clark Ross whom they early on nicknamed Granny for reasons unknown or politely forgotten, Gerald Jones and David Oliver Galloway, Dog for short. They called each other Ole as if they held a first name in common. It was always "Ole Granny" this, or "Ole Jones" that, "Ole Dog done 'er" or "Ole Zee aced it."

He did not often speak of his father but once when they were sophomores Zee asked Dog to hitch-hike with him over the Boston Mountains south to Fort Smith. Zee had been told answers by his mother to some of his questions about his father, but he scarcely knew from the dim picture he was able to sketch of him in his minds-eye, just what kind of person his father was. He was at an age where questions and curiosity about the absent member of their family needed answers. Absent from their daily lives as well as absent with any sort of financial aid.

Zee asked Alicia where he could find his father and she had given him a precise location. "You will find him living in a small white house on 25th, a side street off the main road just past the Buick car dealership. It sits behind a low white picket fence. It's after dark now but I see a light, like there's a large neon sign close by blinking first white then red onto his face as he gets out of a late model car. He's wearing some sort of military uniform. "She paused and scrunched her eyes as if to see closer."Army."

Instead of the usual hour or so it took to drive, it had taken the two boys over three hours to hitch a ride and knock on his father's front door and Zee, by then, was as taut as a piano wire.

They found him exactly where Alicia had envisioned and tried for over an hour to engage him but achieved little more than a semblance of clumsy conversation. Zee, in his naive earnestness thought a light hearted banter would win his father.

At the most Zee wanted to repair the lines of contact long severed. At the very least he held out a fervent hope that his father would be impressed with his spunk and forthright effort. Neither had been forth-coming. In truth, nothing Zee said or evidenced seemed to penetrate the man who stoically sat idly by looking into the middle distance before him. Zee could have endured anything but the total indifference with which his own heart-felt enthusiasm was met. Dog felt his good friend did not in any way deserve the affront.

When they left, Dog thought the very least Zee's unresponsive father could have managed was to stay on the porch until they were out of sight; see them safely down the road. If he had watched them go, the normal politeness afforded even some stranger, he could not have missed the sight of his fine son, a son that any father would be proud to claim as his own, walk stooped shouldered past the wax lavished, highly polished blue of his own car in the driveway. It's shining brightness stood as idle and provocative as a mirror and he could not have failed to see, if he had bothered to look, the trodden expression on his son's face reflected in it as he slipped quietly past the car to stand beside the busy highway, there to stick out his thumb to the on coming diesel choked traffic for the lonely ride home. Instead, not so much as a handshake had passed between them. In fact, the only thing his father reached out for was the door; to shut it behind them before they had ever really gone. Dog's face burned as he looked back at the already drawn shades at the windows and his jaw ached from their clenched tightness.

After that Alicia asked Zee to find her a car; to be her official driver. He, a good two years older than she and both, far wiser than their peers. She would direct it's use and he would have full charge of it's care.

His friends said, "It's time you learned how to

drive, son," and took turns teaching him to drive in their own father's cars. Since they went to school and held various jobs during the day, these "lessons", for the most part, were given at night up and down the counties darkest country roads. Sometimes these lessons were given under the influence of a few beers and so if a stray cow or mailbox loomed suddenly, each was on it's own.

Zee knew that whatever antique automobile he would find for Alicia would no doubt have a standard shift. He must learn to drive well if he expected to earn a chauffeur's license.

On a hot dusty night Dog drove his father's old Ford truck, which by now smelt like a bar with the door open, out past the rodeo grounds and cattle sale barns to the edge of town and stopped where the pavement ended in total darkness. Dog moved on the other side of the gear shift, crowding Clark next to the door while Zee went around and got in on the drivers side.

As Dog issued instructions, Zee began the irreverent procedure of striping gears and lurching the truck into a darkness suddenly made unfamiliar in part by the beer and the loud crunching of gravel and by the angle at which he sat on the business side of the shift column. In the narrow cab his left shoulder, slumped as it was against the door, caused his hands and arms to reach out at odd right angles to grip the steering wheel, which then tended to throw his eyes out of focus behind his thick glasses and the dark world in front of the pale head-lights out of balance. Beyond, in the near distance, could be seen the rushing head-lights of an oncoming vehicle fast followed by a high rooster tail of dust made red in the glowing tail-lights, indicative of the speed by which it approached.

Zee shifted the overworked and shrieking gears in preparation for the onslaught everyone feared coming straight at them, licked his lips and set to singing an unrelenting open air version of *In The Sweet By and By* into the wind. "Oh, godamightytherehegoes!" Dog said. "Keep your foot hard on the clutch!" he shouted. "Shift all the way now!"

"Hold 'er steady in the road man!" Yelled Granny, gripping the right door frame with his sweaty armpit.

"Ohmagod, he can't see the son-a-bitch!" Dog cried. "Zee! Get over damnit!"

Zee only licked his lips between verses, hunched beady eyed and determined over the wheel hell bent for the wrong side of the road like a dog running sideways with a tick in his ear. At least he looked determined as all get out but later said it was just a limp disguise for sheer terror. Suddenly in the place of three husky football hero's there could be seen a multitude of white rimmed saucer eyes and open mouths and all thought of tomorrow vanished as each past indiscretion was reviewed and asked forgiveness of for being so young, dumb and untruthful. Too soon the oncoming truck was upon them and Zee's hands froze in a locked position on the wheel. Giant swirls of dust as horn's blared and spitting gravel flew into the cab from the low shoulder of the road opposite and the truck sped past on the wrong side as Zee took his half out of the middle. Instead of slowing down he finished the chorus, "In the sweet by and byyyiii...., we shall meet on that bea..u..tiful shorrrrr! Yah Hoooo!" No one noticed if he was in tune. No one cared. They were just grateful the other guy had gone low on the other side so they did not have to take out Becker's Machine Shop.

No one said much of anything as they continued at

a good clip into the dark countryside, breeze from the window cooled their faces and dried their wet, nerve tingled underarms. Zee began to feel in optimistic control on the straight-away until Dog had him stop in the middle of the road and practice backing up.

"Look out Zee!" Granny shouted, head hanging out the window. "Oh, sheeeeut! Man, you done wiped out ole man Perry's mailbox!" When they looked back the bashed in side of it could be seen in the cracked red glow of the taillights as it dangled in silent disregard along-side the paint smeared post. They hardly had time to return their attention to the road before Zee had ground the gears in a fast getaway and Dog wondered what he'd tell his father in the morning.

Before long Zee was getting the hang of this driving business and declared his intention of going out to the community of Johnson where his girl friend Amy Joy Bullock lived. They switched drivers to go across town and switched back again after turning off the paved highway onto the gravel of Harmon Schoolhouse Road. As Zee steered, the road, made familiar by all the times he had walked it, suddenly appeared more shadowed and a lot less roomy than he remembered. He hoped to keep to his side of the road, at least until Amy Joy could see him actually driving.

From the dark appearance of the house they had lost track of time and so Zee drove the truck slowly past, disappointed but, practiced and proud.

"Where you headed now Zee?" Dog said as the crunching tires echoed sound along the fleeing embankment and against the palpable darkness.

"I gotta pee." Granny said suddenly.

"Yep. Me too." Zee said. "Gotta make room for more beer, doncha know!"

A familiar road loomed. "Pull off here to the creek."

Dog said. It was to this deep wooded spot that they usually took their girlfriends to park and make out in the dark beside the wide free flowing creek.

They got out of the truck and stumbled off in different directions. When regrouped they drank another beer or two and lit up White Owl Cigars. One minute they were whooping it up, splashing each other and generally "cuttin' the fool" and in the next they were whooping up greasy hamburgers and French fries they had eaten earlier at Jackson's Drive-In, and Zee had disappeared into the darkness.

"Zee," they called finally into the shadows. "Zee, where are you, we gotta go man, it's after twelve."

"Zee?"

Nothing.

"Zee?"

They split up and searched the thick undergrowth on the bank. "I think I see him lying up on the bridge!" Granny shouted and began to cross the swinging foot bridge. Halfway across he looked over the side and saw him floating face down in the water. "Zee....!" He shouted into the night and plunged in after him. As he turned his head to hit the water, out of the corner of his eye he saw Zee lying in a heap back up on the bridge. He had jumped in without a thought to his own life and limb, to rescue a floating log.

"There he is Dog." Granny pointed. "Son-of-a-gun's passed out on the bridge," he sputtered coming up for air. He stood in the waist high water, slung his wet hair out to the side and wadded ashore. "Come help me get him in the truck."

On the way home they stopped in town at a little all night grocery store they sometimes frequented for buttermilk to settle their stomachs.

Before it was done the driving lessons had cost

their fathers a few dollars in repairs to the family vehicles but they were largely supportive of the boy's efforts; sparing with their anger and comments as well. The fathers, for some unfathomable reason, perhaps because of their own unreachable youth in memory yet green, "cut them a lot of slack." Knew they were good boys, good scouts, just doing what boys have to do.

When Zee found the magnificent old Cord for Alicia, he was able, with a new drivers license in his wallet, to take it for a test drive.

Nine

Reckoning

As Alicia watched from the second story window of the hotel Zee straightened from polishing the Cord's side chrome exhaust. Chamois in one hand he tugged his shirt cuff down his jacket sleeve and watched a late model car careen up the hill and brake in front of the hotel. In an obvious rush a young man flung open the car door and was half way up the well worn steps before the engine died. When, in a few moments there was an urgent knock at the door, Alicia knew it was he; knew the reason he had come.

"I've been expecting you, Michael." she said as she opened the door.

"I took a chance that you would still be here." He said, winded. "I remembered you were setting up the studio today." His green elfin eyes shone out below a high freckled forehead topped by a riot of russet-colored hair. His eyes did a quick appraisal of the room. "I like what you've done here," he said. "It's great. The Prentice looks right at home on that wall."

They had found an easy camaraderie when she had walked into his EAGLES RISE Art Gallery down on Spring Street the week before, looking for something special to add the right color and movement to her rooms at the Crescent. After she told him the nature of her work he had suggested an etching by a local artist Pat Prentice which depicted a single tree, bent and reshaped by a century of wind and rain, as much the work of nature as it was representative of Mr. Prentice' talent.

"I didn't like to ask you the other day in the gallery,

Alicia, but I really do need your help."

At twenty two, Michael Patrick O'Shawnessey McKinney had an artist's eye as well as a good head for business. He and his mother had come to Eureka Springs from Sedona, Arizona to set up an art gallery.

Michael's was one of many art galleries in Eureka Springs where some of the finest local artists place their work. Alicia had chosen to enter EAGLES RISE GALLERY for it's powerful emblem. Having been born in November she knew the scorpion was but one of the sign's talismans, the other was the eagle. Michael had added a second line to the outdoor sign board written in gold leaf calligraphy:

Where Eagles Rise By Their Own

Command To Soar.

That day she had been intent upon art as a whole but was caught immediately by a pair of riveting Julian Stanley eagles Michael had painstakingly selected and arranged as the centerpiece of the gallery. "Massive and powerful. Breathtaking," she had said standing in awe before the life sized bronze. She could almost hear the eagles, their black and white bodies caught mid-flight in courtship, scream the age old ritual out at the vast mountains and cold streams above which they flew.

As Michael began to guide her along the outer wall of the gallery he stopped before a brightly lit abstract oil.

"Will Bishop does a superb job of capturing color in his landscapes. I am particularly drawn to this one." He said. "The correlation of hues, his use of green blue to yellow as a vehicle of expression says peace to me. "Something in his voice made her turn and look full at him. He stood against an off-white, matt finished wall. "Bishop favors form over detail, focuses on color and shape."

As Alicia watched, his face and head began to take on a fuzzy outline of itself. It moved as he moved. "Ahh," she said to herself, "Michael's aura is a bit muddy." She saw it as a grey outline fading into tan-ish orange.

"Please, Michael," she used everyone's given name knowing how powerful the sound of one's own name is to the psyche. "If you will permit me to say...?" Alicia paused.

Michael heard in her voice an unexpected kindness; saw in her eyes a deep concern. "Oh," he said, "by all means, do...say what...."

"Color," she said, "is used very effectively in the treatment of illness and the well being of body, mind, spirit. You, I believe, are attracted to these particular colors for reasons you may not be aware of. Together, these colors, Michael, indicate to me, you might be having a problem sleeping at night."

"But, how could you possibly know...?" He looked startled at this perfect appraisal.

"Excuse it, if I have intruded, you see...," she broke off and pulled a business card from an outside pocket of the leather case she carried under her arm,"it is what I do."

Michael accepted the violet colored card:

Energy is All.
All is energy permeated with a Mysterious Music which resonates separate vibrations.
Personality is the vibration; soul, the music.
I read the music.
Alicia Townsend, Crescent Hotel

"I didn't like to ask for free advice the other day in the gallery. It would have been quite selfish of me..., unsuitable." Michael flushed and knew the tan freckles which marked his face from birth telling of his Irish heritage, now stood out against a beet red background and was embarrassed.

He had come to Alicia, he said, because she had been right about his not sleeping well. This was a last effort to understand a strange, recurring dream which had haunted him for several years but, since arriving here, he had experienced almost nightly. His face webbed over with thin lines of fatigue, he looked out at her from eyes sunken in green hollows where they retreated when he'd had no sleep.

"I sensed something was troubling you while I was in the gallery, Michael. Please come in and sit down." Alicia gestured toward the couch and moved toward the stereo. "I was just listening to a favorite piece of music. Excuse me, while I adjust the volume."

While Michael made himself comfortable at the end of the couch Morris watched from one to the other as Alicia slid the CD's volume down to conversation level. She kicked off her shoes and sat in the high backed chair placed at right angles to the couch next to Michael.

Morris, when he was certain she meant to remain in that position, spread himself across the curved arch of her foot until it looked like he'd been poured there from a pitcher of warm butter streaked syrup and began a kind of syncopated purring in time to their heart's rhythm; listened to the smooth give and take of their words.

"Alicia," Michael started, "I don't exactly know what this recurring dream means but I'm always happy when it starts. And it can start in such a benign way. Some familiar setting, anywhere, to catch me off guard, then it's like I sense something coming. Fast! Like I'm being set up for a jolt. A flash slams into my gut." With the back of his hand he blotted the beads of sweat that had started to form on his forehead. "How do I begin to tell you the dread that engulfs me, the terror....?" Cold sweat mopped. "Then, very quickly, before I realize what's happening, before I can back away or rethink my step, there I am in this terrifying free fall! I'm falling from a great height and.... whew," Michael stopped.

"Take a nice deep breath, Michael."

He forced himself to follow her instruction. Closed his eyes and took a deep breath.

"Don't close your eyes yet Michael. At this point it will only make you dizzy."

"Damn it all, just sitting here my heart is hammering so hard it feels like it will explode right out of my chest. Alicia, I've always been afraid of looking down over the side of a building or over a canyon but now I can't climb even the shortest stepladder to hang a painting in the gallery anymore without my head spinning with acute vertigo. I wake up at night drenched in sweat. I am terrified to shut my eyes for fear of falling and crashing into that bottomless, dark chasm." Another deep breath. "Real or imagined, it shakes me so I can hardly function. And now, to make matters worse," he shuddered in mid-sentence, "I have developed this blasted insomnia and fierce acrophobia as a consequence." He seemed to inhale down to his toes and let it out in a long, shuddering sigh. "I don't think I can take much more of this," he said, cradling his head between both hands.

Alicia knowingly helped to fill in the gaps of his story.

They might have so continued, each engrossed in the speaking and listening of the other but for the great hammering at the door. Morris shot straight up as if from a cannon. There followed a small, contained silence while a gust of wind wailed around the corner and likewise beat upon the window.

Alicia barely had her hand on the knob when the door was pushed open by a wild-eyed, blond woman of Brunhildesque proportions who barged into the gentle calmness of the room like a runaway locomotive, steam driven and gaining momentum in a pair of stained, tight white pants and tee shirt, the word H A R K ! stretched across her ample bosom in orange and red day-glow letters.

She entered the room without ceremony as though the words THE LORD THY GOD COMETH emblazoned on her back were invitation enough. A bleeding Jesus Christ was seen draped across every letter T as though they represented crosses and him crucified there three times in the same day-glow paint.

"You can't fool us, you little devil worshipin' heathen!," she spat, breathing hard as if she had spent hours getting up a violent head of steam. Alicia recoiled in alarm, her arms flew up automatically as if she had been struck by the limp concordance bible the woman brandished before her like the charged rapier she intended. The odor of liniment and bleach reminiscent of a horses stall trailed after her and cut into the sinuses.

"Who are you? State your business here," Alicia demanded, recovering.

"Well!" the woman shouted, spit flying without introduction as if it couldn't wait to quit the raging mouth. "Everbody knows who ah am! Ah am Sister Dolly Garvin." But she could see the sound of it fell flat in the lovely room and suddenly she supposed herself to be more inventive than that and so summoned a higher, louder voice to cover the rest of her vital material.

"Ah preach the gospel of the Loward down at the Salvation Abundant Vision Experience Divine

Tabernacle. That's SAVED in capitol letters if you don't know what it is! We done long ago SAVED this whole town from witches like you."

Alicia had the sudden urge to laugh or allow her mouth to spring open in complete disbelief, but she did neither. Instead she said, "You can't just barge in here! I'm with a client."

"Yes! Well! We done saved each and everbody from the everlastin' fires a hell!" Sister Dolly Garvin pushed spent air out through flared nostrils as if in frequent precaution against blowout damage from an over heated boiler. "And you ain't agonna bring your pretty little blasphemin' self around here!" She bellowed down at Alicia. "Nosir! Not here amongst godfearinfolks you ain't! In this town nur any around here where the Loward God will strike you down and lay a brimstone afire around on your pretty little head for practicin' blasphemin' and cast you into a fiery furnace for disobeyin' his law. Praisegodandhisholynameahmen!" Sister Dolly shouted, her face now a study of blotched pink and white rimmed fury. The raging mouth had begun to move before her feet were firmly planted in the middle of the room and her eyes had, like two black struck coals, already tagged each warm body there, separate and distinct sinners all. From his crouched perspective under the couch, Morris finally allowed himself to blink.

As if a determination, not entirely in her favor, had been reached, Sister Dolly caught a glimpse of motion to the side. Her head swung around like it was skewered on a greased turn spit and her eyes looked about to pop when she saw Michael come off the couch and move rapidly towards her. She took a step back and rocked on her heels as if to replant herself and had it not been for her morbid curiosity about such things she would have been terrified that he was going to grab her, throw her down and ravish her right there on the floor in front of 'godn' everbody.'

Sister Dolly Garvin had heard of all such evil, repulsive goings on in circles such as she imagined this to be. Sexual orgies she had heard whispered about; sex acts urged onto people all too willing to do the devil's bidding and had, in fact, waited until she saw Michael go up to the room, in an unacknowledged desire of an opportunity to catch them in one of those profoundly despicable acts. She was sure of the devil's rights, hadn't she often enough preached how he took what he wanted, not what he was offered, but she was not so sure of her own... Michael only stood beside Alicia with his arms stiff at his sides and glared at Sister Dolly with a look reserved for mad dogs and trained lions.

"It's you!" Michael said."You're the one who's been following me. I've seen you peering into the window of my shop every day, leaving your greasy hand prints on the window. Hanging around, pawing at my car. What do you do, hide somewhere to watch me? Does it give you some kind of perverse pleasure to watch me clean up after you?"

Sister Dolly Garvin almost lost her bearing and momentum as she saw Michael's accusing face near enough to touch, the face that had begun to haunt her days and own her dreams at night. The face which had from the first minute she laid eyes on it, like some long sought possession, had stabbed itself into her heart .

Alicia was no stranger to this kind of fundamental tirade. With little variation the same words were spoken with the same intonations by thousands of fired up evangelists at any given time across

America. They viewed themselves as a breed apart, removed from the masses, their mission exempt from ordinary honesty and integrity. Were, with few exceptions, sociopaths loving the sound of their own voices. With little or no provocation they would just as soon start their spiel, "Brother, are you washed in the blood?, "or some such other." self serving utterance, in the aisle at Walmart as in church and once started they didn't seem to know when to quit. If interrupted they were perfectly capable of ignoring any and all reasonable dialog, continuing right where they left off. It was next to impossible to stop them altogether. People could insult them, walk away, faint, or be carried out of tent or tabernacle and it would not even slow them down. Beguiling and thoughtless, they were rapacious beyond all comprehension. Alicia was just at the point of telling her to leave when Sister Dolly took a deep breath and with something like the snap of her backbone jerked herself and her gumption up a notch, dared Michael to stop her and stabbed the evoked bible an inch from Alicia's steady nose."And you! Missy, you will burn in hell forever!" Sister Dolly lifted the book, this time at the heavens straight up, it's worn leatherette cover sagged back over a red knuckled fist, deserted the quivering red and black printed pages in mid-air and Alicia was reminded of what a sheriff's deputy had told her about old hippies and their marijuana. He said that the bible, with it's sheer pages, simply represented a ready supply of rolling papers. Look inside a hippie's bible and chances are you'd find hundreds of pages torn out. Smoked. Inhaled straight into the body of man.

Sister Dolly glared down at Alicia as from an imperious height while keeping a close eye on Michael so that she appeared before them a towering, sputtering, hairy lipped Elmer Gantry descanting a

Dies Irae of judgment and wrath over Alicia's petite frame.

"You! Nur none like you, little lady... Hunna humma...," she was just getting into her groove, "are gonna come around here aforetelling and pertending ahealing right under sweet JEESUS's nose!" Sounds came out of expelled breath. It began in her lungs making pumping, connecting sounds. It was not so much verbiage as it was an overuse of breath like air raking over the reeds of an accordion. Between words, and in mid-sentence, she threw in this "hunna humma" sound helter skelter and just when a person got used to it, you couldn't count on it. "Hunna humma," she continued, "No-sir, you are doing the devil's work!" Giving no one the chance to interject or retaliate she pointed the book toward the window in the direction of the Gulliver sized statue of Christ standing on the top of East Mountain, washed white in the light of the early rising moon. Sister Dolly's curl lipped snarl seemed to draw back on itself as little beads of sweat began to form in the brown fuzz at the far ends of her mouth. "He sees you a doin' all this evil, hunna humma...don't you think he can't!" She looked around in sudden desperation as if trying to find a ready example.

One of Sister Dolly's failings was once she got started, she never knew when to quit. She took it as a high compliment and deemed it part of her success that her congregation squirmed and itched to leave her presence every Sunday afternoon when it got to be 12:30, 1:00 O'clock.

Alicia was incredulous to the point of numbness at the woman's smug, presumptive manner while Sister Dolly Garvin tried to convert her by screaming a diatribe into her face like a 19th century circuit riding preacher in a hurry to get to the next town of unbelievers.

She snapped the book shut once again under Alicia's nose. "You are a blasphemer of the first water, hunna humma...and a thief in the other if you think you can come over here and steal in his holy name! You can't go messin' aroun' in his bidness and takin' people's hard earned money for it! Nosir! Hunna....That money don't rightly belong to you! It belongs to them that has the true, legitimate word of God, hummahuna... and don't you forget another thing, Missy, God says in his Great and Holy book," she gave the biddable scripture another jolt, "if he wants a thing done, he'll flat do it hisself! Hunna humma... it says so right here!" She was working to the heavy rhythm she had set for herself now. She began to fan and thumb alternately through the hapless pages, punched presumably at several examples of his wrath without either looking at them or lessening her stride. "He is doing a fine job of working in his mysterious ways, hunna humma... and you come along here tryin' to make him look slack. You, just throwing it up in his face!" With a loud 'throp' she clamped the bible shut with one red-knuckled hand not three inches from Alicia's face before slamming it like a smoking gun alongside her polyester clad leg and let out a long "hurruumph!" from her continuously loaded throat.

"I know who's child you are! Yesir!" Sister Dolly squinted one eye shut and bringing the bible up into firing position once again pointed with an unemployed long finger at a spot between Alicia's eyes. "You're the devil's own possession, thats who you are, hunna humma..and you got no bidness coming here messin' with this here Gawdfearin' communitee! Go back to where you came from or I'll know the reason why!"

After the woman's initial outburst Alicia had taken a deep breath and let her fanatical rampage play itself out. She realized what was happening and stood perfectly still. It would be useless, she knew, to try and reason with her. But now, she had enough.

"Please leave now," Alicia said quietly firm in her resolve. "Or I will call the police."

"All right then!" The woman flushed angrily, wheezing through white rimmed nostrils, her mouth set only in straight lines now. "All right! I'll go and leave you to your devil work!" She shrilled and turned to Michael, "And you to your devil worship!" Sister Dolly saw him, wanted desperately to grasp his sweet face to her bosom, hold him and croon to him of her saving grace. Save him from his young appetite and Alicia Townsend.

"But, I'm warning you!" She added hotly, shaking herself loose from so velvet a thought and wounded the air again with a merciless jab, this time the tissue thin, red lined and underscored pages waved about heedlessly and it's spine threatened to come apart in her hand. "You will pay the Lowardgodamighty's price if you don't quit the devil's blasphemin' and sinful carryin' on with that black magic and every other voodoo thing I know the devil's got you into doin'! Cuz' I'm telling you now, sister, you won't be allowed doin' all your evil in this Godfearin' communitee! The Loward Jeehova will smite you down, Hallalooya AMEN!"

This last she spewed forth as from a fire in her belly and quaked in something closely resembling an orgiastic spasm, turned and marched out the door, menacing the very fiber of the newly laid carpet, an arrogant, highly absurd caricature, a cartoon likeness totally out of place in the quiet elegance of the room. Sister Dolly's white polyester slacks, long ago rump sprung, shone out a pink and dimpled glow through the thin, threatened fabric and the straps of a black brassiere cut into her shoulders and sucked the tee shirt into deep trenches in her back as she went.

She had come under cover of darkness and into the darkness she returned, the bright day-glow colors of her tee shirt, THE LORD THY GOD COMETH shone out in the direction of her leaving. Alone she walked, her knees and whole body quivered as though she was on a mescaline high and she congratulated herself all the way down the hill. She had done her Christian duty. Marched herself righteously into her all night job at the Speedy Shop Convenience Store on the one corner just as proudly as she would have marched herself through the pearly gates of heaven on the other. Her singular and meritorious battle over evil this evening would most certainly have earned another star in her crown and, something like a sob caught in her throat at the thought, what did that sweet looking boy see in that Alicia bitch anyway; really.

"I have never heard such babbling nonsense." Michael said after she had gone, horrified at the women's outrageous behavior which still shuddered a palpable miasma of rage in the middle of the room. "That was a mean, spiteful woman. She must be mad."

Alicia closed her eyes and leaned her small back against the door, took one deep cleansing breath, and in her mind's desiring the peaceful room was restored to her once again. The negative energy dispelled.

"Michael," she said finally, seeing the utter distress in his eyes. "You must not bother your head about her. Try not to let it get under your skin. Be objective, recognize her for what she is. A scared, wanting human being and if the truth be known there are more like her out there than can be imagined. Somewhere under all that hate there is a great fear; a fear that was thoughtlessly instilled in a once innocent heart and she has hung onto it as if it were her life."

Michael, stranger to this brand of unrecused logic, gasped at her response. "Alicia, she could have snapped you in half! She is trouble with a capitol T!" He almost laughed at the unintented pun. "You heard how she's been following me. Just this morning she was outside my house in an old junky car. I don't know how long she had been out there."

In fact, Alicia had not liked the woman's actions any more than Michael had. "Never the less, there may even have been a twisted element of kindness in her visit here, Michael. Though it was probably the self sacrificing kindness of a martyr. It is all a matter of perception." She recognized the incredulous look on Michael's face and was reminded of something Plato had written regarding reality and it's perception.

"Alicia, either you are a saint or the most naive person on the planet." Michael sat in the corner of the couch and dropped his head into his hands as if his shoulders could no longer support it's weight. "This is all my fault."

Alicia walked to the bookshelf and pulled a small volume from the shelf. She smiled at the top of his head as she carried the book back to the chair. Morris made sure the coast was clear before he rearranged himself at her feet.

She opened the book. "Two people." she read aloud. "Two people are having a discussion. A philosopher and a musician. The philosopher said, "Let me show in a figure, how far our nature is enlightened or unenlightened: Behold! human beings living in an underground den, which has a mouth open toward the light and reaching all along the den; here they have been from their childhood, and have their legs and necks chained so that they cannot move, and can only see before them, being prevented by the chains from turning round their heads. Above and behind them a fire is blazing at a distance.

"'This is a strange image, and these are strange people," said the musician.'

"'Like ourselves," replied the philosopher, "they see only their own shadows, or the shadows of one another, which the fire throws on the opposite wall of the cave.'"

Alicia slid the book on the floor beside her chair. "You see, Michael, there are people who cannot see, and there are still others who will not see. It is the realization of not really seeing what you think you see and the effort to see that makes all the difference."

After Michael had gone, she, promising to look into his recurring dream difficulty, paused to consider one last time, the woman's visit.

People, she thought, seem to be content to go on with old dogmatic views and beliefs which have replaced the doctrine of love and service. She sensed that they would go on preaching hate programs from their pulpits, lashing out desperately, attacking blindly other churches and their religious dogma which they feel to be in competition with their own. Frozen in their dogmas, forever frozen in soul constricting stasis. Fearful of their once gallant and joyous nature. Alicia knew that no matter how well intentioned the woman might have been, she had in fact, become a bitter, spiteful woman in the process. She had become frustrated and angry because it was beyond her capacity to understand. Had become vengeful because not only did she not know any more how the world was supposed to operate, but, may never have known just who was in charge of the world. And she was even more afraid that no one was in charge.

Ten

Thoughts Too Deep For Tears

Outside the wind sang around the corner of the old hotel and rain started a steady pattering against the window. Alicia leaned back in the chair and Morris settled his bulk at her feet once more. She knew that Zee would not disturb her, but wait instead in the lobby downstairs until he could escort her out and drive her home to the lake.

As she sat with Morris at her feet her thoughts were on Michael of the green eyes. She relaxed into the chair and took several deep breaths and felt herself begin the sweet spinning; the familiar spinning which signaled the disengagement of mind from body; approach of the keen, accepted knowing.

She watched as a lighted arch came onto the wall in front of her. Streaked diagonally with light and dark shadows of interconnecting circles of light lifted and separated the perfect triskellins which danced within the arch.

Countless multi-shaded auras began to form and stack their varied vibrations along it's sides like well defined, never ending replicas of itself. As she watched it began to pulsate and climb the wall until it bent itself over onto the ceiling and all at once shot out a radiant beamed star pattern which began to pulsate in time with her own throbbing heart. At it's center the white angel appeared and seemed to wrap the entire hotel in light energy until the room was gradually emptied of it's beautiful furnishings, the walls and floor faded and disappeared. In it's place instead appeared a skeletal room as it had been at the time of the hotel's construction.

She sat very still. In the dark space between shadows she detected dust and sweat more than sound. Suddenly from high above in the rafters she heard a scream falling. Falling as if in slow, drawn out whispers of pain. A pain to last a century. And a body slammed at her feet, sending Morris, fur flying, to cower at the back side of the couch.

While Alicia watched, a wispy white form rose above the still body of a man and materialized itself into it's exact replica before her. An exact replica, an ancestor surely, of Michael who'd just left her.

She sat in her chair in the dark deserted room as he rose, came toward her, passed through her and came out the other side.... and from the prone body before her, he rose again and came toward her, rose and rose and rose.....

The last words that he had spoken in life, 'Kathleen', he said. A keening, 'Oh, Kathleen' came into her mouth now as if in his tortured voice and she felt his lasting despair.

Life had held such promise. He thought he had planned it differently.

The rain had shone a beacon like brightness at the end and beginning of every building as the wind whipped and the driven rain splattered the dark cobbled street and Michael Patrick as he walked home that early spring evening. It seemed like yesterday.

From under the wool slouch hat his eyes shone out a sharp and clear radiance the color of a fresh green meadow and he could not suppress a grin that threatened to overfill his mouth. His thoughts threw a liveliness to his cold wet feet as he made his way from the construction site of the new county church. The new pips on the blossoming apple trees overhung the wall of the near orchard, and he could not have been more oblivious if the trees had rained the streets with seasoned fruit as he turned into his own well worn stoop, lifted the latch of the old oak door and said to his mother's back at the stove, "The devil is whipping his wife out there and fair bless me if I'm not a carin' atal this day. Or very likely any other day soon, for that matter." It was a cozy if crude keeping room he stepped into. A welcoming fire blazed and crackled in the fireplace.

He flung from his tousled head a battered slouch hat and whipped the side of his breeches leg in front of the glowing fire.

His mother turned from the stove and saw his pretty face light into the accustomed lively, crooked smile that never failed to dig into her heart.

"Ah, Michael, 'tis good to see ye face home on such a nasty day as this! And what hae ye so merry this day of all days, me boy?"

"It's nothin' if it's not that I'm off to America in the mornin' to seek me fortune, mum." He kidded but there was the look of total seriousness about his words.

This bit of news was more than a little unexpected. Michael, she knew, was in love with Kathleen O'Sullivan and engaged to be married in a fortnight and it had seemed from the moment they had laid eyes on each other, a team of wild horses could not have pulled them apart.

"Like two peas in a pod, they are. Always were," people said.

"What's it all about then, Michael, what's it to be?" His mother wiped the backs of her hands on her ever present apron.

"Ye know how long and hard its been since the father passed, mum. And ye know it would be harder still to feed one more mouth, even tho she's a pretty lass what sports it." He blushed, ducking his head; his face in the firelight turned the burnished color of his curls and evened out the endowed freckles which had been his legacy before birth. "I canna rightly ask the lass to sacrifice her passion o' me."

"It's true and sad it is ye ha been creepin' alang here, but it ha to be a powerful draw to leave Kathleen an' home, Michael." Her eyes were as blue and round as saucers and as white rimmed.

"Aye, it is that and nothin' more than ithers have done afore me. It's that Pat O'Shawnesey was by the church this mornin' early," he said, swiping the side of his face with a coat sleeve. "He says he's to pick a crew to build a grand hotel atop a mountain in America and get 'em over as soon as ever he can. I'm hired for stone work in a place called Arkansas."

And it was so. His father had seen to his training following the esoteric tradition and at nineteen his love and early knowledge of the incarnate geometry of proportion and symmetry had matched him with any man twice his age and made him into a rugged, 170 lb. man of superior skill at cutting and fitting stone.

Michael had bade his mother a sad goodbye and pledged his never ending love to sweet Kathleen at ships rail in the early morning mist and sailed away to America and Eureka Springs, in the Northwest corner of the State of Arkansas.

To his mother he pledged support and to Kathleen, marriage in America as soon as the money came in.

He was proud to be hired as one of a crew of such known accomplished craftsman, at a fine salary with which he intended to send for Kathleen, but beyond that he yearned, desired unreasonably some have said, for fame as well as fortune. To go to America and build a great hotel in the beautiful Ozark mountains would surely even out the path.

But, as fate would have it, and history will tell, fame did not come to Michael Patrick because of the beautiful and enduring stone work he had done on the Crescent Hotel but what he had purposed in death instead, that sealed his claim to fame there. If fate had meant him to drown or be run over by a train, he would not have fallen into a broken heap at the bottom of the hotel.

An Irish Catholic from County Cork, Michael had more than a passing acquaintance with guilt and superstition and so wore a gold Celtic cross upon his chest, kept himself crossed at all times, but one.

The clouds had opened and a fair torrent of earth plunging rain came down upon the hotel's new roof that Saturday morning. Michael thought it the perfect time to inspect for leaks between the blocks. He began his inspection high in the rafters above the 4th floor of the nearly completed hotel. The day was October 31, 1885; Halloween. As he went hand over hand, his feet supported by nothing more than a wide plank, one alcove remained before he let his mind wander to Kathleen's imminent arrival.

She had wired a date of departure two weeks before yet for all he knew she could be in his arms that very night. The words of her gladness had fairly leaped from the cable at him. She was bringing her hope chest filled with beautiful linens and kitchen pewter, to start housekeeping, and, she said, she had a surprise for him.

His head swam with thoughts of her. He had tasted her sweet youth but once and that so hasty and impulsive an affair as to leave him weak and irresolute about leaving her. They had lain together on a gentle slope beside the little creek in the first lambent light of spring back home in Ireland, could even now hear the cowbells in the meadow and smell the fresh clean fragrance of her as they planned their future together.

As he walked the scaffolds high under the roof he ran his fingers repeatedly over the fine lines between the blocks. Lines so delicate, without the use of mortar, that not a drop of moisture had escaped to the inside wall.

Kathleen would not fail to be proud of his work. Proud as he was proud. After everything she will have sacrificed she would stand and share equally the glory of his work. He would take her by the hand and they would walk as he loved to walk under the bright sun, along the hotel's massive outer walls. He never tired of examining, touching the stone here and there; to touch the fineness of an almost imperceptible line and smooth curve as a man might examine a woman's body with the tips of his fingers.

Sometimes a high vividness would overtake him and perhaps he knew something of fear in those moments but it is doubtful. At such times he would lean with both hands against the wall and kiss the block as if it were the stone of Blarney Castle back home in Cork and he needing all the luck under heaven.

Kathleen, when she came, would stroll with him and he would point to the very stones he had himself trimmed out so precisely and placed in accordance with tradition; each one a loving trophy, a living monument, there to remain for all time. They would walk and he would tell her of how the huge pieces of magnesium limestone blocks, just the suitable density, cut with such precision down at the White River quarry had been brought in by railroad and wagon, how they could then be laid without the use of mortar.

They strolled, in Michael's imagining, atop the mountain in the clean, clear air and every now and then she would squeeze his hand and surely think to herself what a clever lad she'd married.

She might even imagine she saw their lives as he'd dreamed it, together in this great country of America, his thoughts and emotions so powerful as to be forged into the very stones of the Crescent Hotel, there a permanent record for Kathleen or anyone else to read as easily as the blind could read braille. If they walked where Michael had walked.

Kathleen.

His spirits would so lift at the thought of her until with dulcet voice he'd raise a light song of Irish gladness to the hills as he worked. "There's a tear in yur eye, and I'm wonderin' why, for it never should be there 'atall. With such pow'r in yur smile, sure a stone you'd beguile....." Kathleen would draw back her hand and blush.

Kathleen.

To O'Shawnessey and Callahan, fellow stone workers watching from below, Michael stooped under a beam, let go his hold too soon before reaching to connect on the other side and seemed at just that moment to misstep. His feet, even on solid ground had felt heavy and clumsy in the new boots, now his foot appeared to come down a little off center and he toppled over the side in slow motion as if in playful imitation of a free fall.

To Michael it seemed an absurdly high penalty to pay for such a small mistake. A small vanity. How impossible it was to be walking around perfectly healthy one second, feet and limbs intact, laughing and joking. And the next, stumbling, falling, 'can't reach!' Can't grab! Oh MarymotherofGod Maryhelpme...!" and finally, "Ahhh...Kathleen..."

"Kathleen!" he cried in climax to his mortal life.

His loose body hit the second floor like a sack of loam and he knew nothing, felt nothing and he, in his larger part, looked down from the rafters upon his lifeless body and could not bring about the slightest comprehension of fact within himself. He could only realize something was dreadfully, grievously wrong when he heard O'Shawnessey shout his name. "Michael! No!" Heard almost in whispered prayer, "God No! Michael boy!" from above as if he still clung to the rafter and could make the dastardly event right itself, and heard too the thunderous echo of many rushing feet and the shouting of his name, "Michael!" from every mouth, "Not Michael, surely not Michael!" He could not feel his body being lifted, carried and put into the back of the wagon, a heavy weight laid on top of a thin layer of stone dust.

Kathleen.

Kathleen's arriving. Learning of his death from Pat O'Shawnessey. His body crossing the Atlantic back to Ireland even as she with glad heart had sailed from it. The two ships would have intersected at some maliced point between Cape Clear and Halifax. Could she have known in the further reaches of her soul? Had her heart quickened as they passed?

The stricken, unbelieving look on her face as Pat O'Shawnessey placed Michael's gold Celtic cross around her neck and held the weakened and pregnant body of Kathleen to his chest while tears of disbelief overflowed his own eyes and he mistook her sudden seizure of wailing, the holding of her belly as a frightened, unbearable anguish, when, instead, it was Michael's own son coming abruptly into that saddened society.

Kathleen.

Michael watched her struggle with that old,

crashing pain and his soul anguished how to let her know that he was there by her side as always. In so far as he was able, he felt what she felt, wept when she grieved, stayed with her, caressed the two of them and watched his son's pink bud mouth pull at his mother's sweet breast.

He watched them sleep finally. Watched his son grow until, under the love and care of his good friend and mentor, he watched them thrive.

Kathleen.

He watched and was conflicted yet saw truly that it was right and holy for Kathleen to stand beside Patrick O'Sawnessey and pledge her troth; take his name for herself and Michael's son in the small Catholic church down the hill.

Michael and Kathleen walked together now in Alicia's seeing.

"Michael." Alicia eyes fluttered and knew that he had come back from wherever a man goes beyond death and that she had beckoned him. Michael, here in this room yet both of them had for a time escaped beyond it's mortal walls.

Alicia stirred.

Morris, unable to realize the manner by which she had slept, could not yet calculate the pluses and minuses of her awakening. He knew her to have been fixed there in the chair but at the same time was not present in any sense of the word if there is a such a place in the solid world.

Eleven

The Wonder Grew

Still Alicia, at sixteen, had not been able to explain how she used all her senses in understanding the 'otherness,' the smallness and largeness of her divided being; she only knew that being with that 'other' gave her purpose; gave her answers.

Einstein, at sixteen, had written in *The World As I See It* (1930): "The most beautiful experience we can have is the mysterious. It is the fundamental emotion which stands at the cradle of true art and true science. Whoever does not know it and can no longer wonder, no longer marvel, is as good as dead, and his eyes are dimmed."

Alicia stood in her night dress on the deck outside her bedroom at the lake and reached her arms to the southern sky. She watched an eagle, enclosed within her outstretched hands, drift in ever widening circles against the iron colored sky. Oh, she thought, to sail, wind driven like that across the sky, over mountains edged in crimson, gold and yellow. Even in the advancing colors of fall the sense of a broader winter lake was there, sending shivers of pleasure up her spine. The changing of the guard, she called it. The ancient pattern of death and rebirth.

After Rachael and Hank's death, their old friend and neighbor Pernel Frey had asked to buy the home place for his son. Alicia was silently glad to have it so appreciated.

On a steep wooded lot deeded to her long ago by a devoted client, Alicia had a small house built for she and her cousin Beth Anne on Beaver Lake out of Lowell. Entrance into the house was gained from the ground floor off the driveway, the kitchen served as foyer and dining room as well. Beyond, a wide glass and stone living area faced the lake and was flanked by two large bedroom suits which, cantilevered out into space, looked like a large bird sunning it's wings over the water.

Due to the remoteness of the property Alicia asked Zee, to live in a small gate house at the bottom of the hill where he and his German Sheppard "Grouch Gezundheit" could keep a close eye on the security entrance. This had proved to be an all round good solution, for people had, in their enthusiasm, presumed Alicia's celebrity as something belonging to the world and combed the hills to find her.

Below, a blue heron stood motionless in the shallows, one of it's stilt like legs drew a bent shadow on the water as he anticipated another fruitful day.

She thought again of Michael and Kathleen. Had begun in her mind to refer to him as Great Michael. And there was the present day Michael. "Hummm...," she thought and hugged her shoulders. Yes, there was very much the Michael of the green eyes wasn't there? "Hummm...." She felt a small thrill at the sight of him there in her mind's eye; drew in for a closer look. Probed the spot where he, in her mind, dwelt. "Ah, well," she smiled a private smile. There is definitely the beginning of some feelings there. Thoughts of this nature she had never before entertained. However, she must keep everything in perspective, in balance.

Though the spirit of Norman Baker of the white suit and lavender Cord automobile had been the first to summon her to the Crescent Hotel, Alicia had been fairly inundated by others who had arranged themselves in a kind of line or querulous holding pattern according to some atavistic, needy hierarchy. They spoke to her of need; of fine hopes, dreams they intended for their lives and it was as though the near living of these dreams had merely been the planning stage, and, like most dreams, they were fragile. In all these cases the fragile living dreams had been abruptly seized by an august force of unimaginable strength; dashed against a mightier boundary of it's own making. Dreams, she knew, could not be undreamed. Hopes and dreams, the true domain of Will, exist throughout eternity.

Once yearning hearts are set upon a path, in the belly it is like a gnawing hunger. Some lingering spirits, however well intentioned at the beginning of their past lives, had not been Will driven. They had been too easily distracted by that sweet teeming life until they had somehow forgotten or somewhere lost their way and could not rescue themselves. That they then, at the end of it, discovered a basic residual need within themselves caught them off their guard. They clung like magnets to the intimate connection between people and places they had not been able to inform or impact upon while in this earthly dimension. They sought to obtain now some truant bit of information which could in some way alter the way they viewed life, disease and death. For this was the secret, the positive or negative way a person approached life, revered life for what it was, respect for the collective, the exalted love of opportunity to learn and grow in knowledge.

As well, the wishing need of the living now tugged at Alicia from this side of the veil.

She closed the door behind her and went in search of tea. While it steeped she put an English muffin in the toaster oven which she always kept on medium brown, and took orange marmalade and butter from

113

the fridge. These basic, little routine things, required no conscious action and allowed Alicia a few moments of commonality in her very uncommon world. In her mind she was already at the Crescent, anticipating the day.

"Don't worry about who you might have been, Allen, the important thing is to remember *why. Why* you are here now." She stood at the studio's door saying a last minute instruction to a client a few days after moving into room 218 at the Crescent. She looked into the eyes of the tall young man before her. Saw distress there at some unusual early marriage problems.

And, don't concern yourself if Mollie or her parents don't believe in the efficacy of reincarnation. Everyone is entitled to their beliefs and many people choose not to accept the accountability that it implies; the absolute and total commitment it sooner or later requires. Unfortunately for them they have forgotten their agenda, therefore have not experienced or recognized it's reality at work in their lives. They have lost sight of their purpose, therefore allowing themselves to be victims of circumstance, expressing an array of misconception and misinformation. When asked about suicide, for an instance, I try to explain what a belief in reincarnation, life continuing after death, does not mean in regard to taking your own life. Some seem to think it is the easy way out of a painful life. If life appears to be too painful or disappointing, it certainly does not mean you should end it by suicide. That is disastrous. There are no shortcuts. By the way, there are many ways, however thinly disguised, people inovertly commit suicide. Withdrawing and not eating are two of the more common ways. Conversely, it does mean you must work through the challenge however painful. Once understood, the system is unremittingly judicious. It is there to activate memory, turn you around, set you on the correct path. It is there to help you to remember your commitment to Self and help you stay true to it's purpose.

A dear friend, an only child who was profoundly depressed over first her mother's and then her father's death, came to me and as I was beginning to explain that they continued to look after her, guide her, love her, she began to cry as she expressed to me how much she missed them. I truly empathized with her, for I too am an only child who has both parents in spirit. Her husband walked in, saw her distress and without listening or hearing the full explanation of what the reality of life after death is actually meant to be, he assumed I was somehow validating her right to take her own life in order to join her mother and father. Before I could explain what life's continuing did not mean; where it should not lead; what should not be concluded, he whisked her away to sedate her with drugs, which I suppose by some prior agreement between them was his right so to do. She said later that he had sworn to keep her from all harm. She later died under baffling circumstances. As I said, everyone has a choice.

"When people believed the earth was the center of the universe, it did not make it so. And, believe me, that battle was more hard fought. On the other hand, metempsychosis, reincarnation, in ages past, was the accepted belief of the whole civilized race of man. Still to this day it is accepted as Truth by the vast majority of the race. You have awakened to the essence of you, the spirit, and mind of Allen. You realize now that you have always existed and will continue to exist after physical death. For now, it is enough."

"Thank you Alicia. For being here. For making

sense out of things that happened to me. It isn't easy for me to explain or talk to Mollie. I know so little of the way the clockwork of the universe works." Allen Eiesly bent and kissed her cheek lightly. "Thank you. You are a treasure."

"Ah, but that is just the point, Allen. "Things" don't just happen to you. We can discuss more of that later, if you like."

As he walked away Alicia saw a tall woman dressed in a nurses uniform walk past him pushing an empty hospital gurney down the hall. Neither reacted to the passing of the other. "Hmm," she intoned as the nurse came toward her.

Staring straight ahead the nurse walked five or six paces beyond the door before she suddenly stopped, turned and looked back over her shoulder. She wore the old muddled look of doubt and indecision she had doubtless carried with her throughout endless ages. "They are not supposed to die, you know," she said, talking to herself as much as to anyone and solemnly resumed pushing the gurney until they disappeared around a corner.

Soon after Alicia moved into the Crescent she saw the wisdom of placing a heavy oriental hall runner and comfortable seating in the hallway. As she would concentrate on one client inside sometimes she heard the pacing of another in the hall. Or, there would be people lined against the wall waiting, even though they had no appointment. They were just there to take their chances on seeing her, they said. It had been the very reason her father had placed benches outside on the little porch back home. She seldom turned anyone away, even if it meant staying until after dark.

Alicia turned back to close the door and was startled to see a man sitting in one of the chairs in the hallway. He had the pale scrubbed look of a medical man with his shock of white hair and immaculate dress. "Oh! I didn't realize....," she started, "the nurse must have been speaking to you." She recognized Norman Baker at once as the man who had been trying to escape through the tunnel and the man responsible for her being there.

"No," Norman Baker said. "Cassie was talking to you. She was right you know. They weren't supposed to die. We did nothing intrusive to our patients. If they died in our care, which was very seldom, it was because they came to us more than half dead already. The A.M.A. saw to that right and all! Ha! Even then, we still had a high rate of cure and all they had to show for their lamentable effort was failed treatment. No cure, mind you. That word they held reserved for some far distant future when one of their own formally educated and highly trained, "real" doctors could come up with what they themselves admitted might not happen for thirty or forty years. Now, I ask you, in the name of all thats sacred, how can they justify their neglectful actions by not using the cure I have so often offered. Why must even one more trusting soul endure the pain and agony they are needlessly being subjected to while the A.M.A. experiment, "practice." By the way, why do you suppose they "open a Practice," call themselves "Practicing" physicians?" He slapped his knee. "My golly, that's something to think about isn't it? Our cure rate, our success, on the other hand, is an egregious affront and cannot be tolerated. Not on your life!"

Alicia turned, opening the door, "If you will come in..." She began, then realized Norman Baker had vanished. "Oh," she said simply to the empty chair and closed the door behind her.

As she turned back into the room she almost ran into the nurse standing right in her path. "The A.M.A., they're the real culprits, you know!" She said with her arms akimbo. "Mr. Baker was the smartest man I've ever known and his moral standards the highest." She said as if continuing a conversation started decades ago.

"The great tragedy was that the world, or more realistically, the A.M.A. was not ready for the likes of him. He wouldn't give up. But they had to get rid of him somehow. They tried to prove his methods of cure were false and they couldn't manage one iota of evidence against him, we had the documentation to prove our claims, so they had him thrown in jail on trumped up charges of advertising his cancer cures through the U. S. Mail. He was a noble man, ready to do anything to fight disease. They didn't scare him one little bit with all their medical degrees, let me tell you. He was twice as smart and courageous as the lot of them put together! They thought they held sway over everything concerning health. They had no idea what Norman Baker was all about and they didn't care to know. Tell him he couldn't do a thing? Why that was just the ticket! He just waded right into whatever forbidden territory their medical domain had set up. They rewarded his phenomenal success by thowing the book and every political ploy they could think of in his path. Swore to stop his progress, but his ideas and inventions went right on rendering obsolete the efforts of thousands of doctors. He was always miles ahead in treatment and cure. They were constantly threatened by patient's testimony. People were so sick they were literally carried in here. When they walked out into the sunshine of a new life, living testament to this hospital's ability to cure, the A.M.A. not only didn't want to hear about it, it made them desperate to discredit us. Oh, it was so unfair."

"Yes, I agree. Perhaps you're the one then, who needed to talk to me?" Alicia said motioning for the nurse to sit down.

"No... yes, I need to show you something." She swept past Alicia out the door.

"Wait. Cassie, isn't it?"

"Oh, sorry, it's Cassandra Lake, the doctors call me Cassie." She said over her shoulder.

"Cassie, I was talking to Mr. Baker in the hall before." Alicia said, following her down the north stairs toward a red carpeted landing area at the bottom.

"Yes, and he could very well have been addressed as doctor if he had wanted to be. Instead, he chose to play a larger role in fighting disease. He bought this hotel and transformed it into Baker Hospital. He was owner and Administrator and as such took full responsibility for finding and keeping the best doctors and nurses, taking the time and effort to train us in the therapy." Cassie went down another flight and entered a dim room on the right at the bottom of the hotel. "We wondered why he did not choose to become a doctor. We often said as much to him."

Alicia's sinuses were immediately attacked by the musty odor of the dank shadowy basement.

"This is one of Mr. Baker's inventions which played a large part in the cure for cancer," she said, laying one hand along it's side. "And oh, how the A.M.A. despised those words, *cure for cancer!* If they had spent half as much money and time as they spent harassing Mr. Baker on a cure instead of treatment they would have living patient testimonials also." She brushed a hank of blonde hair aside. "Don't get me started. I have stories about their treatments that would curl your hair and make you sick." Cassie ran her hand over the side of the tub. "Anyway," she sighed heavily, "as you can see it is an out-sized galvanized tub filled with water from the Crescent Spring in which we submerged the diseased patient inside this length of coiled wire. A weak electrical current is sent through the coiled wire producing a very carefully measured magnetic field which passed through the patient, creating a resonance in the body. This effected specific molecular changes in the diseased cells without causing harm to healthy cells of the same mass.

"It has to do with physics and I don't understand everything about it's workings but I do know that we have had some miraculous cures, and not just for the five year grace period of remission but completely successful, long time cures here at Baker Hospital."

"I'm truly impressed Cassie, but what about you? How did you fair when it all came crashing down?"

"I had literally devoted my life to the cure of disease. I did not want to be associated with anything that would treat people as if they were sub-human, carving them up like so much meat with surgical procedure after surgical procedure foisted upon thousands which left them crippled or dead. Helping to heal was my whole life. Mr. Baker's cures and advances in the medical field had been so suppressed and maligned that when the day came that they closed down the hospital, I was devastated. I felt so impoverished, so already dead, I could not continue. I had a massive heart attack and collapsed right there in the hallway before I could get to Mrs. Callahan's room to pick up her poor dead body. She had died of a coronary upon hearing the hospital was closed down and she would have to leave. We would all have to leave. Standing outside the door I could hear her family whispering, crying, and I knew as soon as they opened the door I'd have to face her family and I just couldn't face them. It seems like ever since then I have tried to go into that room. I walk to the door and try to go in. Do my duty and go into that room, put her body on the gurney and wheel her down to the morgue in the basement. Over and over I try to make myself face that poor sad family and every time I do the whole thing starts again. It starts all over again, no matter how I battle against it. Oh! I'll never forget it. It's pure hell!" Cassie gasped in unbearable anguish. "When I think of the time, money and mean rotten effort the A.M.A. wasted on trying to destroy Mr. Baker with legal gobbledygook! It has been a national tragedy. We cured everybody in sight, what could he possibly have done to be punished like that? He did nothing to deserve what they did to him. None of us did."

Alicia put her hand out to Cassie. "I believe you know in your soul that it can't be your fault that some people won't take responsibility for their own health." Alicia spoke softly. "Isn't it true that most people came to the hospital only after everything and everyone else had given up on them?" Alicia took Cassie's hand from the side of the tub where it had scrubbed back and forth the whole time she was talking. She looked into the center of her palm and ran a small finger over several lines and smiled. "Oh, Cassie, the good news is, it is never too late. Soon mankind will understand and end it's persecution of these messengers from the higher powers of the universe and learn from them."

Twelve

Cracked reflection

In the next few days Michael McKinney came again to room 218. When she answered the door he stared almost in open mouthed wonder at Alicia, so graceful and serene, when she moved she looked like a young swan, as if on water. Her black eye lashes made little demure wings on top of alabaster and peach cheeks when she blinked her pale blue eyes. The sheer white chiffon blouse tucked neatly into a slim black skirt, sleeves billowing like feathers, completed the illusion. It was all he could do to keep from telling her how beautiful she was.

Alicia talked to him about how she viewed death and it's aftermath; about the circumstance of his great grandfather's death and why the way he died was directly responsible for Michael's recurring nightmare.

"In a way, Michael, your nightmare began when he fell from the rafters up near the roof of this hotel many years ago and he was totally unprepared for the continuation of his mind, his 'self', the actual plurality of his being in real time, for no one had ever told him that there is very little if any disruption of consciousness after the "death" process." She didn't like to place blame on anyone or anything, and would not now. Yet, she had always wondered why organized religion had not seized every possible opportunity to administer this everlasting message of love and hope to the very people who had invested and entrusted them with their most precious possession; the core of their being; the SOUL; the SELF.

123

She had always supposed the august body of divine intercedence, which is "the church", was committed to the care of souls on earth. Every soul cared for, without bias or prejudice of any kind. It proclaims to be the messenger of truth and enlightenment. Why had it shirked that responsibility? Why had the caretakers not shouted this immortal, unshakable truth from beneath their gold encrusted peerage? Or could this truth, in fact, be unknown to the very caretakers themselves? And, if they themselves knew this truth with all it's ramifications, to whom did they pray for release? And what of man, caretaker and auteur of his own soul? He is not blameless in this benign neglect. Blameless in his naivete. It is true, as Demosthenes is noted to have said: *The easiest thing of all is to deceive one's self, for what a man wishes he generally believes to be true.* He and he alone must take responsibility for his knowledge as well as his inescapable actions. Ah, Alicia thought, what a dear price man had paid and continues to pay, for this oversight.

"After the quitting of the corporeal body Great Michael simply lingered here because he had no idea what had really happened to him or what could be done about it. No one had informed him of these things." Alicia said. "At first he stayed because of Kathleen and their son. And, then he became his own prisoner in the hotel."

It was very late. Alicia and Michael were sitting in their accustomed position, he on the sofa and she on his right in the high back chair. Morris, as usual, lay across her left foot and tried unsuccessfully to keep his eyes shut. There was beginning at the back of his head a nameless gnawing in the place where past memory slept or where future memory began, he could not tell which but only that it was fast coming.

124

He rose and without bothering to stretch, began to pace as a tiger might, head down, back and forth in front of the door. His movements did not disturb the two engrossed in conversation.

"But, Alicia, what are you saying?" Michael said. "I was not even born yet! Hell, what am I saying? My own parents were not even born yet, for that matter! What has all this to do with me, anyway?" His brow knit together and his left hand hovered in a helpless motion around his mouth. Alicia leaned forward and took his hand.

"Michael, you are his flesh and blood. You look exactly like him, you're even left handed like him; you love to work with your hands. You could be some sort of gemel twin in waiting." Michael only managed a look of confusion.

"I know these things are very difficult to conceive at first," her voice soft but deliberate, "especially as it refers to our very nature and to our ability to exist apart from our bodies."

"Oh, my god! I just remembered something."

"What?"

"Last year I designed and built a native stone wall around my patio. It was so strange. I'd never done any building of any sort. But, I dreamt how to do it. In my dream every step was laid out in front of me. Even though I had never even touched stone before, somehow I knew I could just get up and build that wall. I itched to do it! I knew I would be good at it before I started." He stopped, incredulous now. "Isn't that strange?"

She smiled and patted his hand, drew her own back into her lap as he leaned back to contemplate the full meaning of the experience.

Morris came and brushed against her leg for assurance and looked toward the door. He knew the big lady they called Sister Dolly was lurking out in the hall. He saw the shadow of light and dark beneath the door but more than that he smelt her. And, the smell of her stung his nose. He sneezed.

"You see Michael," Alicia continued, "you know more than you think about how this phenomena works. Some people think it's merely a coincidence when things like that happen to them. If they think about it at all. You have had other experiences from which you learn, I know you have; everyone has. One is the sudden and distinct feeling that you are reliving something; an event you have witnessed before; somehow you know you have been there, seen that, heard that before, sometimes to the point of remembering exact scenes, clothes, conversation; it's called deja vu and is very common."

"Oh, sure!" Michael smiled at her. "Like while I was listening to you I almost knew what you were going to say next. Sometimes I know when the telephone's going to ring. Makes my head swim. But, I never paid much attention to it..., besides, people are always making jokes about it." He added. "Anyway, I thought that was supposed to have something to do with reincarnation."

"Right, that feeling of lightness is that you've probably experienced a partial OOBE; or out-of-body experience. Sometimes we become aware that something is awry and say things like, 'I'm beside myself with worry,' or, 'I was just not quite myself all day.' Have you never wondered where such expressions come from? There is a partial separation of body and mind; you, the conscious being encountering, experiencing something apart from your body." She reached down and scrubbed Morris' ears with one hand.

"Where did I get the idea that this deja vu thing

was connected to reincarnation?" Michael said.

"It's a common misconception. One which muddies the waters of both, valid but totally separate, experiences. One is not the other. If you will think about the deja vu experience itself, with all the attending data, such as clothes style, buildings and their interiors, automobile make and model, things that are up to date, dealing in "real" time now, engaging you as participant in the event, it could not possibly be reincarnation as such. True, the event itself involves something out of the past. And, you were there, you lived it. However, it is a *flashback of a precognitive dream* you had. You have actually lived a future event. So in that sense, it is a "past life experience." Everyone could literally tell the future if they remembered their dreams. The problem is not all dreams are precognitive. Dreams are extremely important. They are direct messages from the self to you, the aide-de-camp to recognition, and they serve many purposes. You must learn to differentiate between what I call "dill pickle" dreams, the nonsense dreams that could be caused by what you ate just before going to bed, and those of instruction, which will positively or negatively impact your life"

"Wow! Isn't that something to think about!" Michael was already planning a dream journal.

"That is just the tip of the dreaming iceberg. We can discuss this more at length some other time if you like. The other thing is," Alicia continued, "when you are asleep or even just drowsing and suddenly you feel your body jerk awake. You have been out of your body and the jolt you feel is the tremendous spirit energy, which is what I call the larger portion of ourselves, reentering your body. You are literally jerked back into the corporeal body. When that energy is settled down, reintegrated with the body, I call that the smaller portion of ourselves. Smaller, not because of any sense of mind constriction or dimensionality, but in a physical sense it actually feels disproportionately flat and tight by comparison, like the power lessness of a straight jacket, and must mingle with the gross vibrations of the corporeal body. Diluted, so to speak, if it is not recognized, remembered; lessening it's potential, it's ability to function. Functioning with the larger part of ourselves is like being plugged into an A.C. circuit of electricity; the smaller like a D.C. circuit."

Michael groaned, crossed his eyes and stuck his tongue out at her as if all this new information had run together and threatened his brain with overload.

Alicia laughed. "Very funny Michael!" They fit comfortably together.

"Tell you what," she said and walked to the bookcase as she remembered the enthusiasm with which she had entered her own quest for esoteric knowledge, "there are some things I'd like you to read, things about your 'self', your true essence, and later we will talk of how you, me, all of us, fit into the grand scheme of things, of the universe and our role in it."

It was getting late and Zee would be waiting to drive her home. She had many appointments the next day.

As they made sounds of quitting Morris noticed the shadow under the door was no longer there. He did not know why or how far away Sister Dolly might have gone, but knew only that if she had come through the door as before, he would ditch the place in a flash.

"I know this is probably too much for you to swallow in one piece," Alicia was saying, "but, I think, because of the family polarity, your psychic connection to Great Michael, that you will have an easy time understanding what this is all about."

As she drew several books from the shelf Alicia said,"You may read these in any order you choose. However, I began my own study with this one." She held a smallish volume out to him.

"My mother gave it to me when I was having a hard time understanding my own psychic ability. You see, as a small child, I thought everyone could do what I did, see the things I saw, hear and feel in the way I did. It was not until I went to school that I began to learn differently. Not only did the other children not have this ability but I learned that almost everyone, including teachers were not all that enthusiastic and receptive about my abilities. Most did not understand and some were downright frightened in the face of it. This refusal on their part to consider fact was quite a shock to me even when I tried to explain. I asked them why my curing hiccoughs or seeing a person's "dead" grandmother around them, was so different than someone who has great eyesight never needing to wear eyeglasses. Or, like some other animals, to hear significantly better than humans. Because you can't hear what your dog hears does his ability mean he is "weird" or "supernatural"? I told them, "Surely, you can't possibly fault a person or be afraid because that person was born seeing and hearing really well, could you?'" Of course not. "For that matter," I said, "why shouldn't the situation be reversed and considered an odd *deficiency, a handicap,* not to have these and other "natural" abilities? Wouldn't that reasoning be more logical?"

"Well," she said, tilting her head back and laughing at herself, remembering the young Alicia's self-assured innocence, "I tell you, I learned real quick to keep some things to myself!"

"This book, There Is A River, written by a man named Thomas Sugrue who was himself very special, but that is another story altogether; this book, is about a young boy, Edgar Cayce, who was a lot like me. Just a regular kid who grew up to be a very famous psychic." She giggled and looked at him as if to say, 'not seriously!' Her self effacing glee was a surprise to Michael for he always took what Alicia said seriously, but the merriment in her voice and the flash of keen intelligence seemed to be an open invitation for him to relax a bit.

Relax Michael, he told himself. Get with the program. If she can make jokes about a serious subject such as this, at least he could be a little less"up tight". If she could lighten up a bit, show him that she was just a fun loving teenager at heart then so could he. On the other hand, he could not possibly see her as "regular" in any way.

"At all times", Alicia continued, "regardless of the strange information Edgar Cayce received about herbs and cures for his clients while in a somnambulant state of consciousness, he maintained a high integrity," she paused, reflected again. "Many times, he received information contrary to his own religious beliefs, such as reincarnation. Never-the-less much of his advice and many of his cures were based on clients past lives. In other words, who and what you were before can have a tremendous influence on your proclivities, health and welfare in this one. He was such a great help to people that sometimes his own health suffered from fatigue and neglect."

With each new question Michael asked, she would thrust more material at him, until he, mostly in jest, began to think maybe he shouldn't have asked so many questions.

The connection between such seemingly diverse

subjects as quantum mechanics and man's soul was difficult to fathom when Michael began; but, as he studied he learned that everything is connected in one way or another; few things are permanent and those few are rather abstract and intangible. How could an art history major such as himself, he wondered, begin to understand, to equate the reality of the micro world, quanta reality of which Alicia spoke, with the very soul of man? He understood why she was so absorbed in her life's work. Alicia obviously had as a goal something so different, something so truly apart from the ordinary that it boggled his mind. On the other hand, he could not comprehend how one so young and unsophisticated in the ways of the world knew to delve into ideas of conservation, of permanence, as being central to the perception of that world. The natural laws of conservation, she had said, the laws of modern physics states that if an object or quality remained unchanged in any given circumstance, we are taking hold of conservation, of uniformity in time. He would be able to deepen his understanding of the physical world, she said, if he could learn to think in terms of levels of conservation. She spoke of how quanta reality demands the deepest and most breathtaking expansion of man's concept of the world ever imagined.

With every grade of his understanding, she seemed to step up the pace at which she fed him information, urged him forward. Under her guidance he was more than willing to strive toward what she referred to as his unfoldment. So he did the only thing that had worked for him thus far. He asked more questions.

As he walked out of the hotel and crossed the drive to the parking lot Michael thought he saw out of the corner of his eye a slight movement in the shadows.

Thirteen

Transition

An eagle, when he searches, flies in ever widening circles high above the earth. He would not starve if he did not but instinctively knows that if he always hunted close to the nest his chances for survival would be greatly diminished. The concept of needing less food is simply not comprehensible to him. He must fly in higher and higher concentric circles, searching. It is his nature. Man has even more need to search.

Many nights Alicia and Michael sat together talking. It was for Michael a time of exciting mind discovery. Alicia watched as more and more he adopted a specific position on the couch. He would sit with stocking feet drawn up hugging his knees to his chest.

Alicia had discovered as a child divining for water, healing or merely sharing information that the more accurate or true the situation was, the more the area of her solar plexus vibrated. As she gave information she learned to rely on the frequency and intensity of this vibration, hold a respect for it's manifestation and could gage it's accuracy as if it were some truth barometer. This insight she would save until Michael was more comfortable in his skin. She giggled to herself.

Sometimes they talked far into the night. A rhythm of question and answer had been well established. They sat talking and drinking the soothing Earl Grey tea she loved. She listened to the homey sound of it's preparations as Michael puttered in the small kitchen alcove she had created behind a large tri-fold screen. He asked many questions which she answered as simply and accurately as she could.

"But if, as you say, it is not necessarily the reincarnation of Great Michael which I am experiencing," he said coming around the screen bearing two cups, "what else could it be? I've been wondering about a lot of things related to that." He placed the cups on the table between them. "Watch out, it's really hot." He blew across his own steaming cup. "For instance, when you go backward in time to the moment of birth, given all possible scenarios, how can you really be sure you will turn out to be you and no one else?" He put the questions at random as a child would have asked, 'Why is the sky blue and where did I come from?

They sipped tea and munched on crescent shaped almond cookies, while she pondered the question. "Ummm...." She removed a crumb from the corner of her mouth with one pinkie finger before she spoke. "Last question first. It's one seldom asked. Go back to what we've established about agenda, self guided and will directed. If you are not highly motivated or if you feel you've made a misstep in placement, that is you feel you are in the wrong place at the wrong time, you could get bumped." She stopped and smiled at the bewildered look on his face. "What?"

"Bumped?" He looked totally lost.

"Yes, bumped. Just like at the ticket counter of an airline." She saw he was about to crack up."Hey," she said, "Please, don't laugh!" She was a touch out of patience but saw she might have jumped in a little ahead of herself.

"Let me back up, preface that by saying that before you are born there are self evident procedures to carefully consider. Events and consequences that are predicated upon the background, environment you envision for future. Notice I did not say "set future", that is predestination and does not account for free will, which has everything to do with the question. Ideally you've made your parent selection based according to the lessons your self needs for growth with knowledge. So, yes, we can be bumped. Bumped when someone else has higher priority, higher need. I told you people seldom ask that question. It's no wonder they are in the dark about it. Unless it happened to you. You would know if it happened to you. It can be very frightening." She sipped her tea thoughtfully. Hooked one side of her hair behind her ear.

"I once had a woman bring her small son to me. Almost every night, she said, he would wake the household with his screams. Terrifying screams. 'Nooo, nooo!' he'd wail, 'leave me alone, get away from me!' He cried out in the night. In the morning his little eyes would be ringed with fatigue. No one knew what was going on. The mother said when she went in to him, cradled him in her arms, calmed him, he would tell her that someone was trying to push him out. Trying to make him leave. The mother feared possession. I counseled the boy. Tried to give him strength to resist but the next time she brought him to me he was a different boy. Where before, he had been a shy, sweet and considerate little boy, now he was a more determined, energetic child, confidence shone from his brown eyes. It was clear he had bumped the other child. He obviously had the greater need."

"How terrible, Alicia!" Michael put out his hand and took her empty cup. Placed it gently on the table next to his own.

Alicia smiled. "Not at all, Michael. We should use extreme caution when making assumptions of any kind. Don't take them too seriously until all the facts are in. As they say, 'It ain't over 'till the fat lady sings.' I like to think it ain't over 'till it's over, and it's seldom over."

"What happened to the boy, do you know?"

"Oh, yes. It hasn't been easy for him. This child felt guilty as he grew up never really knowing why. He was loved by his family yet still suffered a profound sense of guilt. He is making great strides now that he has learned to relinquish a sense of punishment and internal pain. He has a ways to go but he is learning to turn his attention to nourishing and honoring what is sacred within himself without guilt, without feeling that he had acted selfishly."

"So, he realized what he had done was wrong and he was sorry?"

"It is all a matter of perception, of course. But yes, in this case he did feel guilty of wrong doing but, by the same token he did what he had to do for his agenda. In any case, once it's done, it can't be undone. The other little boy will also be responsible for his own relinquishment. Who's to say whether it was premature or late?"

"Wow, I had no idea. There is so much to learn. The fabric of the real world just gets thinner and thinner doesn't it?"

Alicia smiled her little subtle smile. "As to your first question. The possibility of reincarnation now for Great Michael? Lets say this. As we struggle to grasp the nature of, the true significance of what we are all about here and our relationship to one another, we learn through challenge. We must learn to test the shell we are in, struggle against the cocoon of complacency, against the old way of thinking and acting. Sometimes it's easy, sometimes it is a mighty struggle out of which we emerge a metamorphic marvel! We develop a certain intuition for these things. In your case I did not intuit one spirit but two. Both your's and Great Michael's. Individual spirits. That is," she partially corrected, "as far as any can be discerned apart from the whole."

Sensing his befuddlement, "But, that's another avenue... Let me see...," she hooked a strand of long dark hair over one ear and fixed a look into the middle distance. "Print making is a good example, Michael. You know about fine lithographs. Think about how each completed image is the product of 10 to 12 photo-developed plates, all of which carry a segment or layer of the final image that has been hand drawn, individually processed, and carefully inked to achieve a natural, uncomplicated, watercolorlike appearance. Rather, the responsibly committed artist knows and accepts the highly dichotomous and complicated business as part of the process; something which must be done; knows the finished product lies in her, and only her, hands. And you innately know that the purpose of composing a painting, isn't just to zap you in and out and be done with it. Desirably, no matter the subject, it should invite you into it, keeping you there, to wander, to explore it's every aspect, to delight in it."

"Alright, so... on to another clue which illustrates our wholeness, our connectedness to everything." She said as she crossed to the bookcase and chose carefully among the beloved references. She flipped through the familiar pages and began to read aloud from The Principles Of Nature by G. W. Leibniz.

"'Antimatter.'" He writes. "Up to this time we have spoken as simple physicists: now we must advance to metaphysics by making use of the great principle, little employed in general, which teaches that nothing happens without a sufficient reason. This principle laid down, the first question which should rightly be asked, would be: Why is there something rather than nothing? For nothing is simpler and easier than something."

"Occam's Razor," she added and replaced the book and motioned to Michael. "Lets walk outside, I think we could use some fresh air."

Morris glanced toward the door and seeing no shadow moving under it swaggered ahead as if he knew a better way. "Occam's razor?" Michael said, as he opened the door for the three of them.

Alicia explained as they walked down the stairs. "Simplified, excuse the expression," she laughed at the obvious pun, "Occam's Razor is a principle used whereby if two solutions to a problem are presented, the simplest must be chosen."

The moon had slipped around and they were sitting in the silvery light on the steps of the hotel's veranda. Alicia's hands moved like small birds; her voice sounded like a certain primeval melody, soft and genial. To Michael, she seemed to study something afar off. She, reciting a litany of knowledge and he with only questions as response.

"We come to view the observable material world, as no longer made up of individual objects, but rather as an indivisible whole, sometimes simply as with concentric rings from a tossed pebble on a pond cannot be separated each from the other; or when a woman is pregnant who can say where one life ends and the other begins. They are merely different aspects of the same living thing."

"I see," he sometimes would say, or in chaste consternation, hold up his hands as if in surrender, "wait, wait," he would shout..., "wait! Hold it! I think I understand the big picture, but I still seem to be hung up on some of the traditional ways of thinking, which does not even begin to explain the pain, the struggle I, as well as others, seem to be experiencing just trying to live."

She would then stop or continue smoothly aligning her thoughts into expression or back up and begin again, take a different avenue or show by new example how, in her knowing, the world was put together and how they were in fact, responsible for how the world turned.

"I respect your deep connection to your great grandfather. But Michael, while in this dimension, you are an individual." Alicia looked fiercely into his clear green eyes. "You are not some collated echo of him. You know that no matter how many times people tell you that you look like pictures of him, no matter how empathetic and helpless you feel to stop this spiral of negative activity, you are your own person and if you have suffered another's pain it is because you have 'taken it to raise', to own, so to speak, not the other way around... and only you can disown it."

Sometimes she would stop and close her eyes as if seeing and listening to inner extrinsic council; speak then with her eyes closed and gesture emphatically with her hands offering a certain notion. They went on like this for hours through the calm night, Alicia sometimes using words and movements not her own and once or twice even in masculine tones unraveled and explained mysteries as old as the world is old.

In those moments Alicia realized as never before, if the ties, the bonds of family are that strong, how much stronger must be the cosmic. Michael was somehow possessed of his great grandfather's residual fear of falling to his death and he was experiencing this fear because he had somehow needed that protracted psychic connection. Yet, she could not make him know it for what it was; understand the purpose it served in him. Nor could she make him feel it was valid despite the logic and rightness of her intuited knowledge. If it did not somehow ring true to him, resonate as truth deep within his heart and soul; she knew it would then pass undetected, remain incomprehensible and be left unresolved for the rest of his life. The goal, his agenda to be seen only as valid in his between lives and though he might vow, though he might strive mightily in another lifetime, he would be striving against odds, against a strong urge to sleepwalk through yet another life. When we lose track...., 'now that's another one of those things we say unconsciously yet is so meaningful, she thought to herself.' For, in truth, we have actually lost or forgotten which "track" we are supposed to take in order to reach our destination, fulfill our agenda. We have forgotten the reason we chose to be here, live again. And end to end filling our lives with busywork. Killing time, we call it. How sad, she thought. Cramming it with senseless causes, egoic vain glories. She remembered Walt Whitman had written many times on this most important theme,"That shadow, my likeness, that goes to and fro seeking a livelihood, chattering, chaffering, how often I find myself standing and looking at it where it flits, how often I question and doubt that it is really me."

"In my work, Michael," she said, "communication is everything. It is sometimes hard for me to choose the right words or thoughts that will make a difference in another's understanding. Oftentimes I take the simple, straightforward, approach. Sometimes it is enough. At other times I find I must back up; take another tack entirely."

They sat that fall cooled morning in a final silence drinking tea and watching the rising sun. Alicia, with Morris at her feet on the veranda steps, trailed a slender hand across his back and scratched behind his ears.

The whole of Eureka Springs, in beetled gradations of autumnal color, spread a dew laden celebration of roof tops before them. The one, a tribute to the recent ingenuity and expertise of man. The other, a fitting example of nature at it's eternal best. It is difficult for the unlearned to grasp the fact that the mountains beyond had formed themselves some 600 million years before during that vast, ill-defined period of geological history known as the Precambrian era. When the Ozarks were being formed, the vertebrates had yet to emerge.

Alicia stirred herself. "I once wrote a poem for a person in which I tried to explain the importance of being quiet, stilling the mind; of not having a constant background of sound, radio, television, whatever. It was like an addiction, just for the sake of noise always around her. Silence makes some people highly agitated. Silence is so much a part of outer space, until astronauts are tested to ascertain how much they can tolerate. Sound deprivation is real and threatening to some.

"Anyway, when external sound, noise, was not present, this person even hummed monotone tunes, actually they weren't tunes at all, but just some low frequency tones repeated over and over. When I told her she was doing a natural mantra and it was the soul's way of trying to get in touch with her, she just about freaked out. She had no idea what it was all about. It has strictly to do with vibration"

Michael looked aghast. "Well, that makes perfect sense to me. My mother does it all the time! Walks around humming unrecognizable tunes to herself. She is so zoned out sometimes I don't think she knows who or where she is!"

"Exactly." Alicia stood suddenly. "I'll just be a second," she said. "I have a copy of the poem in my files and I want to get a sweater. It's a little nippy."

When she returned she saw Michael sitting on the veranda with his back against one of the white columns at the top of the steps. Morris had arranged himself in his lap while Michael smoothed his ears with both hands, "There Morris, ole boy," Michael crooned into the squinting golden eyes, "you are a good fellow to have around."

Her mouth framed a little crooked smile at the total pleasure she read on both their faces. She sat on the step directly below Michael and looked down at the slightly limp paper in her hand. She had not thought of the poem in ages. It had been typed on the old Underwood her parents bought her while she was in junior high school. Strike marks on the left side of the letter W could always be seen on the reverse side of the paper.

"I had filed it under reincarnation. Cracked Reflection, I call it."

"Sounds intriguing." Michael said, slowly stroking the length of Morris' back.

She looked down at the paper suffused with the golden light of that October dawn and cleared her throat.

It strikes me now that nothing is without symbol
But then, ah then, it was all so simple
A thing was only a thing, after all, what else could it be;
You heard what was to be heard and
Did what was to be done, and now, yes now

Before you step into the cracked reflection
Make sure you see what you think you see
And not just a symbol of that which is.

The door with nothing behind it but busy
Opening into a frenzy of activity
Without cause, without pause to consider
And listen, ah, listen and listen
And know behind which door
Awaits clean blank
Think carefully before you enter for

That which is thought
Begins immediately as if writ by mind's magic plume.
And again comes 'round the cracked reflection
And the door with nothing behind it but busy
Opening into a frenzy of activity

Without cause, without pause to consider
And listen, ah listen and listen
And you know behind which door
(You've been there before?)
Awaits clean blank
Think carefully before you enter

For that which is thought
Begins immediately as if writ by mind's magic plume.
AND AGAIN COMES 'ROUND THE CRACKED
REFLECTION
LISTEN OH LISTEN AND LISTEN

Alicia folded the paper into her sweater pocket and
sighed. Michael made a husky "Umm," contemplative
sound deep in his throat. "It looks like I'll have to give
this reincarnation stuff another chance." The trio
contented, simply sat and watched Eureka Springs

143

emerge from the dark side of it's path around the sun.

"You see, Michael," Alicia said, scant altering the natural ease of the moment. "Your great grandfather, whom I now call Great Michael, has not been able to move on; has not realized a progression, but has continued to walk instead among the rooms here, walk on the rafters under the roof and continues to fall to his execution over and over again. Each time he relives the dreaded event, he actually builds, however slightly, a more mired and gross vibration; much as a mud dauber returns to place layer after enshrouding layer of mud; tirelessly building it's nest. If something destroys the nest in his absence he continues to fly back and forth, tries with every ounce of energy to find what he so diligently placed there until finally, finally he realizes it is truly gone and begins the labor again using the old foundation as base for the new. In this same never ending cycle of activity Great Michael returns here again and again; walks in the basement, in the rooms, especially room 218, because he is looking for something; he is missing some 'thing' and his need for it has trapped him here. It is some 'thing' other than his mortal body. We know of his continuing search through guest's clothes, in their dresser drawers and closets. He has disturbed people, pushing them out of bed in the middle of the night, even as they sleep behind locked doors, searching the bed linens and they hear him walking about. Walking," they say. "Always walking."

"He is so obsessed by this searching that his 'WILL' has created an energy strong enough to move furniture. He thinks that if he returns everything to it's former placement in the rooms he will be able to find what he's looking for. He examines guest's luggage and jewelry cases. He never takes anything or does any harm or damage. He only does damage to his 'SELF' each time he relives the fall; injures no one but himself, until now; until you."

Alicia became agitated now; the solar plexus vibration strong. She stood to relieve the tension and began to pace back and forth, along the top step at first, then up, down, up, down; two at a time until her legs were stretched unnaturally out and she looked ready to go off balance. Michael, alerted to the danger, stood apart, confused and frightened now. He did not know what was happening as he watched her pace on the very edge of the gray veranda floor twelve steps above the sidewalk. She tread with a vengeance now, to and fro until she began to gulp for air and her eyes glazed over. To Michael, she seemed to have stepped into another world. He stood shivering a little although the sun was beginning to warm the morning when he realized that even though her head was inclined toward the steps, in fact her eyes were closed. As he watched her pace back and forth on the steep stairs high above the ground he saw her begin to slip sideways and her hands to grope frantically at the air as if reaching for support. His own feet moved quickly and before he knew how it happened he had grabbed her to his chest. She shook in his arms as great sobs of anguish rent the air.

"Alicia!" He cried. "Whats wrong? Talk to me!"

"Michael, oh, Michael I know what it is!" She opened her eyes to his frightened green ones and said breathlessly, "I know what he was looking for. I know what Great Michael was looking for! All those years, walking, and walking and searching; I know what he was agonizing over!"

She took a deep breath. "Michael, it's all so

145

romantic and tender and sad;" she didn't stop long enough for him to ask what. "It's his father's gold cross! He needs his father's gold cross that his mother took from a locked chest of his father's things and hung around his own neck when he left Cork to come to America and he simply can't find it. He is literally lost without it. That cross represents peace to him now, in a sort of transubstantive way. Though he has searched throughout the years he cannot find it. He thought if only he could find the cross here where he last wore it, everything would be put to rights."

Alicia felt Michael tense. He held her suddenly back with one hand and with the other groped along the opening of his shirt and slowly extended an intricately carved gold Celtic cross which he let dangle in front of her eyes.

"This cross?" He said, as astonished at himself as he knew she must be and bent to kiss her wet and tumid eyes.

Alicia stared at the cross he held out to her on a heavy gold chain. She traced the intricate circle with one small finger and leaned her head against Michael's chest and wept. For all the years of torment and discouragement that the long ago Great Michael had endured, she wept. For the futility of his search, and finally for the misbegotten life without Kathleen, she wept.

Michael felt her heart beat against his chest as he held her like a small fragile bird. And if she sensed the drama, the adventure of it all, how much more must he.

Fourteen

Chattering: The Shadow Goes

When arriving at a building on the one side while the other faces water or a view of such extraordinary proportions it is difficult to say which is the front and which is the back. To arrive at the Crescent Hotel by carriage or automobile, as had presidents, governors and leaders from around the country, is to drive under it's specious porte-cochere, unload passengers and baggage and enter the ground floor through glass protected double doors into the lobby nearest the front desk. You may enter where they entered at the height of the Victorian era dressed in unsurpassed finery to relax, drink the healthy waters, and bask in the sunshine of distilled mountain air. You may walk on the broad expanse of polished wood floor where they walked, past the large fireplace on the right, which serves as divider between lobbies, out another set of double French doors onto a wide veranda which rises one floor above ground and the sight is like walking into a boundless hall set for a lavish banquet. The visitor is offered the immediate feast of formally laid paths through colorful, varied flowers and shrubs as prosciutto ham slices might be arranged with melon and fruit on a festal board. The central display reveals roof tops scattered among giant oak, maple and magnolia trees for your pleasure, like tiny parsley and broccoli trees might be found nestled between cherry tomatoes, mushrooms and radish roses on a relish platter. The further mountains might resemble a spectacular earth work of goose liver pate' spotted with almonds as if it surrounded a miniature Eureka Springs on the hors d'oeuvre tray. At the top, the star of the banquet, you might see as the crowning touch, an intricate ice carving of the Crescent Hotel from whose balconies one might heap with chilled, silver spoons Beluga caviar onto points of toast; for like the finest caviar, there is no building in Eureka Springs on equal plane with the Crescent Hotel.

To walk out onto this or any of the next three verandas, stacked one on top of each other like tiers on a Lady Baltimore cake, is to face every nuance of this scene and the immediate, natural tendency is to feast your lungs on fresh air. To take great heaping gulps of it. Breathe as deeply as if you were directly connected to a pipeline of pure oxygen and your life depended on it.

"Have you noticed how wonderful this air smells?" Michael said. Alicia and Michael stood on the first floor veranda and faced the new day as it was. The first of their lives together.

Alicia opened the door to the lobby where Zee, slouched with his hat covering his open mouth slept on an antique settee throughout the night, jumped awake. She said she was sorry he'd been inconvenienced but, they were starved and would he please bring the car and join them at the bakery down on Spring Street. They would walk down. Once again she marveled at the patience of the man.

Michael took her arm and led her down the steps and across the wide garden. Morris did not try to follow as he might have if he were younger and did not suffer from arthritis, but, turned instead to push open the cat door and walk stiffly across the hall to his pallet behind the reception area in a kind of large closet affair off the main lobby. Old habits can be relied upon to comfort age and aching bones.

They walked down the steep slope and soon realized the lawn ended across the cap of a stone wall which bordered the hotel property on the east. At the bottom the five foot wall rimmed the second tier of streets and they saw there was no way to gain it's access without jumping off so they turned to the side in the direction of a steep set of concrete steps but soon found these barred by iron railing, their safe purchase of the street could not be gained without going all the way back up to the hotel. Instead they chose to continue down the hill which gradually became more precipitous as they went until one foot had to be put sideways in front of the other to prevent pitching headlong over the wall.

Michael went the last six feet alone and by using one hand as a reverse vault jumped off the wall at the streets edge and turned to coax Alicia down. "It's o.k., come on, if I can do it, believe me, you can do it." He said. Alicia had watched his jump in amazement. But, how soon he had forgotten how far and steep it might appear when looking down from a height. "Just take it easy and you'll be fine." His own heart a furious staccato beat.

Alicia was, in fact, at that moment not at all sure she could manage without slipping. There was nothing, not tree nor bush; nothing, to grab or break her fall and from where she stood she wished he'd just sail his able body back onto the wall and help her down and was about to say as much when she took another tentative step sideways and started the dreaded slide down the slope, over the wall she went, flailing arms and grabbing air in broad jump fashion; with a loud 'whup!' she landed right in his arms, almost knocking him down.

"Wow! Sorry!" She cried while he yelled something like... "otchit-uff!" into her ear. She saw her reflection begin to disappear in his green eyes as they softened and he bent his head toward her mouth.

"Ah, Michael." She said, drawing back her head a little. "Ah, it's too soon for me to know what I feel. Can we please just be friends a while longer? In her eyes he saw a gentle pleading.

"You're right, Alicia." He said light heartedly. "Let's not rush things. It's only that you looked so cute and helpless flying through the air with that terrified look on your face!" They turned and began to walk down the quiet tree lined road laughing and swinging the hands they held between them.

The road followed the rock wall, from which every other road in Eureka Springs seemed to spiral down and was, in reality, little more than a broad paved path, barely room for two cars to pass. One car with two women in the front seat came toward them and passed, braked in the middle of the road behind them.

"Uh, Oh!" Michael mouthed to the side. "It's her. Just keep walking. Whatever you do, don't stop... come on." He pulled Alicia by the hand and began walking fast.

"That's it you lil' harlot! Run away and hide, we seen you!" They heard her before the car had stopped. Her mouth was the only thing that could be seen or heard out the car's window, shouting as if to the trees and the birds in them. They all knew instantly who it was bellowing down the morning at them.

Sister Dolly Garvin stuck her head and the omnipresent bible simultaneously out the window at them and yelled a new string of black and blue remarks, some they believed were coined on the spot: "Devilgoatmiss! and Sheanticris!" Until, to paraphrase Emily Bronte, "She was and is yet, most likely, the wearisomest, self-righteous pharisee that ever ransacked a Bible to rake the promises to herself and fling the curses on her neighbor." She was so fine an example of profound ignorance for all the world to hear that it seemed a shame to disabuse her of the notion on this fine morning and, as they were fast walking in the opposite direction, they chose to ignore her. Sister Dolly liked that even less.

"Come back here!" She screamed in a pitch higher and more deadly than the electricity that skittered in the wires overhead and tried to grind the car into reverse. The motor died instead. She did the next best thing her tantrum charged self could do; flung herself out of the car and kicked the door with all her considerable might and while white lightning pain shot up her discharged foot, her mouth never missed a beat.

"We seen you all scrunched up together back there, girly! We seen 'em I tell you!" She yelled her head around to any and all who were within ear-shot. She aimed the poor flaccid bible at Alicia, that same abused bible she used as a constant reminder of her righteousness and screamed another scripture as if it were a sacrosanct bullet into Alicia's departing back. "She had her dress up over his head in front of gawdeneverbody! We seen 'em!" The woman in the passenger seat had not said a word and still did not and it was only when Sister Dolly's great toe commenced to throb and swell inside her thin blanched tennis shoe and only when a bright red stain began to blotch the surface did Mayleen Huff invade her friend's deranged pique.

"Sister, get back in the car," Mayleen begged. "I do believe you have broken your great toe." This, to the babbling marauder she knew had lain awake half the night agonizing over Michael being with Alicia.

Now, on top of everything else, they would be late for the special church meeting sister had called.

The steep grade of the road helped Alicia and Michael gain an intersection of sorts on the downward spiral and they practically dove into a narrow footpath which opened on the right and quickly began its own hidden course around and down west mountain. In a matter of seconds they were out of sight and alone but for a feisty red squirrel who chattered at them in no uncertain terms as they ran down the dappled shadowed path where the hotel's guests long ago walked or rode horses as a short-cut down into town.

As they slowed finally, Alicia said, "I'm so sorry Michael. I feel partially responsible for your having to go through all this." Grasshoppers flew from branch to bush, their beating wings signaling an impending visit upon each other.

Michael's hand reached to brush skeltered hair back from her face. He spoke softly. "No Alicia, it's all my fault. I just hope she's not stalking both of us now."

Sister Dolly Garvin had managed to put her feelings for Michael aside while she rushed home for an ice pack to put on her toe. The top of her foot was already beginning to swell as she cursed Alicia, the car, the day, the mocking sound of her own anger inside her head. To all these and more she sent living sparks blame and received nothing save bitterness and vexation in return.

She sat with her injured foot on a chair and thought how to even the score when all she really wanted was to send him flowers, show him what a really kind person she was...

"The abuse is getting worse Alicia. She is a sicko, and I do worry for your safety." He hugged her hard against him as if he thought she might disappear as had Great Michael. "I'm the one who should apologize. After all I feel as though I have been treading water all my life and you have just rescued me."

He held her away. "I feel I could not breathe if anything happened to you."

"Oh, Michael," she drew back and looked into his eyes. "Sometimes things can get pretty hectic around me!" She motioned with her head back up toward the road and laughed. "Even now I feel there might be trouble, but isn't it all so amazing how everything has a way of working out?" He twirled her lightly in the bower of his arms, and his laugh could be heard over the early morning train, whistling itself a safe arrival at the station far below.

The trail was steep and their heels dug into the rocks as they made their way down and out of the deep shadowed tunnel-like overgrowth. Midway down the mountain a set of worn and scabrous steps led to another street level and they paused to drink from the fountain under a beautiful green and white gazebo. A sign proclaimed the water to be that of the Crescent Springs, another of the continuously flowing natural mountain waters in the area.

They stood together in the portioned shade, the spring's continuous flow made sweet water music as they looked up past the high stone bluff, through trees and dense undergrowth. Up through the towering oak and magnolia trees, though it could not be seen from this vantage point, they knew the Crescent Hotel to be up there and it was hard for them to believe, standing in so serene a place as this, they had, just moments before, escaped from a raving mad woman.

As if by unspoken agreement they caught hold of each others hands and began to walk, and, as if they

153

always had, start to whistle "Greensleeves" at the same instant. They looked incredulously at each other and broke off laughing so hard at this flukish synchronicity that their mouths could not perform again the recognizable notes.

They walked under the first autumn sun and felt a kinship with everyone who had ever awakened to a promise fulfilled. Past the old Carnegie Library and up onto Spring Street they walked; in front of the post office, the law offices of Eply and Eply, and peeked in the window of Michael's EAGLES RISE ART GALLERY which he would open in an hour. They ambled past jewelry, book and kitchen shops and just as they were about to enter the bakery, Zee pulled the Cord up to the curb and they all were in time to witness a young girl dressed as Alice In Wonderland, blond curls swinging like bells in unison, skip merrily toward them down the sidewalk with a pink plastic flamingo slung like a golf club over her shoulder. Quick on her heels, as if they were both late for a dress rehearsal, a very short March Hare, ears flopping maniacally, bounded at a set distance after her.

Alicia and Michael exchanged a look of open-eyed acceptance and shrugged, "Works for me!" he said and Zee collapsed onto the bakery's stoop laughing until he cried. When they last looked down the street after the pair, they had gone around the corner or somewhere and they were not quite sure if Alice and Company had not slid down the proverbial Lewis Carrol rabbit hole. It was, after all too early to tell.

Fifteen

All Her Paths Are Peace

They watched the leaping chiaroscuro of the fire in the grate and waited. An early winter bluster had appeared straight out of antiquity on that All Hallows Eve and straight into the open windows and doors of the drafty and, for the most part, dark Crescent Hotel; sending a flurry of hands to push and tug them shut but not before the cold surreptitious sharpness of it had marked the room's periphery; crept along the baseboards in gross reminder of how little chill the mortal flesh could tolerate.

A small table had been placed before the fire, but for that and the eldritch light of tall white candles, the room would have been in total darkness.

Alicia and Michael sat opposite each other in straight chairs, hands flat on the table in front of them and waited. Morris lay with his annatto colored back arched over the curve of Alicia's foot and drowsed while their shadows played out the flickering drama against the opposite wall.

Great Michael had been there many times before, indeed at times it seemed he had never altogether left. He had been there with one major difference; at all other times he had, for all purposes, come alone. Alone he had been in his suffering; alone in his need. The difference now was that he was drawn into this approachable circle of light by an indescribably pure and loving kinship between himself and the energy that had recently come to be there. He could no more have resisted it's influence than a feather could have gained control in a whirlwind.

One instant he was not there and the next his entire focused presence was totally there. Just there.

Alicia said, "Hello Michael, we have been waiting for you."

"And I you, lass." Great Michael said with a sharp fear and eager relief at her acknowledgement, testing the so called 'reality' of the situation. He was fearful that he might himself become extrinsic, feathery again; fearful he might suffer a quick return to that old repeated pattern of himself; and eager to gain the wherewithal that would release him from it. He most desperately longed for release.

"Michael," she said, "say hello to your great grandson, Michael Patrick O'Shawnessey McKinney."

"Aye, I thought it likely he." he said looking to Michael. "For tis like glancin' in a bright glass and he havin' the same countenance as meself." He saw that what Alicia and he had talked of in the dining room about young Michael's coming to Eureka Springs was true; and it was right and sane that this night, on the anniversary of his death those many years ago, the three would meet together and attend to the unfinished business between them. This night, Alicia had promised, it would finally make sense.

"Michael," he said, "we hae grave business to attend this night lad."

"Is he real, or is he not?" Michael gasped as if asking the question of the universe, and he may as well have done. Asked it of whomever or whatever was in charge; asked it to disentangle the seeming disparity of common knowledge of what it was like to be 'dead.'

"Yes, I am real," Great Michael said, "but are Ye, lad; real or are ye not?" And looked as baffled as ever a wanderer might when happening on a bright unexpected light from a darkness complete.

This, from a seeming ghost sent Michael's senses

reeling as if he fought a swift current which threatened to suck him headlong into a black hole. This, he could not fathom. This, for all the perplexed questioning and Alicia's patient answering, he could not absorb as reality. To acknowledge this presence; the absolute, unmistakable presence of the seeming mortal who stood essentially a stranger before him, bringing such a sweet and caring manner with him as he did; this, instantly riveting, instantly commanding persona in work clothes and scuffed brogans from another century, this, he could not get straight in his head. That this was, in fact, his own venerable great grandfather did not make matters easier.

Michael spoke from the fringe of an illusory vortex as if testing the solid ground for quicksand. "Hello, great grandfather." And it was like nothing he'd ever dreamed of saying in all of his life.

The fire made a sputtering sound as a log burned in half and collapsed into the ashes sending small orange and blue sparks like miniature Roman candles against a dark sky and no one took notice at all. Their inspection of one another could have taken a second or even a lifetime for all that it mattered.

Alicia spoke quietly to the standing figure beside them, "Michael has something for you."

She watched as Michael stood and pulled the chain over his own head and placed the Celtic cross with deliberate care and emotion around the neck of his great grandfather.

"Great grandfather," he said, "my mother gave this cross to me on my thirteenth birthday, as her mother had given it to her. When it was given they recited the story of how you had come across the ocean from Ireland to build this fine Crescent Hotel in Eureka Springs and told with great sorrow of your untimely death when you fell from the rafters and so the cross and the story were handed down from generation to generation."

Great Michael closed his forest colored eyes to the light and his great fist over the cross. On another level of being he felt the long absent imprint of the cross with it's sacred circle against his own long suffering heart as imponderable aeons of time beat in his chest. As simple a thing as that, as natural an act as that, cast shadows far across the decades as Sinclair Lewis' "Rosebud" has from the voice of citizen Kane.

Alicia broke the silence. "Michael wore the cross with great pride and respect but because of this intimate connection to you he has experienced himself falling, as you have, over and over again to his death but, until now, he did not know the reason for this unending cycle of terror."

Alicia read the unasked question in the silence between them."How is this possible?" She scanned their faces for verification and gazed down into the fire as if the actual words could be read in it's surreal amber colored light.

"Of all human fears," she said presently, "the fear of falling is one of the strongest; because falling has, at it's core, death. Yet most people do not realize that it isn't death they fear as much as it is the separation at death." She was not looking at Great Michael and was surprised when, after a long silence, she felt his hand on her shoulder. It was a kind touch. When she looked up his face was kind too; she had not seen recognition and knowing in his eyes before. She did now.

She smiled up at him and despite his anguish he smiled too. "Are ye sayin' lass, its not the dying that's the cause of me misery, but its the fealty to me flesh I canna' give up? Is that what you're tellin' me now?"

"Ah, Michael, something tells me you had it all figured out a long time ago." In his eyes she read fear and uncertainty poised as old adversaries.

Alicia stood and faced them. Morris sat at her heel. "Somehow, we have forgotten the basis for our real strength," she said, "our substantive energy. I refer not to your old body which returned a long time ago to the natural state of all things; but to the wild flow of pure energy within that body which was created purposefully, willfully, by the real you out of a certain need for expression; our SELF's need for expression; not the gross body, which is revered for the work it allows us to do but which is, in truth, merely a container for kinetic energy. It is by means of this residual kinetic energy that the terrible helplessness you must have felt became emblazoned on the cross as surely as if it had been carved there. The absolute horror of being grabbed by the incontrovertible strength of gravitational power as you plunged to your death embedded itself into your consciousness, went through you, directly into the actual chain and cross around your neck, into your clothes as well but metal seems to hold the imprint of this energy longer. It was after the cross had been placed around the neck of young Michael here," she motioned a hand in his direction, "that he came to this nightmarish impasse with his dreams however slightly it began. The stronger the experience, the more lasting the memory that was imprinted on the cross for all the world to read as surely as we can feel and read your thoughts in the granite blocks of this grand hotel."

Alicia sat now in the dim light of the shortened candles and dwindling fire, her voice, always a gentle and solacing particularity, assumed now a kind of tender authority.

"Michael," she spoke to Great Michael first. "Now, you will no longer be pulled into the never ending cycle of old pain. You can, by realizing what it's all about, release these thoughts as your prison, tell them to take a flying leap." She giggled at the unintended pun; at the unexpected lightness she felt.

"Pop them like the bubbles of hot air they are!" She snapped her slender fingers as before a paper tiger, her mouth set in the firm hard line of a trainer and herself so ordered: "You have control over whether you stay or go. It is strictly up to you, Michael. It's your choice... it always has been."

She let a smile play across her face and made an unfolding motion with her hands as if to release a bird held slightly. "Just... let... go..."

Great Michael put his face down as if to receive a benefaction through the fontenel spot at the top of his head and if it is true that the eyes are the windows of the soul, conviction could be seen in their depth as he raised his head and looked first at Alicia and then to Michael and as simple as that, he was gone.

Sixteen

Budding Morrow In Midnight

Morris's arthritic pain had eased. He drowsed peacefully before the fire after Great Michael had gone. His was the perfect relaxation; soothed to the marrow of his bones. Now, as if a cold sharpness had suddenly entered the room, the fur across his back raised as his ears picked up the sound of rushing feet and the door burst open.

"There she is, the little she devil!" Sister Dolly Garvin directed a dirty jagged fingernail above the biddable bible as though the one supported the other and shouted as if long rehearsed, "I demand, by the word of Gawd, arrest her for the devil worshiper she is!" Sister Dolly turned in sated action to the two men left standing behind her and gave her best "Hurrumpf!" for the self-serving entitlement of it.

Alicia sighed back into the chair. Her doll-like face in the firelight shone a combined look of astonishment and relief as the men walked forward and handed her a warrant for practicing sorcery. She began then, to be a little out of patience with Sister Dolly.

Her lawyer was called to the station downtown and almost before he had finished reading the warrant a commotion of car doors slamming and high excited voices set up on the street and sidewalk outside. The old fashioned screen door swung open and people in all manner of costume and dress began to swarm through: Two judges and their wives had come in tux and gown as though interrupted in mid-waltz; the owner of the Crescent Hotel wearing blue jeans and a plaid shirt had brought along the manager who was outfitted in an olive colored silk jogging suit and a couple of people Alicia recognized as hotel employees out of uniform; five children dressed in Halloween costumes accompanied by a lady in orange cotton sweats and a very large buff colored dog; an elderly couple with kind twinkling eyes came in house shoes and had to be helped up the steps under the lit balls of justice. In all, there were some twenty people along with Mayleen Huff who Alicia and Michael recognized to be Sister Dolly's friend; and, of course Sister Dolly herself was there looking smug and self satisfied despite an all too obvious case of hiccoughs she had acquired somewhere along the way. She may have been awash with liquor for all anybody knew. Certainly the moist air around her smelled to high heaven of something strong and alcohol-like. And the checked mood of the crowd left no doubt as to where this was all headed. A perfectly good celebration spoiled. Looked like the frivolity of Halloween would have to wait until next year.

All but Sister Dolly and Mayleen Huff had come from parties or scavenger hunts; from watching television and handing out Halloween candy at their homes; some even from their beds and all but the two had come in support of their great friend and confidant, Alicia Townsend. And all together they, in their separate manner of expression, set up a rushing demand to know at once whose idea it was to arrest this dear girl and what could she possibly have done to deserve such humiliating treatment anyway and the large buff colored dog began to howl and was sent to await his owner outside. The children took to unwrapping and sniffing each piece of candy and the youngest opened the door and fed the dog a piece of purple bubble gum which he accepted gratefully, without question. It was such a merry-andrew circus that Alicia and Michael could not look at each other without great restraint; a shortage of solemnity was just that eminent.

One of the judges walked to the back of a desk and pounded on it with a thick metal paper weight in the shape of an Oklahoma inscribed oil derrick and everyone jumped as if a gun had gone off.

"Now," he said, peering at the arresting officer over the top of his quarter moon glasses perched across the bottom half of his nose, "are you going to tell us what you are charging this young lady with?"

"Well sir, your Honor sir, Miss Sister Dolly Garvin here," he pointed one thumb over his shoulder in her general direction as if he were hitching a ride out on the highway. "Sister Dolly came in here and demanded that we go up to the Crescent Hotel and arrest this little lady," he nodded at Alicia.

"Your Honor, Miss, Dolly... er Sister... em... had a copy of a statute which states that anyone practicing fortune telling or sorcery in the city limits will be prosecuted."

The room suddenly became a tomb of stillness. The judge looked pensive while his brain rummaged around as much as it could in those ancient files he knew were no longer valid and turned his gaze on Sister Dolly, "Have you proof to substantiate these accusations?"

"Yessir, I surely do! I heard 'em first behind closed doors up at the hotel the other day, and tonight, well, let me tell you what, tonight being Halloween and her being a witch and a blasphemer, they was a-settin' in the dark with candles lit all around like a sayence talking to the spirits! I couldn't believe it myself but I seen it with my own eyes! And I heard with my own ears that she was blaspheming our sweet Jeesus by practicing witchcraft and healing like only he'd a done if he thought it was the right thing to do at the time. If he needed to." She had worn her good polyester flowered blue dress for the occasion and so took as deep a breath as her tight girdle could withstand and did the only thing she knew how to do. She raised her voice alongside the bruised bible and plunged ahead.

To say Sister Dolly was enjoying her role as avenger would be an understatement bordering on fiendishness and at that moment it would have been easier to stop the lion from eating Daniel than to negotiate her out of anything.

"He said right here," she poked the scarred bible with a stiff middle finger as it was her constant wont to do, "that it was always him to decide who gets healed, ('hiccup!'), and who don't!" Sister Dolly nodded her head around the room to make sure no one missed this very salient point. "And not nobody can, ('hiccup!'), ask the reason why neither!"

Reading more apathy than sympathy in their faces, she darted her head down to whisper to her friend Mayleen Huff as if she had just remembered the main point of her accusation. Mayleen leaned herself out from behind the total bulk of Sister Dolly's form to look at Alicia as if she couldn't quite believe she had actually showed up and whispered something behind her hand into sister Dolly's ear.

Sister Dolly nodded and bent down and very gingerly removed one tennis shoe from a swollen and blood cantered foot. The crowd gasped at the bared foot and held their hands over their mouths. It was an ugly sight. And the fly that had been here-to-fore ably entertained by the children's suckers and orange marshmallow peanuts, suddenly did a fe-fi-fo-fum turnabout and headed for the wider selection.

"She done it, she's the one! She done this to me!" Sister Dolly exploded at last and hopped up and down on one foot while a loud 'hiccup' erupted of it's own free-will out of her mouth. Children and old folks scrambled away as from a diseased person.

Sister Dolly pursed her lips and pointed the bloodied shoe at Alicia. "I warned her!" she hiccoughed. "I told her she couldn't come around here spreading her evil," 'hiccup', "around these gaudfearin," ('hiccup'), "folks! She done what I said she done and she's the devil's own handmaiden on top of it!" ('hiccup').

As one, the crowd pressed forward again to get a closer look and began to mutter various intimations of distrust toward Sister Dolly and call for forbearance on the part of Alicia. There could be no doubt on whose side lay their allegiance. They separately and together let the judge know they did not even know who this Sister Dolly person was. "Who is this woman?" They said to the judge and to each other." Where did she come from? She's not from around here is she? With certainty they said that this Sister Dolly had no right or permission from their community to speak on their behalf.

Alicia glanced at Michael and with a confounded look toward the judge took a step forward and said, "I think your honor knows, I have never intentionally caused harm to a living soul, my work here is quite the opposite. I would suggest you ask my friend Michael McKinny to tell what really happened that morning and for that matter, ask the lady with Sister Dolly to tell the truth of the incidence she witnessed." She leaned out and met the eyes of Mayleen Huff.

Michael first said he wanted to clarify that Alicia was not practicing sorcery but, helping his own energy to rid himself of terrible nightmares. She was merely doing an act of kindness. He then repeated the actual scene with Sister Dolly on the road.

The judge asked Sister Dolly's friend to tell what she had seen and instructed her to be very careful what she said because if it came down to it she would have to swear it as truth on the bible in court."

The lady hesitated and looked again at Sister Dolly's foot and perhaps it was the refinement and calm of the young Alicia, or maybe the sheer circumvention of facts by Sister Dolly, but, whatever the reason, the lady told the judge shamefaced, that Sister Dolly had kicked the car door with her foot and that it could be proven by examining the car. But, she said, she wanted to say something on Sister Dolly's behalf. Her friend Sister Dolly, she said, was a well meaning person at heart, really. She told of her being a good person, really, it was just that sometimes, when it came to her religion, she really lost all control, and no one could reason with her.

Sister Dolly held her unhinged jaw in that position and her eyes in white rimmed surprise until her friend said quietly out of the corner of her mouth, "Well, it really is the truth, after all."

"Whaa...!" Sister Dolly's jaw remained unhinged.

After this spoken defense Alicia cupped the elbow of her attorney and by her hand motioned him to a corner of the room where they bent in sotto voce conference; he shaking his head disapprovingly and she nodding affirmation until he seemed to sigh and shrug into a kind of reluctant compromise.

Alicia walked forward and placed a small hand lightly on Sister Dolly's arm. It was not in her capacity to hate. She saw only that Sister Dolly was a suffering human being and began in her mind the same calming ritual she did for anyone in pain. In just moments the crowd began to see the swelled face of the accuser yield it's unreasonable anger and it's need for great gulps of air ceased in mid-hiccough as she faced the judge with her eyes closed. Alicia had never tried to cure hiccoughs without the person's knowledge or permission.

There could be heard in the near distance the lonesome sound a train makes when reaching the last stop of a successful journey; something like a huge sigh in the night when all challenges of the trip have been met and the route book cleared once more. The dilatory fly buzzed the sticky sacks of candy and the children's mouths opened and closed automatically around chocolate filled suckers.

"If I can say, your honor I am impressed by the sincere testimony given by the friend on Sister Dolly's behalf." Alicia had often chosen to side with an adversary, understanding the fear and need behind such behavior. "I believe her when she says Sister Dolly is basically a good intentioned person. But Sister Dolly must understand that she cannot continue to stalk me, interrupt my business by barging in on my client's private counseling sessions. In this and every other conflict we must seek a harmony with each other; study and build on our likenesses within the universe, recover a oneness which has been shattered by warring religions with a false concept of what sin is. Realize, as the great Thomas Mann said 'He who believes in the devil already belongs to him.'"

"I cannot deliberately change Sister Dolly's concept of God anymore than I can deliberately change her concept of sin, that is not my province. But, if we are, as a diverse people, opposed to one another's goals and motivations, we must understand these concepts are the credo of institutions that are provided in our society and we generally behave as our institutions suggest. It is difficult for anyone brought up under their power to look at them objectively. Because of this, most people cannot see life except as a series of rivalry situations, wherein success is measured by humiliation of one's fellows. No one wins in this kind of situation and you end up feeling more powerless, more the loser, than ever. How can you win when you give up your power to an institution? How can you be happy and joyous if you are constantly labeled a loser, a sinner?"

"As from a height," Alicia said, "the turmoil below cannot be seen, so too the turmoil is itself involved. The astronauts from their vantage point in space told us that the swirled blue-white elegance of our water planet cannot be seen by those of us who are lost in the dust of it's surface. We are as self-absorbed as King Kong must have looked to Faye Ray, an unbelievable apparition of power out the window. Those of us who have forgotten that spark of creative energy which brought us to life, cannot perceive that life clearly. On the other hand, because we may temporarily have forgotten it does not mean we have lost that intrinsic quality, for it, by definition, cannot be lost or given; cannot be wrested from us or bartered on our behalf, as is so often published, but, must simply be remembered by us in order to reclaim it. Wherever it goes, driven by whatever emotion, intent or will, we go. Where it is, we are."

In the warm room all motion had stopped. Even the flies were silhouettes on the screen and the children, already thinking of Christmas trees and stockings filled with striped ribbon candy felt a nameless significance to the young girl's words, stopped chewing and allowed their mouths to be dulled by brown candy circles.

Alicia continued to face and address the judge and

the group as if they were a kind of gestalt alone in the world. They sighed as if they had held a collective breath as her words now filled the chamber. Her words fell in odd numbers, a kind of rhythm set, as soothing as a mourning-dove's call in the woods. Words of affirmation. Words deeply satisfying.

"Nosir! No!" Sister Dolly burst into the calm, the flowered dress hiked itself from beneath her tight belt scrunching up on one side as if to give full meaning and support of the bible she suddenly thrust up and set the overhead light to swinging. "Nosir, your worship!" She shouted without a sign of hiccoughs and made the crowd recipient of an 'I told you so' smug look around.

"See there," she positively beamed, "I told you that girl was a blasphemer and a lying, thieving blasphemer at that! You heard her say our swaweeet Jeezus lied! Lied, mind you! Said he didn't sacrifice hisself for our sins there on the bloody cross! She said he never could die on the cross to save us from our everlasting, burn in hell, sins, and that's just a plain, flat out lie!" With this last outburst a vein began to swell and visibly throb at her right temple and she withdrew her eyes into their sockets like a tiger after striking it's prey.

Everyone began to frown and grouse among themselves and with confounded words shout at each other for they had surely heard this kind of talk before, this Sister Dolly kind of talk; known this talk from the cradle, from their parents; known their own minister's to talk this talk from the pulpit; unkind, hurtful, uninvited and sorrow filled talk. They felt cornered. Pinned down like butterflies on a specimen board. On the other hand Alicia's way of seeing and putting things together, this way of love and unbiased understanding, this full comprehension was surely more life validating, self responsible talk and gracious. And, to them, it had a ring of bountiful truth for they knew in their hearts that had they been given the choice, it surely would not have been to have Christ or anyone else for that matter, put to death on their behalf. Knock on any door and the man, woman or child who answers will be appalled at the idea of a neighbor put to death on his own lawn to atone for... their what? Irresponsibility of birth? Should we be ashamed for being born? Did it mean no one should be born? Come one come all to circus of sacrifice?

To them at that moment, it was an insanity.

One little tow headed boy sporting a superman cape around his shoulders, after hearing Sister Dolly's twisted mean hearted rhetoric, jerked the trick or treat sack away from his sister who set up such a caterwauling until everything and everybody was flung into their own separate brand of chaos.

"Order!" The judge shouted, blew his nose into a white linen handkerchief and took up the oil derrick and made a new dent next to the previously walloped one. "Order, now I say! Or you'll all have to leave!"

"Now, Sister Dolly," he said over the top half of his eye glasses after the room calmed, "you have gotten clear off the subject and gone to preaching something else entirely and instead, I believe, you made a false accusation against Miss Alicia Townsend because you couldn't control your own temper and did bodily harm to yourself and if Miss Alicia's helping another human being through rough times is a crime, then I'm a monkey's uncle." No one moved while the judge continued. "And Sister Dolly? Don't bother this court with any more folderol! Charges dismissed!" The Oklahoma oil derrick hit the desk again and every-one watched Sister Dolly's flowered print dress disappear out the door as if the one action had caused the other.

"Hurrumpf!" she swept over the dog, "You just wait and see!" He held his teeth out to her in reply.

In the car, Michael once again voiced his concern for Alicia's safety. "That woman is mad, I tell you! There is absolutely no way even you can reason her out of the insanity she preaches."

"Alicia will be alright Michael." Zee said from the front seat. "I get concerned every now and then myself, but she knows how to handle herself. Besides, I'm always within earshot."

Michael sighed. "Well, it's a fact you have to go about your daily business, Alicia, but promise me you will not take any foolish chances."

"Emmm." She said and laid her head back against the seat. "Zee's right Michael, I am ultimately responsible for my own safety. Responsibility makes you see things in a totally different way. Responsibility for your own actions is the ultimate freedom. That's really what I wanted to get across tonight.

"I'm beginning to sense that for the first time and you're right," Michael said. "It's not nearly as frightening as it sounds. In fact it feels some kind of wonderful to know that I will advance or fall on my own merit. Why do you suppose people shirk it like a plague, resist even the idea of that kind of independence?"

"Ah, Michael," She laughed, "that kind of logic, that magical reasoning, my dear sir, will get you everywhere!"

Zee drove into the parking lot at the Crescent Hotel alongside Michael's car.

"No, seriously, Alicia, why has responsibility gotten such a bum rap?" Michael said. "It seems like more and more people are just shrugging their shoulders."

"Well..., maybe we can apply a little more of that logic here. The trouble, Michael, is that when we are awakened to responsibility we must continue in accountability. Simple. Responsibility, accountability. Some are made uncomfortable by this most equitable and reasonable of measures and seek some relief from the self imposed burden of responsibility their actions have assigned them. But, however painful, however great the exigency it imposes upon us, until the commitment is satisfied we cannot be freed from it and as handy as it would be to be delivered of this responsibility, safe to say most would conspire to evade liability, imprudent actions on our part cannot be passed on or taken up by any other than ourselves. Abdication is simply not an option, sorry." She crinkled her eyes and kissed him lightly on the mouth. "Sleep well, Michael."

"Oh, what magic doth ye weave, me darlin' girl." He reached for her hand and pressed it to his cheek. "Good night." He said, half out of the car. "And Alicia, thank you forever for what you did for Great Michael and me tonight. Even though I feel naked without the cross," his hand went automatically to his chest, "it all felt so right! It was quite an experience. I'll never forget it!" And as if he sought a private inventory added, "I do believe I will sleep the 'sleep of the just' tonight."

From her hidden position behind the shrubbery Sister Dolly Garvin saw the car's dome light come on and Michael lean in to kiss the hand of Alicia and it might as well have been someone else that crouched in hiding for all the control she felt over the situation. From somewhere deep within that other person a silent tortured scream began. She had rushed out the door of the police station a jangle of nerves and hormones and dropped Mayleen off at the corner instead of taking her home. Had come immediately to the Crescent to crouch desperately in the dark and watch Michael's car and would have waited all night for him to return if that was what it took.

As Michael started his engine, before he turned on the headlights, he glanced into the rear view mirror. A glint of light came off some dull metal behind the trees.

"Oh, Hell!" He slammed his right hand into the steering wheel. "Will she never stop?!!"

"What...? Why is she doing this to me? What is going on?" He tried to calm himself when what he really wanted more than anything was to feel her mashed red face under his fist and gave the steering wheel another hard whack. Crack! The automatic adjustment shot the wheel into it's highest position. 'Whoa! Take it easy man! It can't be your fault. You did nothing to encourage her. That's true,' he thought, 'I didn't. The first time you ever laid eyes on her was when she skulked by the gallery... no wait... wait a minute... wasn't she the clerk at the convenience store a month or so ago. She gave me change for a twenty instead of ten and was so grateful when I pointed out her error I thought she'd come unglued.'"

"O.K. That's it!" He started the car and moved away from the sight of Sister Dolly's bumper gleaming out at him in the moonlight. "That's it, I've had enough of this. And I don't care what Alicia says I won't let her be subjected to this crazy woman ever again."

As he turned into his driveway he heard the light ping, ping, ping sound of gravel in the rim of Sister Dolly's tires as she drove slowly by with the lights off. He closed the door to his ivy swarmed cottage and told himself no matter, he had made up his mind.

Short of strangling Sister Dolly he could protect Alicia by leaving for awhile. Tomorrow, in fact. He would make arrangements to go abroad tomorrow. It was time, past time really, for him to go in search of. That is what his mother used to call it. 'Go in search of.' It meant to forage the unique art and antique pieces out from wherever they happened to be: in little out of the way places, seek the museum quality under the dust and grime of ages in attics, back rooms and barns. "Always expect the unexpected Michael," she'd repeat the cliche with a twinkle in her eye.

After their father died she had taught him and his brother Shaun everything she knew about form and style as they were growing up in Sedona, Arizona. She would have them stand before a painting or piece of sculpture and tell her what they saw. Explain what was right about it; what was not so right. Michael had an eye, she said, and the patience. Shaun was otherwise suited. She sent one to art school and one to study law. One was definitely right brain dominant, the other, left, she said.

Their's had been a prestigious fine art gallery in Sedona. Perched on the rim of Oak Creek Canyon, it's red adobe walls looked carved, an integral part of those mighty earth works whose buttes and canyons are as sought after by movie makers as the energy from the vortices far below attract so many tourists that the motel/hotel rate of occupancy stays at a strong 98% year round.

His mother had sold the gallery at a handsome profit when she was told of the great healing waters of Eureka Springs, Arkansas. Her arthritis was acting up and besides, she said, she needed a change. She needed greener air, greener pastures she laughed. Together they bought the building down on Spring Street, leased out one half and Michael set up his

Eagles Rise Gallery in the other half.

It was while furnishing his house that Michael came to discover the rich and varied antique shops in Northwest Arkansas. He found and purchased his first piece, an 18th century Provencal walnut chair with it's original rush seat for his accounting desk in the gallery. That was 8 months ago. Now that he'd met Alicia things were almost perfect. Almost.

Why not, he reasoned, travel to France, find a few good pieces, a chest or two, armoire, desk, tables and whatever else he thought might appeal, to hang paintings above, place sculpture on and inside, showing everything to better advantage.

He had studied and read of such fertile areas in Aux-en-Provence, Ansouis, Avignon, Arles, where one could find the best eighteenth and nineteenth century antiques and paintings. A broad selection of paintings from seventeeth to nineteenth century were to found at ateliers which often host open-air markets that draw buyers and sellers from far and wide. One only had to know the difference between the rare find and junk.

Yes, he would leave the gallery in the very capable and experienced hands of his mother, and kiss Alicia goodbye. Be gone a month or two if necessary, whatever it took to get Sister Dolly's attention away from Alicia.

Suddenly lighthearted he began to sing in a fine baritone, "Love lift us up where we be---long! Where the ea....gles cry on a moun...tain high," from *An Officer And A Gentleman,* as he fixed himself a peanut butter and grape jelly sandwich and went to telephone his mother. "Far from the world we know; up where the clear winds blow, Hello Mother o'mine? Will ye tend the gallery while I go across the sea in search of?"

Lesley McKinney laughed. "Michael Patrick! Where's your head, son? What's got you so full of blarney this time of night?"

"Well, as you always say, Ms. McKinney." He said around a mouthful. 'Keep a fresh stock. The more variety of related merchandise the more repeat customers.'"

Lesley laughed and stuck out her tongue to the phone. "You're eating peanut butter and grape jelly aren't you Michael?" She asked about his comfort food, didn't wait for an answer. "Of course I will, Michael," she continued. "You know I will, son. But, what has got you in such a rush all of a sudden?"

He told her then, about Alicia. How and why he'd gone to her for help. About Great Michael and the gold cross. How much she had come to mean to him, and how he cared desperately for her safety. About how his presense in her company had absolutely incensed one Sister Dolly Garvin. He told her about the stalking and the absurd and dangerous behavior and of how he hoped his absence would put Sister Dolly on to some other, more harmless diversion.

Alicia had made and kept true to her pledge to see the spirit of great Michael calmed; the rest would be up to him. However, her work in the old Crescent Hotel was just beginning. There were others in need of assistance and she deemed not to leave them to their sorrows.

With Michael off to Europe she felt something like a leveled relief. Time was needed to sort out her feelings for him and he most assuredly could use some time away from the now drawn, haunted face of Sister Dolly she sometimes saw crossing the street at the post office or sliding by on the street below her window at the Crescent. But for these brief unobserved glimpses Alicia did not see her and

176

quite forgot she was still around.

People continued to come to her from everywhere. Most could not altogether understand why they came. They seemed to float about the hotel in a kind of curious waltz with the long departed as if they half expected to meet their own future dimensionless selves along the dark corridors until the floors and walls seemed to emerge and recede in a certain bioplasmic strangeness. Haunted, as it were, by spirits who had deviated from the path as though interrupted in mid-conflict, without common resolution.

It was during the first lull in days, Alicia let Morris out and closed the door. Each morning he waited at the hearth in the lobby. And each morning he saw her approach through the glass panel doors his ear's shot forward and he made a soft safe purring sound in his throat. This morning he escorted her into her rooms as usual but was not allowed to lounge about for very long. She had a new client coming in a hour and she wanted a quiet time in which to prepare herself.

After first taking generous swallows of mineral water from the bottled Crystal Springs water she always kept for herself and her clients, she leaned back in the chair and closed her eyes. The deep, measured breathing began automatically to clear, cleanse; prepare her for a new start. She began to see shadows moving behind her eyes and hear quiet foot-steps approach and retreat, felt an immediate, threatening presence in the unfamiliar room in which she found herself.

Seventeen

To Win Or Lose It All

The young man's choked breathing was rough like something pulled through tightly packed gravel and in sudden sharp peaks his skimpy chest rose and fell into the sunken valley between his ribs. His ragdoll-like stupor atop the mattress spoke a raging fever as Doctor Moore entered the small stuffy room.

"Could I get a cup of hot coffee?" He said to the nurse. "I've been up all night and this dastardly wind seems to be blowing influenza germs in over the Mississippi River faster then I can wrestle them out." He shrugged out of his heavy alpaca coat and handed it to the nurse. Making house calls at eleven o'clock in the morning was nothing out of the ordinary, but this was St. Louis in January in the middle of the worst blizzard he could remember and his joints were cold and stiff with arthritis. The new year, 1904, had been a doozy thus far for weather and sickness. The rooming house, thank God, had been on his way.

He heard the rapid voice of delirium as he approached the shallow folds in the bed. The young man's red mottled cheeks and hair plastered stiffly to his temples were typical of many he'd seen throughout the long night.

"Purple light projection, that's the ticket." The young man licked his parched lips, spoke and paused, frowned as if listening into the void. "Could be that luminiferous ether!" He exalted, eyes ablaze with light as if he'd just discovered a great truth. Knew an answer in the midst of unbridled adversity.

179

'All these phases of dying.' Doctor Moore shook his head gravely, there was no telling what one might hear at a deathbed. He saw his own brand of proof in the patient's glowing eyes. Prolonged, elevated fever in one so pitifully frail was always, in his experience, fatal. The metal corners of his large black medical bag made a tap dancing sound on the bare floor as he plopped it down beside the chair. With the ends of the stethoscope hanging from each ear he flicked out a thermometer and inserted it between the two flaccid lips; lifted the slack wrist and almost winced at the heat.

"Racing pulse," he said listening. "Temperature 106 degrees." The nurse made note. 106 degrees. She had guessed within a tenth of a degree. Critical for a child, deadly in a man.

He palpated the young man's chest in several places and listened. He shook out the thermometer, placed it onto the worn red velvet lining in it's leather case and with a finality all too familiar, snapped the lid shut and folded the black wriggling stethoscope back into the bag. As the nurse handed him a cup of hot coffee he whispered to her over the steam. "You might as well notify his people." He shrugged hopelessly. "Unless a miracle occurs he's a goner."

When Doctor Moore returned that afternoon at two o'clock he was shocked when the young man grinned, albeit it weak, and with a"Hullo Doc" sat up in the rumpled dank bed. "What in the world did you do to him?" He demanded." I never saw a fever break that fast!"

"Nothing." Said the nurse. "Except I gave him a dish of ice cream."

"Why you could have killed him! You don't give ice cream to a person with high fever!" Doctor Moore was scandalized when he thought of what could have happened to his patient. "Who told you to do that?" He demanded. The nurse pointed to the Jewish landlady.

"Don't you know a person that sick hasn't a chance in a hundred of living after eating ice cream?" He glared at her. Suddenly the doctor realized how ridiculously moot his senseless tirade had been when he saw the beginning mirth pass between the patient and his two care givers as if to say, 'What difference does it make? He's going to recover, isn't he!' It was obvious something had literally saved the life of twenty two year old Norman Baker.

"You keep ice cream in the dead of winter?" The doctor took another tack.

"Ya, vintertime, sure." Said the landlady. "That's nothing doctor, I alvays give to my children ice cream when they got a fever."

The landlady's dish of ice cream may have helped to break Norman's fever, however, there had been another particular factor to consider in his cure.

Before, in the pressed heat, the galling ever spiraling heat of Norman's body had drifted him alternately close and far away like an exhausted bird whose wings beat fervently upon the windowpane. Voices in the room could not be distinguished from a radio playing next door; a buzz and hiss of garbled messages through which the voices crossed and recrossed themselves and mingled with cabbage and onion smells from the kitchen and when the doctor came through the door the odor of ozone filled the room and lay manifest along the folds of his snow sprinkled coat. Norman became aware of every sensation through the pores of his scalded skin. Aware and highly sensitized so that when the doctor's hands reached to examine and probe they felt like needle points, and he winced at the slightest touch as if he could not easily bear the shape or weight of these antiseptic hands on his sensitive skin.

All that morning he had slept fitfully, and through the fevered confusion a ferment of dreams drifted. His own voice came over the radio,"Hello folks, this is Norman Baker the voice of XENT in Mexico," and while the U.S. Ambassador to Mexico, Clayton Powell told of his interest in Eureka Springs, Arkansas, from the elegant Crescent Hotel, Norman found himself in a crystal lighted ballroom singing "Happy Birthday Clayton Powell", along with a crowd of political dignitaries and prominent people from the around the state.

"You will own that radio station and this hotel one day." The voice said into his head simply and without preamble.

Yung once said that any essential change of attitude signifies a psychic renewal which is usually accompanied by symbols of rebirth in the patients dreams or fantasies.

Norman Baker had asked himself more than once that winter of 1904, what was he out to prove. The answer was always the same. He did not labor, as some people supposed, for money or celebrity. He worked diligently, with wholehearted enthusiasm for his ideas because he knew he must. A perceived idea is a priceless thing. These things come unbidden to fertile minds. They come for the benefit of mankind. Dreams or fantasies, it made no difference to him, he knew them as important problem solvers. Each of his inventions arose from a direct need. Each was needed to solve a specific problem. Norman came by his inventiveness early.

Born of poor immigrant stock, Norman's father had

come to America from Germany as a stowaway at age eleven and renamed himself John Baker. After fighting heroically on the side of the union in the Civil War, in 1865, he married Francis Anschultz, a cultured woman who contributed poems and stories to magazines of the day. He started the first sheet iron and boiler machine shop in the little southeastern river bend town of Muscatine, Iowa just below Davenport. At the time of his death John Baker held one hundred twenty six American and foreign patents.

Norman had been a brilliant student. Youngest of ten his mother spoiled him and his father could not do anything with him. Even at a young age he seemed to have his own agenda.

"But Father," Norman said time and again, "I don't want to go to college." It was a continuing battle of wills.

It always began with his father's small, placating, "What are you? Afraid? The others could not go, but you Norman, you can go to University anywhere in the world you want." His big powerful arms stretched over his shoulders and came together with clasped hands in a pleading gesture. And end in a shouting match, "If I say you go, you go!"

Norman thought it was in his blood to be a machinist. However, it took a lot of persuasion on his part to be allowed to leave high school after one and a half years.

His life was to take a strange turn because of a physical quirk. Young Norman was noticeably pigeon-toed. He was teased constantly by a popcorn salesman called Popcorn Jim. "Toes out, bud!" He'd shout from a safe distance. "Toes out!" Norman could not bear his taunting; heard his teasing even in his sleep. So, even though it hurt mightily, he began with all his strength to walk slower, to deliberately concentrate on every step, forcing his toes out. He cured himself and the power of suggestion was born in his mind.

This first lesson of mind over body was to help him throughout his life. Besides being pigeon-toed Norman was a stutterer. Time after time he was rendered helpless by a workman in his father's plant who would wrestle him to the ground, straddle him and tickle his ribs until he was faint and nauseous. He learned to steel his mind and soon conquered the affliction but, why, he wondered, did grown men behave like this? Where did this compulsion to tease small boys come from? Inane stupidity, boredom, what? From the looks on their faces they looked like overwhelming fiends ready to pounce on the weaker more helpless segment of society.

Norman went to work as a machinist and tool and die maker for Kerr's Machine Shop where Paul Baker, an older brother worked.

Since 1891 Muscatine had been the center of the fresh water pearl button industry. The buttons were made from clam shells dug from the bottom of the river. This required 5 to 8 operations to make one button.

When the German engineer in charge of the Boepple Button plant resigned, the position was offered to Paul who turned it down. Norman hounded his brother until Paul recommended him for the job. When asked if he thought he could handle the huge machines, Norman brashly said he didn't know who they'd had in charge but if he were handling the shop the owners would certainly never see them operating with a brush adjustment as they now did. He told them he was surprised the machines were not burned up in the process. They hired him. Norman had bluffed his way in.

He not only made a good first impression but soon proved his worth by clearing up a static problem in an unused button machine. He knew that static electricity would follow a charred wood line and so by connecting such a line from the machine, over the top of the bench, down the leg to the floor near a ground connection alleviated the problem.

Still, the shop was working inefficiently. The machines were inadequate. Norman put his productive mind to the invention of an automatic button machine. The company agreed to finance the patent while allowing Norman to build the machine, retain 50% ownership and pay him three dollars a day to boot. Beyond that, the best Norman could secure "up front" was a promise that as soon as the machine was operational he would be given a new contract. Not so, said a girl who worked in the factory. She told Norman she had overheard a conversation between two men which indicated that they intended to bamboozle him out of his invention. Norman walked into the office and demanded the contract be fulfilled as promised and they simply told him to go back to work and finish the machine or they would force him to. His first inclination was to walk out but he realized if he quit they would take his tool chest and make it impossible for him to work elsewhere. He went back to work and began to smuggle his tools out of the factory and in a few days he had them all.

When, on the last day Norman walked in the house carrying his tool chest his mother said, "What?" He told her of the intended swindle and she asked if the men could complete the machine without him if he quit.

"Yes, with the blueprints." Norman said.

"Ah," she said." Only if they have the blueprints.

You bring me the blueprints, then quit. "She told him never mind, he needn't worry because he was a minor and the contract was worthless without her signature. If they came with a search warrant she would take care of it.

So, with blue prints in hand, Norman went to the German American Bank, spread the blueprints on the president's desk and told him the story. In return for half interest in the button making machine he was lent the money to complete it.

His brother Paul had faith in Norman and the machine so the two of them rented the Vance and Myers Boiler and Machine Shop, and into it they moved the incomplete machine. However, Norman was not "fast enough" for the bank's taste so they told him to forget it. A friend of his, Nick Barry who manufactured button making machinery had often seen the incomplete machine in Kerr's Machine shop, duplicated and completed the invention and so reaped all the benefits. Norman was taken completely by surprise. He could not believe he had been betrayed by the bank, that most trustworthy of institutions, and a friend had been bribed to rob him of his invention. Another valuable lesson, learned the hard way. Better to let an invention lie dormant until one has the finances to manufacture it oneself. He never forgot this.

However, Norman was learning the much more valuable lesson of a door never closing without another one opening. He could not forget his success with mind control. He had effectively cured his pigeon toed walk and stuttering speech and with it the embarrassment and frustration. All around him he began to see evidence at work of this strange power of mind over matter.

Born under the sign of The Archer, Sagittarius, he

was never quite convinced of the efficacy of astrology but was totally intrigued by the idea that his whole personality was so adequately described by it. ".... an inherent faculty for amassing wealth." He read. "They throw their whole force and strength into whatever they are doing. "More..." Self goals give you a sense of individuality, separateness and freedom from the crowd," it said. And these were but a glimpse of what had opened as possibilities for his life.

He inherently knew that to define his life, find the real self he longed to know, he would have to leave home and the embrace of his large comfortable family to discover what he was all about.

As he traveled in Illinois, Ohio, Indiana and Missouri he sought employment in the largest machine shops but soon grew tired of the sameness. There had to be more to life, he intuited, than these dead end jobs. He wanted and needed something which matched his expansive, soaring spirit.

Despite his small stature he first aspired to public speaking and oration. He noticed that on stage people loomed taller, commanded attention. He perfected and then embarked on a round of mental telepathy stage performances inspired by those of a man named Herbert L. Flint, a stage hypnotist he admired.

He was determined to best Mr. Flint in his own field. Little did he know that this urge to do a thing better than anyone else had done it before was also a Sagittarion trait. With advance publicity the first night drew thousands from the town and miles around. After a shaky start, he was so nervous, so afraid of loosing his place with the memorized speech he threw it to the side and looked his audience in the eyes and began again, "Folks," he said, and the homely word broke the ice. With one hundred and fifty dollars to the good that first night he went on to town after town until they began to blur in memory. He had learned how to reach the people but mismanagement landed him in St. Louis in a depression year where he had to pawn his watch for room and board. It was in St. Louis that he took the job as a moving picture operator, caught pneumonia and almost died. Twice. Norman never forgot that it wasn't the medical profession that saved him. It had instead to do with the Jewish landlady's dish of ice cream and his own iron will to get well.

He willed himself out of bed and marched out into the cold grey January day and found a job as a sign painter despite his sunken cheeks and sickly appearance. On the second day the owner handed him a doctor's card and a five dollar bill.

"You sound terrible and you look worse." He said. "You can't work in this condition."

The doctor examined Norman thoroughly, putting the cold black stethoscope more than once to his back. "Tuberculosis." He said finally."You have the one lung that's bad and the other's not worth a plug nickel. You won't last six months, son, I'm sorry to say. "He gently put his hand on Norman's shoulder. "You better go home and arrange your earthly possessions." Norman looked alarmed. No matter how firm his resolve, no matter how iron his will, the human psyche can still be traumatized by words of this nature delivered by such an authority.

"You smoke?" The doctor said. Norman nodded.

The doctor sighed. "Go on smoking cigarettes and they'll bury you in three months!"

Norman knew the doctor's words were true. He knew a friend in Muscatine who had been told the same thing. The boy had given up the fight and died within three months. Norman determined this would never happen to him. Ever the practical one, he did not simply sit down and concentrate strongly on the fact that he did not have tuberculosis nor did he go home to die.

Even though he was broke he decided to move. He had been sharing a room at a dollar and a half a week with a man who continually coughed and spit on the bare floor. At the end of the first week when his six dollars came from the sign painting job he moved into his own room. He took no medicines and relied on mental concentration.

"A natural inclination toward purity of thought and action, the fundamental cause of their physical power and endurance." His horoscope had read. "Their physical strength is greater than that of any people born under any other sign....they throw their whole force and strength into whatever they are doing...." Powerful words he took to heart.

Within a few months he returned to Muscatine the perfect picture of health.

Norman had money in his pockets and experiences more outreaching than any of his family. He gave no hint of his bouts with illness to the family for fear they would not let him leave again. Instead, he talked to them about his success as a stage mentalist. Mental telepathy, he called it. He had proven that if he had a person of high sensitivity to receive the wordless messages it worked repeatedly well. He told them it was like what some people called inspiration, or to having a vivid dream as to what was about to happen. Doing things on a hunch or intuition. He practiced this faithfully and knew without a doubt his hunches proved valid. If, on the other hand he allowed himself a sober, second thought, it did not work.

He then launched another round of highly successful tours featuring Madame Pearl Tangley, a cryptic magnetic name he invented to bring him good luck.

They were on stage in front of hundreds of people at Lowe's Theater in New York City. Just as Madame Tangley correctly read the message on the board behind her a professional debunker of such acts jumped up out of the audience.

"You're a fake!." He shouted. "It's all a hocus pocus trick!" He shouted to the stunned audience.

Norman whirled around, "That's a challenge if ever I heard one!" His blue eyes were steely and he pointed directly at the man with an unwavering finger. "You there sir, do you dare to call Madame Tangley a fake?"

"Yes sir, I do! It is impossible to read minds! It has to be a trick!"

"You have one chance to prove your accusations. Name your conditions."

The man waved a paper tablet in the air. "I will write down a set of numbers, unseen by anyone, and lay the covered tablet face down on the stage. She must read the correct numbers, in the correct order."

"Done!" Norman shouted. "Provided the audience write down every number as Madame Tangely recites them and they, not me, compare the numbers to those you have written down as she calls them out."

She did not make a single mistake. As a result Norman had all the contracts he dreamed of.

In New York Norman advertised for a secretary to travel. Many applied but he chose Theresa Pinder a recent graduate from Wooster College, in Massachusetts. She could take dictation faster than anyone he had ever seen.

For weeks she did the office work from a hotel room on the Wilbur and Vincent circuit and showed no interest in the theater. Norman finally convinced her to attend a matinee and critique the act.

Afterwards, she said the act was fine but that she could not understand how they had been so highly successful when they used such atrocious grammar. "You murder the English language." Theresa said.

Norman's mouth hardened stubbornly."What do you mean?"

"I don't want to make you angry, but since you ask, you and this young lady say things like 'I seen him do this or that.' The word is saw. You say them numbers when you should say those numbers."

Even though it hurt his ego Norman did not like to think he had made such glaring mistakes in public. He asked Theresa to be their watchdog and correct their grammar in private. The act was immediately improved.

When the first Madame Tangley retired Theresa reluctantly took her place and the act was better than ever. Together they found a rare compatibility. In fact they got along so well that they decided to get married in Buffalo at eleven o'clock in the morning, continuing the act at that afternoon's matinee. They crossed the country several times before renting a house in Muscatine for a summer vacation in 1914.

Theresa's English father, a minister and musician, as well as a piano and organ repairman, was invited to stay with them. He had played the organ at their wedding. They were scheduled to resume their act in Chicago in the fall. Norman wanted a musical instrument to be used for outdoor advertising. Ever a believer in publicizing, he began a search for the right instrument. The only thing available were

191

hand organs or electric bell instruments which were unsatisfactory.

Norman, having no musical education, was no doubt a little intimidated by a wife who was a pianist and a father-in-law who was an organist, and set out to prove once again it was simply a case of mind over matter.

His brother Paul still operated the machine shop so Norman began tinkering around and quickly invented what he named the Tangley Air Calliope played with air pressure rather than steam. Crude as his first instrument was it was sensational from the start and without the mess of coal. One day as he was tuning it a carnival owner two blocks away heard it and came running. James Patterson bought the first instrument from Norman who thought since it was only June he could produce another before the Chicago opening.

He built another, then another, improving as he went along and sold each one as they were completed. When September rolled around with the opening not far off he had several orders to fill. At the urging of a few young Chamber of Commerce friends, Norman dropped out of the theatrical business and started the full manufacturing of the Calliaphone which he had renamed it.

He put Theresa in charge of the office and soon, assisted by ads placed in Billboard Magazine they were grossing millions. To this day the distinctively unique sound of the Calliope immediately creates a magical environment for circus and carnival, skating rink, amusement park, state and county fair, to name a few, around the world.

Norman and Theresa were amicably divorced after five years. They admitted to each other finally that the marriage itself lacked excitement. They felt they were too much alike. Ironically, after five years without so much as a quarrel, by Iowa law their divorce decree had to assert incompatibility as proper grounds.

The Calliaphone business continued to flourish however, until in July, 1920, while Norman was sleeping in a back room of the building, a fire destroyed the building and everything in it. The insurance company could only pay back advance deposits on the Calliophones ordered. Norman was lucky he had escaped with his life.

On a hunch he next tried his hand at tinting pictures with oil paints and was again highly successful. He envisioned an art correspondence school whereby he would teach students to tint black and white Kodak pictures and make a tidy profit. Before long the Tangley School was in full swing and for three years students were ordering from him all their brushes, paints, enlargements, frames, glass, everything to make themselves and Norman Baker, successful.

Even though he had quit high school after a year and a half this was by no means the end of his education. His interests and hunger for knowledge were so diverse that no one subject or school could feed his curiosity fast enough. He had by this time taken and mastered correspondence courses in engineering, advertising and law.

Through research and experience, there came a time when Norman felt a strange thing happening. Information seemed to split, expand, becoming an adventure in and of itself, surprising and insightful. Yet, as eager and needful as he was, perception was only as sharp and on target as his experience allowed.

Up from the ashes the Calliaphone business grew

again, fanned by it's unusual sounds, and it's exciting and colorful presentation. Despite everything, orders kept pouring in and Norman was forced back into business. He would not buck what he called his hunches and so bought a three story building on Chestnut Street in Muscatine and within a few months the factory was running two shifts a day until in one year it grossed two hundred thousand dollars. The Calliphone, the only new tone keyboard-played instrument invented, in the forty years before that, was designed to be played by hand but later Norman added an automatic player, with both types guarded by seven patents.

Norman appeared a miracle of human energy. To accomplish even one of his feats, people remarked, would have taken any one of them a life time of work. It was not work to him however, as he told anyone who asked how he managed to find the time. When they complained about not having enough time to complete their own simple everyday tasks he told them,"Well, I suppose you have all the time there is," he would quote Emerson. If there is doubt in anyone's mind as to whether you make your own reality, try doing little or nothing for a week and see what transpires. Not only will nothing ensue, you will find you have lost incentive as well. Inertia and a negative attitude begins to develop. You feel powerless, helpless. Conversely, energy is multiplied in direct ratio to expenditure. The more you use, the more is generated.

It was as if the energy of Norman Baker had exponentially increased, elevated an inherent vitality within himself, until he held by the tail a business tiger in each of his hands while reaching out with a third. It was too much, even for Norman to wield at this juncture so he let go of the Tangley

Art School. It had served it's purpose and it wasn't until he quit the overt advertising months later that the purchase orders dwindled and finally stopped.

Norman began more and more to rely on his intuitive hunches; going on instinct and inspiration for direction and knowledge. He was encouraged and inspired by others who had become highly sensitized to their surroundings. This sensitivity gave him a powerful weapon most people lacked. He always listened and acted on his prophetic dreams; awareness of things to come helped enormously in his daily life.

James Watt was best remembered as the inventor of the first practical steam engine but in Norman's wide variety of reading he came across another dramatic account of his ability to gather ideas seemingly out of the ether.

With his steam engine James Watt had certainly helped to revolutionize the civilized world. However, true to the inventive mind, another equally lasting contribution was attributed to a dream.

Mr. Watt was vaguely aware that the process of making lead shot for shotguns was long and involved. Lead was rolled into sheets and then the sheets were chopped into bits, or drawn into wire which was then cut into short segments. Either way, performance was highly unreliable and the resulting high price prohibitive.

According to his own account this had been the situation when he began to have the same dream every night for a week. It was always the same. He said it seemed he was walking along the street in a heavy rainstorm but instead of rain he was showered with tiny leaden pellets that rolled around his feet. Others might have dismissed outright such a bizarre scene, put it down to a heavy or exotic meal. In that case, why the same dream seven consecutive nights? Watt, knowing the value of dreams, questioned it's significance. Did it mean that molten lead falling through the air would harden into tiny spherical pellets?

Watt took his experiment to the tower of a church which had a water-filled moat at it's base. He tossed a few pounds of melted lead from the belfry into the water. When recovered from the moat he found it hardened into tiny globules. Thanks to James Watt's dream all lead shot is made by this process, however simplified sans church tower and moat.

Norman too, was becoming highly sensitized to his surroundings and acting on this sensitivity gave him a powerful tool.

At Toronto in 1916 he had occasion to observe the shell shocked veterans returning from the trenches of the World War. As he watched and listened with grateful compassion to those so afflicted he was moved to recommend mental suggestion assisted by diet, spinal massage, clean water and air and plenty of sleep, as a cure.

So strong were his feelings that he offered the prescription to the Surgeon General of the Canadian War Department, as well as to those of the United States, England and France and received no acknowledgement; not so much as a thank you for your concern. Perhaps they disregarded Norman Baker's advice and perhaps not. A later report from the U.S. Medical Department published their methods of cure: 73% by mental suggestion, music and rest. 11% by diet. 3% cured by medicine.

Norman also presented to the U.S., England and France and Thomas A. Edison the design specifications for a submarine bombing net, to be placed across the English Channel, effectively preventing

German submarines from entering the channel. This time he received a polite thank you and a caution that if in fact they were to follow his suggestion, it could not be published for security reasons. He never knew if they employed his solution.

Four years later, in 1924, Norman Baker had a hunch to build a radio station in Muscatine. He had never forgotten the voice out of his delirious stupor that had told him he would one day own a radio station. The whole idea of selecting voices, speeches, events out of time, capturing and releasing them for all the world to hear and enjoy sparked his imagination and set his mind to reeling. Just imagine it, he thought, the air is filled with sounds floating in the ether. What if they were never really lost? Could they be recovered? Hadn't he read somewhere that, theoretically at least, it would be possible to recapture and broadcast these errant sounds. Think of listening to Lincoln as he delivered the Gettysburg address. What would Lincoln's voice sound like? The Sermon On The Mount. Would Christ's voice sound like that of a great orator or an ordinary man, he wondered. Would we think it was his or some actor's voice best suited the role?

His wish was to give constructive talks to the masses, farmers, laborers and business people, humanity in general. Knowing his own nature, a lot of the talk would be political and information offered would be highly explosive. In a rush of intuition the call letters TNT flashed across his mind. TNT, an abbreviation for trinitrotuolene, one of the worlds most powerful explosives, seemed to be just the ticket to hoist Muscatine out of the Iowa cornfields and into the international scene.

He bought property on the highest hill, 150 ft. above the river, and as construction began he built his own transmitter in the Calliope factory but was refused an operating license. After much lengthy political debate and reams of red tape the final result was an opening on Thanksgiving day, 1925. His opening speech informed the people of America of his fight for freedom of the air, of his struggle against political graft and monopoly in the radio industry in general. He was proud to have already contributed seven recommendations which are part of the Dill Radio Law.

The architectural design of Norman Baker's KTNT Radio Station was unlike any other. Since it was from this edifice his voice would inform the world, Norman reasoned it's design should combine American, Moorish, Spanish, Egyptian and a little freeform imagination. The station was dedicated to the common folks and the homey atmosphere invited them to come and sit in the broadcasting room and wander at will throughout it's doorless rooms. Crowds averaging five thousand would visit on any given Sunday or holiday. When the studio, which was built to accommodate no more than five hundred, was invaded, people stood on tables, chairs and even the upholstered furniture in their zeal to see as well as hear the guest performers. As can be imagined this led to crowd mania. The rest room facilities were rendered useless.

Rather than bar the crowds Norman constructed an extension in the form of a three walled studio on the lawn. Benches and folding chairs were set up in the open air but people complained of the hot sun so a thirty by sixty foot tent was erected. The best-selling Calliaphone provided musical background for the festival like atmosphere.

Even as the nation was held in the firm grip of the great depression, so compelling was the idea and reality of a champion of the people in the live broadcasting radio phenomenon that crowds swelled to fifty thousand one Sunday in May, 1930. From early afternoon cars arrived and parked anywhere they could; streets, alleys and vacant lots for a half mile around; the largest number to visit any radio station anywhere in the world. In Norman they had a man on fire with selfless ideals. Practical plans for which to better all of their lives.

Norman Baker was no stranger to the public at large. In the meantime he had taken up the fight against ignorance by arming this vast public with information of another sort. The ignorant, he speculated, were merely the uninformed. In 1929 he had increased the odds against lacked opportunity by publishing a new magazine. TNT: The Naked Truth which he replaced with Mid-West Free Press in 1931. The 1929 May issue dealt with the poisons of aluminum ware.

Norman had had another one of his hunches when he began to suspect the coffee he loved was contaminated by his aluminum percolator. He sometimes drank seven or more cups a day, but could never make it taste right. Then noticed when he made coffee in a granite ware pot at his mother's house it tasted perfect. He bought an enamelware coffee pot and thereafter made very satisfactory coffee. Needless to say he investigated, tested in his own laboratory and found that aluminum pots while they did not rust, did develop holes whose missing particles obviously contaminated the cooked food.

He could not get the large magazines to publish his articles warning the public of the hazards of poisoning from cooking in aluminum vessels. The new magazine TNT would publish the articles.

The aluminum cookware industry came down full

199

force upon his head warning Norman if the articles appeared they would break him financially. This threat only served to make him more determined. As a consequence, not only did he publish his own findings, but also those of Dr. Charles Betts of Toledo, Ohio. Norman backed up this campaign with vital facts broadcast over K-TNT. Ever the fair minded one, he urged people not to take his word for it, but to conduct their own tests. As a result they destroyed about a million dollars worth of aluminum ware, replacing it with enamelware.

When Norman Baker was accused of driving aluminum ware from the midwest stores, of ruining businesses, he dug deeper.

He discovered that the United States Government not only permitted the use of aluminum in the city water of almost every city in the U.S. but suppressed the facts concerning aluminum poisoning from the public. Docket # 540, November 12, 1925 published by the Federal Trade Commission showed the alum in baking powder to be poisonous. Alum is an aluminum derivative: sodium aluminum sulfate.

Many doctors testified under oath before the Federal Trade Commission corroborating Norman's findings. Dentists showed records of cancers in the mouths of patients wearing aluminum dentures.

He put up a valiant fight but in the end high pressure tactics the likes of which even Norman had never dreamt from the overlords of the aluminum industry were brought to bear upon the news dealers throughout the United States and Canada persuading them to discontinue handling the truth telling magazine.

In the summer of 1929, while the magazine was enjoying immense popularity, Norman and his editor Murray King were looking for other serious matters about which to inform the public. They decided to take a closer look at cancer. Like most Americans Norman had been led to believe that cancer was incurable. People were frozen with horror at contracting the insidious disease. Of unknown origin, it crept out of nowhere and before anyone knew what hit them whole families were destroyed by it. Tales of horror and destruction grew until no one was immune from the epidemic of fear.

Norman recalled that there had been a doctor who had treated cancer for years and had reportedly made cures. Norman also found that as a consequence of fighting the American Medical Association, which denied without equivocation or investigation cancer could be cured, the doctor had mortgaged his home, had lost everything battling them in court for his license to practice medicine.

Norman invited the doctor to Muscatine. If he could stand up under investigation Baker and TNT would taut him to the world. If the reverse were true it would be his demise.

Norman had encountered a similar story in 1926 when an Iowa physician, a Dr. Barewald, who had practiced medicine for more than twenty years said that he had a cure for varicose veins. When interviewed he showed Norman some of his proofs. Encouraged by his honesty and forthright manner Norman talked to some of the doctor's patients. One was a carpenter who had suffered from large protruding veins on his leg. He, even with the aid of an elastic stocking which was the only thing his own doctor had prescribed, could not climb a ladder, essential to his trade. Dr. Barewald had treated him more than two years previously and Norman could detect no trace of the gross veins.

Norman talked to more of the doctor's patients and

they convinced him that he had a cure. At this time the medical profession claimed there was no cure for varicose veins; they were operating to remove part of the veins or resorting to elastic bandages to keep the veins from protruding too much and bursting, causing leg ulcers and the condition called milk leg.

Norman went into partnership with Dr. Barewald calling the clinic the Tangley Institute for the treatment and cure of varicose veins by a simple method of painless injection.

When the Davenport newspapers ran a big feature story about Dr. Barewald's discovery of a cure by the injection method the A.M.A's president denounced the cure in a Chicago paper. The doctor was highly distraught and expressed his fears to Norman. They had the power to revoke his license.

They answered the accusation by offering to cure any patient sent to them by the A.M.A. The newspaper attacks ceased, though for a long time the national and state journals of medicine stated the fallacy of treating varicose veins by injection.

He started his own investigation of the alleged cure for cancer in the same wholehearted manner. Norman heard about a doctor in Missouri who had, reportedly made cures. But, he said he would do nothing unless the (undisclosed name) doctor himself requested the investigation to which he summarily agreed, giving Norman a list of more than twenty patients whom he said he had cured of cancer. He went on to describe at length each case and urged Norman to call or talk personally to them as many lived within a hundred or so miles of Muscatine. However compelling the statistics, Norman knew he would have to conduct his own full scale investigation.

TNT's own committee would select five cancer

patients and send them to the doctor in Missouri. They would monitor and judge his success. If these tests proved satisfactory they would investigate his previous cures.

Announcement of the investigation over K-TNT called for volunteers of cancer patients in advanced stages of the disease who could produce proof they had been to the Mayo Clinic in Rochester, Minnesota, the Iowa State University Hospital, or any other reputable institution which had pronounced their cases as cancer. From these, they vowed, only the five most extreme cases would be chosen for their investigation.

Treatment consisted of an herb based formula taken orally, a specific diet and exercise. The patients progressed so rapidly toward wellness that some were dismissed from the Missouri clinic after a few short weeks. They were, however, to adhere to the A.M.A.'s own criteria of five years free of cancer before declaring a complete cure, yet each exuded so healthy an early confidence that word began to spread immediately.

As Norman obtained and refined the herb formula, Dr. Barewald of the Tangley Institute began treating victims of other types of cancer in Muscatine. None were turned away on basis of payment.

Norman Baker challenged the Iowa Medical Society as well as any other to investigate and disprove by facts that the Tangley Institute had indeed affected cancer cures. He further proposed a hospital be set up and the Missouri doctor to teach any of the A.M.A. the technique and thus to make Muscatine a world center for the cure of cancer. They turned his offer down cold. Baring heart and soul, he pleaded compassion for the unfortunate patients. His pleas were ignored.

"You can't possibly mean you're not going to even look into it." He said waving the thick report. "Did each of you not vow to heal? Give your very souls to the cure of disease? Cancer is the most feared, insidious disease on earth. This exhaustive investigation proves we have a cure. I will give you the information and the opportunity to heal, simply and painlessly."

"All I'm asking you to do is investigate as I have done. If you find merit in the treatment I will give you the formula. Not sell gentlemen, give it to you to start your own hospital, for humanity and the world.

When they turned a deaf ear he opened his own hospital.

"Cancer Is Conquered." proclaimed the December 1929 TNT headline. Patients were now to be treated at the Baker Institute which opened to the public on November 27, 1929. "The worst cases of cancer can be permanently cured."

A sign above the front door proclaimed the glad words, "Cancer Is Curable." As the first patients entered and were admitted on December 14, a large picture of Norman Baker, handsome face shining out from a broad forehead, blue eyes ablaze with intelligence, looked them straight in the eye as they entered the lobby. His bold hand had inscribed diagonally across the left hand corner," I'm in this fight to the finish for humanity."Signed, N. Baker.

Soon there were more than six hundred cancer patients from all parts of America and Canada, eleven licensed physicians and fifty nurses had joined in the fight to eradicate cancer. As quickly as a patient was pronounced cured, no trace of cancer remained, they wanted to tell their story on K-TNT and the stories spread until the hospital overflowed and nearby hotels and boarding houses were jammed. Over the air Norman begged the people of Muscatine to open their homes and make room for the sufferers.

As the town physicians drove to their own offices down Mulberry street they were confronted with and chagrined by the sight of hundreds of patients waiting at the front door of the Baker Clinic each morning. They lined the sidewalks, filled the broad steps and porch waiting for the eight o'clock opening of the hospital.

Their own practice's were suffering mightily, for not only was the Baker Clinic treating and curing cancer but it was also taking care of all the traditional ear, eye, nose and throat problems; stomach, gall bladder, kidney, appendicitis, tonsillitis, hemorrhoids and still treating varicose veins successfully, all of these without operations, X-ray or radium.

At first doctors were anxious to work in the Baker clinic but soon they began to receive threats. Every threat carried basically the same message: work at the Baker Clinic and you'll never work anywhere again. Doctors would come and work a few weeks and then leave quickly under odd circumstances.

The town doctors, the Iowa State Medical Society and the A.M.A., felt if they could somehow prevent Baker from broadcasting; squelch his K-TNT voice from advertising his cures, silence the excited patient's voices describing to the world how they'd been given up for dead by their traditional doctors but now had a healthy new life ahead thanks to the Baker Hospital, all this threatened to deal them a fatal blow. Their weapon, prevent him from broadcasting and it would close down the hospital.

They collectively and efficiently applied pressure tactic's to the Federal Radio Commission and

Baker's license was revoked. By June of 1930, despite unprecedented crowds, K-TNT was shut down. However, like cutting off the heads of Hydra, Norman Baker and the Baker Hospital was still flourishing and the valued patients were cured of cancer. All available rooming houses and hotels were packed and as many as four patients a day left the hospital, cured. They were walking advertisements as they told everyone they met in all parts of America and Canada. And he still had his magazine.

Other minor businesses were taken up before and sandwiched in between those more important healing enterprises. Ever the energetic optimist, no one could squelch Norman Baker's zeal for progress, he persistently rushed forward with new products and ideas. His motto was always to sell the very best, whether it was the best coffee, the best bib overalls, the best patent medicine or the best tires. These he advertised in a friendly folksy manner, as for his Tangley tires, "Highways or Byways are Happy Days on Tangley Tires, every ounce is pure gum rubber." The cryptic word "Tangley" had always brought him good luck.

Most days he could be seen driving the gentle hills of Muscatine in his lavender Cord automobile which folks said was the first to climb Main Street Hill. His favorite attire was a white silk Shantung suit, lavender shirt, purple tie with the ever present horseshoe of sparkling white diamonds pinned upside down just below a four-in-hand knot.

Norman Baker did not spend much time lamenting the loss of K-TNT but simply took the radio broad-casting business where the A.M.A. and the Federal Radio Commission held no influence. He crossed the border into Mexico and built another more powerful radio station XENT in Nuevo Laredo.

Gaining strength from this victory, the"American Meatcutters Association," as Norman began to refer to the A.M.A., now concentrated their every ounce of influence and considerable weight against Norman and were successful in closing the hospital.

In an effort to battle this "Medical Octopus" Norman Baker ran and was defeated for Governor of Iowa on the farm-labor ticket in 1932, as was he in his bid for United States Senator in 1936. "Small wonder," he said and moved himself and his hospital to Eureka Springs, Arkansas.

He purchased the Crescent Hotel. It's elegance and aloof height appealed to his inner nature; it's open balconies and large windows provided an irresistible invitation to his patients to lounge and recuperate in the clear mountain air.

As he was still involved in six separate enterprises he had a six sided desk custom crafted to his design and specification which made it convenient as well as efficient to roll from one side to another as business dictated.

Here Norman Baker added a new dimension to the already proven treatment of the desperately ill. Here he treated mind as well as body. He realized through his own empirical experience in healing himself that both thinking and feelings are intimately connected with physical ills, and that in them lie the cause and cure of the disease.

He had the balcony floors reinforced with concrete to support the beds and gurneys. All interior doors were removed to provide a more feng shui balance to the flow of energy throughout. He recognized the value of music and color as important for the purification and well being of mind and body. Here the generous use of certain colors played an important part in the art of healing.

To some, Norman Baker's habit of surrounding himself with the color purple or any of it's delicate, almost tenuous tones of violet, orchid or lavender, may have on the surface, seemed trivial, effete. In truth, color in nature has always had a deeper purpose than the mere decorative.

He had the rooms in the hospital painted shades of this rich purple so that the walls would reflect and cast a jewel-like spell of healing on whomever it touched. Along with the basic regimen of treatment patients were calmed with baths scented with lavender salts in lavender tinted spring water.

In addition, the esthetic value of music to soothe and heal was not overlooked.

Norman hired a classical organist as part of the staff. Each day the Calliophone was wheeled out onto the lower balcony and the doors on the other three were flung wide in glad celebration while nurses wheeled forth the patients into the sunshine and fresh mountain air to the uplifting and mollifying strains of Wagner's Der Ring des Nibelungen. It was as if the vibrations of the music formed colorful streams of light and as from some familiar motif floated and became a part of each other's and the patient's very living anima.

Norman Baker's innovative ideas for treating and curing the cancer patient had been outstanding so it came as no surprise to him when the A.M.A. found him once again and objected to his method of treatment.

They called him a quack. He called a conference. To his doctors he said, "Well, here we go again. It's the same old story. We cure, they slice and dice. It's all that they know how to do. They cure no one and they are embarrassed by our success rate.

What possible objection could they have if we are

successful in curing this dreaded, nightmare disease?" He raked his hands through his premature white hair. "Damn it, aren't we all working diligently toward that end? And, how does the so called medical profession view their role in my business?" But, in 1937 the A.M.A.'s answer was still surgery and radium treatment, therefore no one outside their province could possibly have a cure for cancer.

At that time too, it was considered a gross naivete to imagine that the here-to-fore unexposed life of plant and animal was deliberately involved in the high scheme of things. Man was assumed to have the greater intelligence. Man, they say, is the only creature who 'knows that he knows'.

Prometheus, it is written, supplied fire to human beings for which he was egregiously punished by the infuriated Zeus who was the chief god. Chief gods will broach no usurping. Especially if the mystery of what they do is exposed, like the real identity of the man behind the curtain in The Wizard Of Oz.

If Norman Baker was guilty of anything it was that he attacked the curing of ills as he did everything else. With nerve and enthusiasm. His answers were viewed as unorthodox, absurd, they said, bordering on the ridiculous.

His methods were too simplistic. Treat the whole person he said. Use a healing touch, color, and music to lift the spirit together with the use of herbs and certain other health promoting procedures and people will naturally begin to feel better. After all, if speaking of love and encouragement works for plants and lower animals, it would work for people.

Ideally, he asked himself and others, what ought the practice of medicine be like? Wouldn't anyone get well, he reasoned, if they were taken out of the environment or situation which led to their disease?

In his research and in-depth studies he came across an account of the way the"practice of medicine had painfully evolved." How long must it be painful? He wondered. The practice of medicine had not progressed or changed dramatically since the Middle Ages. He read the rules of a handful of doctors: John of Gaddesden, a court physician; John of Ardere, a surgeon; John of Mirfield, of the priory of St. Bartholomew in London. All were in holy orders and had a definite code which may or may not have originated with the physicians of Ancient Greece. The rules contained maxims which amused him, yet at the same time were a sad commentary on how the professional men of medicine comported themselves:

"Dress soberly like a clerk, not like a minstrel." Norman could imagine what they would say about his lavender shirts and purple ties.

"Keep your finger nails clean." He held out his own well manicured hands and smiled.

"Don't be in a hurry to give an opinion on a patient. Tell him that with God's help you can cure him, but tell his relatives that he is in a serious condition. This will safeguard you if he dies, but if he recovers you will get more credit."

"Do not look lecherously upon the women of the house. To do so would fill the patient with suspicions and retard his progress."

"Tell the patient droll stories as well as quoting scriptures."

"If you don't want to take a case, pretend to be ill."

"If you find the patient dead on arrival, express no surprise. Say that you knew from the account of his symptoms that he would not recover. This will enhance your reputation."

Prescriptions contained some concoctions such as the ashes of roasted cuckoo mixed with the milk of a brunette. This, Norman read, was a cure for consumption. If these and other obnoxious remedies worked it must have been due to suggestion. Some patients, he supposed, must have recovered in spite of the prescriptions rather than because of them. "Healers" on the other hand, were denounced as quacks.

It was still an easy way out for them all these centuries later, he thought. He did not feel so alone when he read how people like Anton Mesmer had been regarded as outcasts and charlatans in spite of the evidence to testify to the truth of their discoveries. Although Mesmer was, like countless others, at first rejected, finally his theories were accepted. There might be hope yet, Norman reasoned.

The A.M.A proceeded as they always did, however. Their intentions was clear. Make a mockery and example of him to the public and he would cease to function. When that did not work they got him on mail fraud.

Norman Baker, despite evidence that he was already in trouble with the government, and with the American Medical Association denying all his claims of cancer cures, still had the support of thousands. Yet, there was no way the public could denounce his cures, which were seeming more and more miraculous. If the great body of medical authority could not in any way duplicate the cures for which Norman Baker was responsible, they reasoned, what else could they be?

One of a chain of Baker Hospitals and Clinics in America, Mexico and Australia, the one in Eureka Springs enjoyed a certain rate of success with many cancer patients affirming a cure. However, in 1940 Baker was arrested and charged by the U.S. Post Office Department for using the mails to defraud.

His enthusiastic cancer cure advertising, among other things, caused him to be fined and sent to Leavenworth prison for four years.

Robbed, as he was, of one of his stellar accomplishments Norman Baker retired in 1958 to the three story yacht Niagra, which had previously been owned by multimillionaire Jay Gould moored in Miami, Florida where he rocked in a cradle of vexation and regret until he died at age seventy nine of jaundice. His remains were buried in Greenwood Cemetery in Muscatine with only ten people in attendance.

"Norman," Alicia called his name. "Norman!" Her voice resounded in the hollow space between orbs of light.

He was in the tunnel beneath the hotel running..., running..., toward freedom. Running toward the light of day. Oh, how he longed for the sure light of day. He could not take in the full significance of this moment and wished he could come out of the tunnel into a whole new world. Could not believe that this was his last battle with the A.M.A. He had lost. Their political gains and egomaniacal gratifications had won. He took a few more tentative steps before his momentum could be entirely stopped and looked around. Dank air, dripped with an eerie quiet until suddenly "Normannnnnn....!" Like some high throttled freight train rushed past him and the walls shimmered and faded and he saw Alicia sitting in her chair, watching, waiting.

"Norman," she repeated softly, "how many times over the years have you rushed through the tunnel only to find there is no outlet? No escape?"

"Uff," the young Norman said. Only that. And fell into a chair as if he'd been punched in the stomach and put up his hands as if to say, "I give up, I surrender!" and bent his head into his arms and sobbed. The young Norman Baker of the intense blue eyes who had vowed to the world, "I'm in this fight to the finish for humanity," after all the years of heartache and struggle, was himself finished.

"You know what this is all about Norman, I know you do." Gently, ever so gently, she brought him through the pain, through the nightmare of disappointment and melancholy. After all he had been through, he suffered no regret. Never regretted one invention, one cure. No, never regret, he said. "It's just that I despise having to let people down, go back on my word. I promised. I made a promise I simply could not keep and that's what hurts."

I see it all so clearly now. He brushed damp hair aside, blew his nose. "If I had gone to school as my father, over and over had insisted... gone to medical school I could have helped so many more people but no, not me, not stubborn Norman Baker, I had to do it the hard way, and, as it turns out, it was an impossible way!"

"Don't beat yourself up with this coulda, woulda, shoulda, stuff, Norman. Take it as it is, a great loving award from your self, to your self. As a matter of fact right now across the country and the globe as more and more people demand alternatives like Acupuncture, Chiropractic, Yoga, herbs and a myriad other so called "unorthodox" treatments there is greater incentive for doctors to reexamine their dependence on surgery and chemical treatment in place of cure. There is no "time" constraints on you Norman. You won't short circuit yourself again, I'll bet. And one day, one fine day there will be a real doctor, not a "practicing" physician, but a profession-al man who will cure disease, not treat symptoms. I'll be looking for that man. Oh, lets say in about twenty five years?"

"Ha!" He jumped up laughing. "Thank you, thank you, thank you," pumping one hand of hers in both of his. "Words fail me."

"Ha!" She mocked. "That'll be the day. Go get 'em Norman Baker!"

Alicia's heart was gladdened but only for a moment. For truly one must grieve over the senseless fall of such a man. The inhumane treatment and so forlorn a close of such a life. Nothing is so inspiring, more affecting than the undaunted energy, hopefulness, trustfulness, cleanness, patience, compromise with which his spirit sustained itself under that barrage of selfish, depressing fortune. The heart of Job himself was not so sorely tried, nor did it pass the trial better. Through the many innovative inventions and enterprises none were so outstanding in their intent, so constant in steadfastness as his cause to wipe cancer from the earth.

"I'm in this fight to the finish for humanity." Norman Baker. He lived his life for it. He gave his life to it. Perhaps he will again.

His life, after all, was his greatest invention.

Eighteen

Who Rush To Glory, Or The Grave

In a society for which education exists only as a minor motive among the college bound, Alicia was a major throwback. She belonged, in the larger sense, to that time when natural talent and abiding interest was of prime importance. That activity to which she was most drawn was the guiding force in her life; to know herself, thereby knowing others and their need for expression was her goal and true purpose.

Some cynics may have said she was naive in her assessment. Impractical in her approach to scholarship. But none could accuse her of misdirection. She was a marvel to watch. It was as if she were following a singular track in space, illuminated by her own light.

Alicia dreamed of a device which would enable anyone, no matter how skeptical, no matter how blind or stubborn, to witness the gathering energies as she did. Those spirit energies which came to her on feet of clay as they had been in this life, with specific, recognizable vibrations; a concentration of energy which was both intelligent and coherent. She longed to enable anyone with the desire, the ability to recognize as their loved ones the individual energies. Realize for themselves the evidence of life after death and more; enabling them to communicate with those who had passed into the next dimension and beyond. Not unlike many others before her, she wished to see life eased for others even if it meant making her own work obsolete.

She dreamed of a device which could produce the

spirit likeness, onto a screen or holographically, from the particular vibratory oscillation which each of us emit from birth; that spontaneous recognition and knowledge which enables all animals to identify their young.

She dreamed of a device which would identify and measure this vibration as surely as fingerprints. She called this device a sine/cosine accelerometer or SCAN.

The N as representing a triad: an indefinite number; the orthographic aspect of it's sound, much as an Escher painting represents a three dimensional view; a constant integer or a variable taking on integral values.

It was to be in the shape of a standing triangle, a pyramid of two A shapes (for accelerometer) seven feet at it's apex with a frame of silver because of its high electrical and thermal conductivity.

As so often happened in Alicia's 'dreaming', she was shown a problem and a solution. The problem happened not to be hers but was tied instead, to the device's solution in an unexpected way. A way which turned out to be the most economical for the overview; a solution found whereby a man's reward was irrevocably bound to his responsibility towards himself and all humanity.

There is a sound the night makes. Peaceful, earth, water and air sounds. Unsparing, collective frog sounds. Sounds made in compliance with species requirements; no doubt some long ago 'up to code' standard set for achieving maximum volume which only incidentally beckons night to fall. A kind of no nonsense, changing of the guard ceremony which never varies. One frog puts the question while from the other side of the lake another answers until questions and answers are flung out so fast it's a wonder any species member can interpret them with anything resembling accuracy. Harmonious sounds mingle and rush forward in undulating waves of exuberant celebration up and down the lake until they sound more like basso profundo stockbrokers calling bids to each other than they sound like short, fat, four legged, leaping animals.

The nocturnal ease of raccoon and armadillo, low slung and plodding through the underbrush, sound for all the world like Babar and friends escaped from a three ring circus for the noise they make. Flying water fowl skim the heads of their cousins wading ashore. Katydid, June bug and their ilk, the kind with small delicate, see-through wings of miraculous design and color set up a high vibratory, sing-song soughing all around until you would wonder as Charles Fort must have, if it rained a merry band of Arkansas fauna down into a board meeting of similar Egyptian wildlife somewhere on the banks of the Blue Nile, could they understand one another? To an amateur, at least, they sound alike. To an amateur, the steady direction-less chireeping of a Florida cricket sounds exactly the same as a caged one in Chongquing, China.

Sound the night.

Alicia dreamed she was swimming in a moon filled mountain lake. The dream was as all dreams are: multilayered and transparent. She had learned to be highly observant and attentive to everything in this state for much of her knowledge came from this level of awareness.

As she swam she became aware of a kind of shimmering, feathery light along the shore. Ah, a waterfall she thought. Moonlight reflected a shower of spring water which spilled from a hole in the rock high overhead. Where before the mountains between which she swam had been softly contoured with horizontal rock ledges overhung with oak, maple, sweet gum and cedar; now, a sharp superimposed outline of towering pines and vertically sloped boulders, snow capped and jagged, began to take shape as if the very air had been stirred with a stick and another scene settled in it's place. As her body hung in the quiet water she watched the transition and filled her lungs, again and again. Breathed air as sweet and pure as if filtered through vast conifer forests. Now the cool spring fed lake seemed to mingle with that of a more invigorating Rocky Mountain water as she slowly and deliberately stroked her way across it's buoyant surface toward the cleft. The calm divided as overhead an eagle called. She saw his reflection in the water, watched as he circled the full moon above the sky colored night water and flew straight into the cleft in the rock. The falling cascade spangled like a thousand little cold stars into the water.

Alicia swam to within a few feet of the lapped surface and her heart raced in her throat as she watched in place of the expected waterfall, the unbelievable sight of thousands of silver coins crashing into the water; did not lose their brightness as they shot below the silvered cold surface. Her eyes followed the bright circles down where she expected to reach out and touch an underwater mountain of coins but instead saw that, a few feet below the surface, they dissolved into what appeared to be man made structures not unlike other ruins of antiquity.

Without hesitation she slipped below the surface and dove toward the ruins. Several shadowy concrete-like chambers whose oversized doors could be seen to be sealed now but obviously had once opened onto the wide, tiered platforms which stretched along the broad walkways. She swam across narrow bridges which spanned a moat and crawled up the side of the mountain touching as she went the rows of spectator seats and couches built into the side of the hill in amphitheater fashion; the whole of which gave onto a central staging area with it's own monumental sized couches and chairs wide enough to accommodate several players. What manner of thing is this, she wondered. What has all this to do with silver coins?

The walls became transparent and she saw within the chambers a time capsule of some kind. Inside were placed items of a particular past vintage meant to show how and by what methods the people had lived; what tools had been used for the building of such fantastic dreams; aspirations to be shared; information to be imparted.

When her head broke the surface of the water once more Alicia saw no floodgate of coins; the mountain and crevice had given way to the familiar Beaver Lake shoreline and a fresh wind dimpled and moved little fresh eddies across it's surface onto her face. She quickly looked back down into the water. The static ruins lay undisturbed on their foundation in keeping with their restricted commitment. The lone eagle circled above and cried into the clouds, "Monte Ne! Monte Ne!" as if publishing a sacred creed.

"Monte Ne." The man standing at waters edge said.

"Monte Ne." He repeated when she stood beside him in the moonlight.

Alicia saw a tall, slim figured man dressed in a black suit, white stiff collared shirt with black bow tie slightly askew below a prominent Adam's apple. His solemn face was underscored by a prominent chin with a just so, heart shaped clef in its exact center. Even in the scant light of the moon she could see his high forehead bore the white demarcation of a man who is accustomed to wearing a hat out of doors. His close set blue eyes, though covered by wire rimmed glasses, seemed to pierce the darkness between them.

"Monte Ne is Cherokee for mountain water." He said, a generous dark moustache masked a thin upper lip. "The Cherokee came through here on their forced march west from Echota, Georgia, to Park Hill, Indian Territory out of Tahlequah, Oklahoma. You see, they were almost at the end of their trail of tears when they reached this place. It was here," he waved the black fedora around the shoreline, "they rested for a time and made it forever Monte Ne. It was also a very special place to me from the first time I laid my eyes on it. It became the focal point of a dream of mine. I'd like to tell you about it and what I'd hoped to accomplish here." He waved a half circle with his hat. "And then I think we can find a way to help each other."

They sat on a log at waters edge. "I am William Hope Harvey," he said. "I've done many things in my life that I am proud of, but this," he nodded his head around, "is the one thing that I wanted with all my heart to see done and I simply ran out of money and, just coincidentally, ran out of life." His voice trailed a sarcastic chuckle.

He told how as a small child he had to sit at his desk at the little school in Buffalo, Virginia, West Virginia today, he said, while the world around him went mad.

"I may not have been born in a log cabin like our president was but there were days when I could hardly keep in my seat in the little log schoolhouse for the commotion set up outside by the Civil War. It seemed like people talked of little else. Somebody or other we knew was always settin' off for it. Having been born in 1851 I was of course too young but my oldest brother Thomas went off with a couple of his friends from across the Kanawha River, from Pliney and Fraziers Bottom and wound up as a color bearer in General Lee's Army until he was wounded. The war pulled boys faithful and true to it like a magnet. Why, those boys could no more have resisted that unadulterated beguilement than a mule can defy his urge to head for the barn after a hard day in the fields." He said, laughing at the imagined absurdity.

"After the war brother Thomas got his law degree and I, at 16 became an elementary school teacher, educating myself beyond a common knowledge at the same time. When I was nineteen I had read the law as well and passed the tests to get admitted to the bar in West Virginia. I had done very well. Went into partnership with Thomas and met and married my wife Anna Halliday while practicing in Ohio. With our first two children Mary Hope and Robert Halliday we moved to Chicago where our son Thomas William was born."

"When I was thirty two the notion to mine silver in the mountains of Colorado struck me like a bolt of lightning! So, in 1884, off we went to Colorado, Anna and me and the three babies, with another on the way. I took over the mining operation of the Silver Bell but it wasn't long before the rough climate proved too much for Anna and the children so I took them to live on the California coast to keep them from freezing in that harsh mountain weather and went back to mining the great veins of silver. With them away I moved myself into the engine house so I wouldn't have so far to go when I had to get up in the night to restart the winches when they shut down. I was fair cold, I tell you, and I could have used a little of that California sunshine myself. Seems like it was at that time my terrible rheumatism commenced. However, it was worth all the pain and effort. The Silver Bell became the second largest producer in the Ouray area. And that's going some." His said as his eyes twinkled a merriment almost as bright as the silver.

"When the price of silver fell I moved the family from California to Denver where I practiced law and tried my hand at real estate and sold a tonic I had concocted called the "Elixir of Life." His eyes twinkled and he laughed deep in his throat which set the rather prominent Adam's apple to jiggle his bow-tie up and down."

"Wasn't nothing much more than a double dose of anisette and good mountain water but folks made fools of themselves over it. Why, they thought nothing of tossing back a few saying, 'Here's mud in your eye! They liked it more for it's recreational value than any took it as a serious regimen of medicine!"

"Ahem." He cleared his throat and with three fingers swept back his moustache as if the thought of it had made him suddenly thirsty.

"Say, listen," he continued. "In those days it seemed very easy to turn a profit. Houses and businesses were going up lickity split so I invested in a lumber business that covered Colorado, parts of Wyoming and New Mexico. I was instrumental in opening a Mineral Palace where everyone could come and marvel at Colorado's mining interests. Why, I even had a statue of "King Coal" carved out of a block of coal that weighed a ton and a half. "Ha," he said abruptly. "It was a eulogized spectacle."

"We then moved to Ogden, Utah where I made some real swell real estate investments. Why, I guess

I must have been up and down financially so many times it never ceased to amaze me that there seems to have been something of a 'mystery of life' underlying my every move. Honestly, my Scott's grandmother used to tell me about the 'wee folk' and how they latched on to help certain people. She said I had a wee good faery sitting on my shoulder and I believed her. With me, it's this way: even when a thing folds, I know there's something else out there just waiting for me to do 'er.

"Like the time after the price of silver fell I moved the family back to Chicago and started the Coin Publishing Company. You see I have always had an abiding interest and fascination for silver. Never gold. Never. Wouldn't have a thing to do with it. Only silver. There's just something about the way silver looks and feels. I know it has much more potential than a medium for exchange or jewelry making. I have always known that."

"On the other hand, because of the financial aspect of the coinage, I then began a weekly paper and wrote several short books on the subject, even conducted a school of finance. Anyway, people began to call me "Coin" Harvey and the name has stuck with me ever since.

"Oh, I had a peach of a time! There was never enough hours in a day to cover all the things I wanted to do; what with writing, publishing, lecturing and the like. Oh, I had a grand old time!"

"And say!" He suddenly stood, hat in hand, and began with energy to pace up and down in front of Alicia. "I met a great many influential and prominent people, some I was even proud to call friend. But probably the best and most famous of them all was ole' Willy B., William Jennings Bryan. I got him all fired up about silver. We became fast friends. I called him Willy B. because he always had "a bee in his bonnet." Yes, he was a good friend and a great states-man and speech maker. Say! His speeches always packed a wallop! For his Democratic nomination for President of the United States in 1896, as the party's Ways and Means Chairman I helped write his Cross of Gold speech. When he was defeated in his effort to become President the party blamed me for making such strong points against gold and I just threw up my hands in disgust at those namby-pamby's. They always want someone to stick their neck out on their behalf; can't wait to get behind someone who has the gumption and fortitude to get out and do something and then they can't wait to throw you over for some-body else when you fall behind or lose altogether."

"What a disappointment that was! Say! We thought to help the people get on the plus side of prosperity and live a good life. Well, I couldn't help feeling sunk. I don't like to bellyache but I wanted to get as far away from them and politics as I could get."

"Well, now don't you know the wee faery was still hanging on to my shoulder for dear life even though the whole country had been in a wild panic when money got scarce. Banks closed, and businesses and factories went bust, I still remember the sore, defeated look on people's faces. It's a thing you never forget. Never-the-less, people by the thousands began to buy my finacial advice books again." The twinkle flashed blue-white in his eyes, "I didn't do too bad!"

The night was one for sitting beside a mountain lake in the moonlight, listening to someone's fine dreams. The soliloquy fine tuned. Generally Alicia did not hear many such upbeat and alive depictions of a life well spent. Coin Harvey warmed to his subject and her heart.

"After winters in Ouray, running up and down the

224

mine shaft at all hours of the freezing day or night and winters in Denver, then Chicago, my joints began to hurt real bad from the rheumatism. I began to hear from some of my banker friends in Chicago about a swell new health resort in the Ozark Mountains in Northwest Arkansas; heard that a one-of-a-kind hotel called the Crescent had been opened in Eureka Springs. Ole' Willy B. and me had a notion to take a look see around.

"It turned out to be a grand hotel alright. Not bush league at all as you might expect for it being stuck so far back in the hills. We came down on the Frisco Line, stayed and nosed around some. It was fortunate, we said, how very fortunate, that they had discovered all those fresh water springs around Eureka. However, we said, maybe we're not sunk yet. Could be there were other springs nearby. Sure enough the luck of the wee folk was still abroad in the land and I was told of another large spring forty miles south called Silver Spring. And here it is where we're standing. You were swimming in it. Well, I don't have to tell you, something powerful went through me on hearing those words, "Silver Spring!" Now, there's an omen for me, I said to Willie B., an omen if ever there was one!"

Alicia could not see the light in his eyes but from the sound of his voice knew it to be there."Imagine me," Coin continued, "with my utter and complete devotion to silver, imagine the thrill and excitement I felt on hearing of a place called Silver Spring!"

"It was something to see, even in it's pristine wildness. I envisioned a resort even more remote and rugged than Eureka Springs. As elegant and grand as the Crescent Hotel was, this one, I was bound, would be rustic and practical. It seemed to take shape before my eyes that first time over there," he pointed in a southwesterly direction, "in the valley beside the glorious Silver Spring, whose water turned out to be as near distilled as had ever been found. It contained natural ozone and earth's electricity and it tasted like nectar from the gods. It was truly glorious!

"I had quite a plan. A plan whose design had rushed seemingly full blown out of nowhere into my head and if a schematic transparency of my life could be overlaid on the land around Silver Spring, each with it's specific topography, peaks and valley's, laid one on top of the other, I believe you would see they fit together perfectly."

"We built houses, hotels and banks. We raised money for the Frisco Line to build a spur between Rogers and Lowell. Nothing was forgotten. We attracted many influential people from surrounding states and abroad. Why, it was the nicest little town anyone could hope for. Monte Ne." His voice held an uncommon pride.

"But there was always something lacking. I had a lived a good life. Good family, even though my wife, Anna Halliday divorced me and I married my faithful secretary of many years, Mae Leake. I suppose my wanderlust was too much for a little lady from Delaware, Ohio to take. She did as well as she could and our children Mary Hope, Robert Halliday, Thomas William and Annette were something like miracles to me but when in 1903 Robert Halliday was taken from us something just went right out of me. We buried him in a vault on this spot right here." Coin waved his hat in front of them. "I made the vault for the two of us. In life he had been my shadow. Followed me everywhere. When they flooded the lake the vault was moved up there on top. I suppose they thought it was the least they could do for destroying a man's fine dream." Coin waved the hat up to a darkness beyond. "There the bones of our mortal bodies lay side by side forevermore. But, I'm getting ahead of myself."

"My life to this point had been lived with a no holds barred, unconstrained attitude, there seemed to be time for everything I wanted to accomplish and with every night's fresh dreaming a new scheme would urge itself upon me, until I felt I was going off in too many directions at once, as if I were truly running out of time. An intangible hunger began to hound me and nothing I could do would satisfy it until I hit upon the idea of a lifetime. My whole life had been in preparation of this."

"What I am about to tell you will be an incredible relief to me for until you came along I carried the knowledge of it around for so long I thought I just might have to give it up for lost. Over the years the torment of that possibility gnawed away at me like a disease. It involved the most important thing I felt I could do for my fellow man.

"I had seen the great Pyramids of Egypt and although archeologists have unearthed a great many spectacular things, we are left to wonder at the true meaning of their existence. Babylon too, Carthage and Rome had fallen without leaving any detailed story of their accomplishments. I determined it would not happen to Monte Ne. There would be a history of our civilization stored in a time vault at Monte Ne.

"We had dammed the main spring and diverted it's water through a network of canals and began to build a concrete amphitheater I designed to be the base of a large pyramid. While in Egypt I experienced first hand the necessity for something like our own version of the Rosetta Stone which, with it's

Egyptian and Greek together supplied the key to deciphering the hieroglyphs. I hoped to place a similar "key" to English in the Monte Ne pyramid so that if, in say three thousand years, English is not spoken in Arkansas the inscription on the cap will be understood.

"The amphitheater was the first part to be built. It was built of a certain privately known mixture of concrete for strength and durability to form the base of the pyramid which, when completed, was to rise above the mountain 130 ft. The height was necessary because the earth was sure to be filled in around it, like the sphinx, as the ages passed. By the time a future civilization would find the obelisk there would only be a portion of the top exposed, therefore, the inscription:

WHEN THIS CAN BE READ, GO BELOW
AND FIND THE RECORD OF A FORMER
CIVILIZATION

would have to be engraved on the most enduring metal known and placed at it's very apex.

"It was a simple matter to reinforce the concrete vault and disguise it as part of the amphitheater which could seat 1,000 people. We built it out of solid concrete 8 ft. thick and before sealing it up I personally placed there a large cache of silver. It happened that I never did trust it to the banks. Most of them started closing by then, and anyway, it would have stirred too much publicity.

"But the idea of a different kind of 'bank' got me to thinking about how the pirates of old solved the problem. They sometimes rigged elaborate tunnels and traps to keep their gold safe from treasure hunters.

"I believe you make your own luck and all you have to do is recognize opportunity when it's presented. As luck would have it one day I happened onto one solution the pirates used to secret their plundered gold up on the coast of Southern Nova Scotia that so captured my imagination I could not get it out of my head."

Coin stopped and looked to Alicia for support. "Please, do go on." She said.

"Well, as the story goes, three young men rowed out to Oak Island, a tiny rock knoll sticking out from the water of Malone Bay that nobody had paid much attention to until this bright Sunday morning in April of 1795. If memory serves their names were Jack Smith, Tony Vaughn and Danny McGinnis who knew that Oak Island had been used by pirates, free-booters who infested the seas in those days. They would anchor in a deep cove on the north end, post a lookout in one of the tall trees and commence the reparation of the ships without detection.

"Notorious pirates went there, Teach and Morgan and Steve Bonney. But, by the time Smith, Vaughn and McGinnis rowed over to the island the pirates had long since been driven from the seas, caught and hanged one by one it was told. The men knew that the freebooters had been gone from the island at least seven years but had left evidence in the form of knives, pistols and a few gold coins that had been found on the beach where they had made camp.

"Supposedly, it was Tony Vaughn who first noticed a worn place on the limb of a huge oak tree and a depression in the hard packed soil directly beneath. All agreed it looked like heavy ropes had been looped over the limb to lower something into a hole that had been carefully filled in.

"Those men worked quietly in their spare time for

several years until they discovered several layers of coconut fiber about thirty feet down. Smith told a Dr. John Lynds of the strange find and for the next several years spent his entire fortune probing it's depths for the treasure it promised.

"At successive ten foot levels, workers pulled out layers of heavy oak planks, a layer of Ship's putty, more tough layers of coconut fiber which had been brought from the West Indies two thousand miles away. Finally, at the eighty-foot level, beneath another layer of oak planks they found a flat stone that was covered with some kind of hieroglyphics.

"The frustrated, almost broke, Dr.Lynds resorted to a large hand powered drill. Down through brittle plaster and more hardwood they drilled to a depth of one hundred feet from the surface until water began to rush into the pit, but not before they had brought up a few scraps of gold and paper did tragedy strike. Water rushed into the pit and three men were drowned.

"Dr. Lynds had spent a fortune and nine years of his life proving there was gold in a man-made vault about one hundred feet below the scarred oak tree. Still, it was forty-six years later, in 1849, with the help of a small group of backers before his workman reopened the pit. They dug ten feet deeper than before and hit a layer of cement. The drill broke into the room again, they were able to retrieve a piece of gold chain before water flooded in again. As far as I know, the treasure still remains intact down in that vault."

"So you devised a similar trap for your silver cache." Alicia said.

Coin nodded. "Now, mind you, I did not want to simply dig a hole and bury it on the banks of the lagoon here. I kept mum about it. While the time vault itself and most of the items placed there was no secret, no one, not even my family knew of the silver hoard.

"I knew from the start that one day our civilization would be destroyed, and the valley here would be filled in." Coin waved an arc in the surrounding moonlight. "The whole project had a high sense of urgency about it, still, little did I realize how soon the end would come."

Alicia was by this time completely captivated by this talented, personable apparition standing before her at lagoon's edge. "Monte Ne." She breathed. "Mountain Water."

For his part William Hope "Coin" Harvey had recited his life at a brisk pace and hoped he still had sufficient energy to set everything to rights. It was not an edifying recital of his achievements so much as it was an urgent use of opportunity.

Towering ambitions of fame, power, fortune and greatness aside, these would have to stand or fall on their own, these were already entered into the record, these then, he could not edit or change. One thing remained.

He radiated now a growing confidence. However, he needed Alicia to perform certain functions he could not. Ever the man of singular action he said at last, "Oh, would that I could alone prevail against the odds." He had chosen to forget how many fine schemes, how many good intentions had passed into the grand dark swirl of time. William "Coin" Harvey did not now pause to consider who might get the credit or who the debit. In the end, he believes, when all schemes are accounted for and added to the totality of human endeavors, his will be a significant contribution.

As if to take a less compelling inventory now Coin

fell silent while Alicia studied the shimmering energy above the watery Monte Ne ruins and waited.

"I breathed my last mortal breath on February 11, 1936. 'Mae,' I said finally to my wife. 'My teeth are rattling and I'm cold down to my bones. I can't stop shaking.' "Coin said." It seemed on that blustery winter night I had been cold for more than half a century and I simply could not face another freezing winter. I don't think I was ever in all my life warm enough to suit. Why, my mother told me that before I was a year old, I had pneumonia three times. She said she did her best by stoking the heat and keeping me bundled up warm and toasty and the thought of anyone opening a window or door sent her into such a fright that except to go in and out, no one ever did. She said she could not bear to expose me to the elements, life being that fragile, she said. So, to my wife Mae I said finally, "Bring on the darkness."

"There was nothing more I could do here. I had seen my children to adulthood, all but Robert Halliday whom I missed with a fierce vengeance. Monte Ne was as near perfect as I could come to it without the money to complete the pyramid. It was the best I could do. I did not want to split open the time vault and take back my own silver, for what purpose would that serve? So, the silver cache remained undisturbed, hidden inside the watery time vault to await a future of uncertainty, but a future no less. Then, it came upon me that for the first time in all of my life, that I was at a complete standstill. Cold and tired. I was all done in.

"Now your's, Alicia, your's is a grand, humanitarian scheme. Of far greater use than any I've yet heard. There is enough silver to produce your SCAN mechanism. I knew there would come a time when silver would come into it's own; be recognized as the precious metal I know it to be.

"I remembered how! I found my way!" He shouted suddenly to the star crazed sky and raised a fist as evidence against reproof to old accusing men who might be hidden behind the still bright moon. He now knew it was possible after all to fulfill so beneficial a purpose as he had dreamed from the beginning, no matter how daunting the task or how long it took to realize.

William Hope "Coin" Harvey had through some tenacious act of will, or untapped resource, reached down and snatched his memory back from the sanctioned abyss and in so doing held and wielded the greatest power of his life.

He looked at Alicia and pulled from the inside pocket of his jacket a yellow edged paper and laid it on a log between them. In the fragile light of dawn Coin pointed and explained the blue lined angles of entry, mathematical calculations, as the two bent in quiet conference beside Beaver Lake. She, asking copious questions as to the opening of a room that had been hermetically sealed, and he answering, supremely content in knowing the silver would be recovered to good use at last. Happy he was! Scottish jig happy! Uproariously drunk with the power of aforethought, he was that happy. "At last. At last!" He crowed and swelled to the morning.

Happy and relaxed enough now he could even tell and enjoy the irony of the close call that had brought him back to the Crescent Hotel one fateful day in 1963 when the new owner of Monte Ne, a Mr. W.T. Whorter, promised he would dynamite part of the amphitheater to get to the articles he said Coin had buried there. Among whose treasure, it was rumored, was a spanking new Model "T" Ford driven into that very same concrete garage mausoleum as big as you please and sealed away on the very day of it's delivery from the factory. "What a shame!" Some shook their heads as they watched what seemed to them a foolish expenditure of good money, "Who does he think he is anyway, John Jacob Aster? A sacrilege beyond imagining. After all, it had only once been proudly driven from the train station, across the lagoon over wide sturdy planks and straight into the prepared vault to be hidden away for eternity for all anybody knew.

"Oh!" They said to each other more than once over the years. "Imagine! A car like that sealed under tons of concrete." They seemed unable to breathe properly with the mystery of it all. "What a waste of a perfectly good automobile." They had said, shaking their heads. "Imagine that! I can't even afford a car like that to drive around in, much less one to bury for no useful purpose. What must that man be thinking of? Do a thing like that to a brand new car! Well, I never!" And some had eventually worked their imaginations around to thinking if a man like Coin had conceived of preserving for posterity all those wondrous things then it was not such a leap to see his mummified self sitting upright with his hands on the wheel driving through the Pearly Gates.

Rumors, well oiled with innuendo and speculation, grew as rumors will, in quality as well as quantity until, over the ensuing seven decades, people came by the hundreds to walk among the remaining gutted buildings of Monte Ne above the underwater ruins. They could stand, peer down into the clear lapping waters of Beaver Lake, hoping to catch a reflected glimpse of the concrete tiered amphitheater or the enigmatic vaults that seemed to contain every dreamt of possibility. Fantasy soared with each visit, took on a night before

Christmas vividness. The thought of what might lay just inches below the surface, sometimes caused young and old alike to jerk anxiously awake in the middle of the night as if they had suddenly found themselves behind the wheel of that brand new car. Or run their fingers through countless silver coins they imagined in their underwater coffin, and the whole idea, like finding Ali Baba's cave was made more mysterious and splendid with each passing year.

"The land had already been sold to the U.S. Army Corps of Engineers for use as Beaver Lake reservoir." Coin said. "So on the day Mr. Whorter was to use his dynamite to get his mitts on the contents of the vault, I, in this my full suit of burial clothes and in the risky condition you see me in now," he waved his hat the length of his body head to toe, "I was at the Crescent Hotel bright and early waiting for the Corps' attorney to come downstairs and get himself over to the railroad station and Monte Ne in time to stop the destruction and rape of the vault. Say! Was I ever in a stew! He was my only hope!"

An element of surprise was seen to cross his face as if he suddenly recalled a flash bulletin. "It was while waiting in the lobby for the solicitor, I had just come down the stairs from trying to arose him, that I remember the clerk behind the desk looked straight at me and seemed about to say something so I said, 'Good morning!' without thinking. It was a natural reaction for me. Well, the clerk's face immediately drained of color and froze in slack jawed panic. Oh! My! I guess I must have given him quite a start. Was he ever frightened at the sight of me! He had seen a ghost sure enough! In fact he had seen in me a true haunt, right and all! However, before he could recover, the solicitor came down the stairs and with never a glance in my direction, went out the door. When the clerk looked back for me, much to his horror, I was gone, as well.

"We arrived at the scene on the banks of the lake here just in the nick of time.

There was a swarm of curious people gathered around, including reporters from surrounding area newspapers, but they were all disappointed. There would be no disturbing of the vault on that day the solicitor told the crowd, and, because of it's perceived potential for damage to the environment, likely there would never come an appropriate day." Coin breathed a shuddering sigh of relief.

The same event has been recounted in mysterious tones scores of times by one of the Crescent Hotel's new owners who was behind the reception desk the day Coin Harvey waited nervously in the lobby for the lawyer to come downstairs. To him, the man in black had just disappeared into thin air!

Resort Enterprises, Inc. had taken over the operation of the Crescent Hotel in 1970 after the hotel had suffered a fire on the fourth floor in the south wing. Which in turn sold out to Crescent Heights, Inc. in 1972. Among the new owners was an architect and developer from Wichita, Kansas. Robert T. Feagins had an eye for a more modern structure and so regarded the Crescent's chateasque style outdated and worn. He planned to tear it down and build condominiums on the sight. His wife had other plans for the grandest hostelry west of the Mississippi.

As the restoration began in the winter off-season Mr. Feagins happened to be behind the front desk when he saw a man wearing black trousers and long black frock-type coat, high starched white collar, sporting a moustache and mutton chop sideburns and small wire rimmed glasses, walk leisurely from the south hall, nod his head and say, "Good morning." Mr. Feagins reportedly said the man's face had an unusual ashen look as he stopped in front of the fireplace in the middle of the lobby, turned toward the front window and stared beyond it for some seconds, turn back the way he'd come and as he walked toward the second floor stair, vanished into thin air. Mr. Feagins' report of the man in black was the first sighting of the "apparition" to be documented.

Before going, Coin gave Alicia explicit instructions he had filed, in accordance with the law, many years ago, giving permission to open the vault. Many had searched over the years for just such a document but when recovered it's wording was seen to have been so encouched in coded banter as to be made unintelligible to all but the forearmed.

For a man who once ran for the highly visible office of President of the United States, Coin Harvey was in many ways a very private man. When he died, his dreams, his Monte Ne died with him. He was one of those people who always kept his plans secret, to the almost disastrous extent of taking some of them with him to his grave.

Physical life, to a skeptic, is all there is. Departing from the physical after death is as natural a process as being born into it. Physical life is a tiny segment of a vast circle wherein there is no beginning and no end. The spirit, or energy, which is self, existed before the start of that segment and will continue after it's end. To achieve dignity and a sense of purpose, man must know that he is more than a body, he is a powerful spirit, energy, which existed before his birth and will continue after death. Some call this process reincarnation. In writing his own epitaph for his tombstone, Benjamin Franklin at the age of 21 wrote:

The Body Of B. Franklin,
Printer,
Like The Cover Of An Old Book,
It's Contents Torn Out
And
Stripped Of It's Lettering & Gilding
Lies Here
Food For Worms.
But The Book Shall Not Be Lost, For It Will As
He Believed
Appear Once More
In A New And More Elegant Edition
Revised And Corrected
By The Author

The laws of the universe, of science, are exactly the same as the laws of life: For every action there is a reaction; for every death, a rebirth.

Nineteen

For Ye Are Living Poems

Newspapers published Alicia's success at solving the mystery of the underwater vault at Monte Ne and, as with so many major scientific breakthroughs, no one realized at that moment just how successful the venture was and would continue to be. They thought her efforts were of a strictly historical nature.

The law had been specific as to the recovery of the contents and the absolute minimum of damage to the underwater vault had been done. No one was the slightest bit curious about the refrigerator sized crate, the weight and number of old farm, carpenter and plumber's tools found inside. They did not realize there was more to these mundane implements than met the eye. They were too busy admiring the newly emerged Model A Ford, which had to be brought up first as it had been driven into the vault last, to notice how quickly the large crate had been spirited away.

On one hand Alicia wished Michael could have been there. She knew he had taken the notion of going to Europe to divert Sister Dolly Garvin from the escalating harassment and she silently thanked him for it. Still, she missed him in a way she had not missed her devoted parents. A very different kind of emptiness began to fill her heart. She smiled to herself. He would have found these cloak and dagger proceedings exciting, on the other hand she was secretly glad she had kept him in the dark as to their true purpose. More times than not, to declare another to secrecy is not a strong act of will and might even set them in harms way. They had spent more hours on the telephone than she cared to speculate about. While she missed his light hearted manner and good humor she knew there was an underlying seriousness that was not merely gratefulness on his part.

Alicia began work on the SCAN design. With the assistance of Dr. Toni Marcelletti, a friend from the University of Arkansas Physics Department, they soon had several students as well as professors trekking in and out of the old warehouse down by the railroad tracks at the edge of the campus.

Like attracts like. Alicia seemed to be a magnet for creative energy. She attracted those most likely inventive souls whose links to the one energy were the strongest, most productive; those souls who never hesitated to follow the creative impulse.

She had given some thought to setting up the laboratory in the basement of the Crescent, however, there was the very real issue of security.

To say there was secrecy and jealousy among corporate thieves in the early stages of computer development would be like saying they made great bedfellows compared with Alicia's troop experimenting with natural laws of the universe. As word got out as to the nature of her work, all manner of established authority came down on their heads and the rest came to spy. She was eventually forced to a method of circumvention which so confused the enemy as to render them ineffectual, and broke.

The 'A' device was simplicity itself. Having neither switches nor gears; no buttons to push, no knobs to twirl or handles to grasp. No 'whistle and bell,' gee whiz hard or soft ware, as most 'new' technology possess. This was not a machine in any sense of the word. More, it exhibited no apparent source of power.

Instead, the 'A' device appeared as the great pyramid Cheops appears to the neophyte: static, devoid of all earnest vitality; a curious artifact in the desert sand but bearing no significant message out of antiquity for us today. Rather, the "A" device served as a receptacle activated by a self-referencing, self-actualizing, "guest mind/energy" invited to appear in the instrument.

Alicia had discovered in working with implacable spirits that many either could not or would not come forth when invited to participate, or appear, which led skeptics to equate absence with fraud, or failure; their notion of constancy being the only acceptable criteria. She found, however, if these spirits had been stubborn, shy or selfish, i.e. all habits positive and negative in life, they usually carried these traits right along with them into the afterlife.

On the part of the conservative skeptic, even the hardest head, the most closed mind does not have to believe in 'ghosts' in order to believe in 'selves' which can be identified apart from their living body. And, Alicia learned that not even the most close-minded of skeptic would declare 'life' to be immutable. If a person had not in life awaked to certain agencies at work within themselves, they usually did not suddenly develop a higher degree of knowledge in the afterlife and would proceed totally unaware of the self's power to reflect itself. Therefore, they would not, could not, be conscious and alert to the invitation to appear to her or any other sensitive person.

The new science was fast changing everyone's notion of what is real and what is not. Those who still believed that consciousness does not play an essential role in the nature of physical reality are ignorant of the most convincing evidence provided by the quantum theory of physics.

The objective in this case, was not so much to locate a specific person or "spirit" in time but rather, "time" would locate them. It was not valid to speak in terms of a find/cannot find perspective, for that implies active searching, but instead, a passive expectation must take it's place. This is what is meant "to appear by invitation." Others, more formally trained, might never have embarked on such an ambitious quest. Having little classic scientific training, Alicia was not bound by it.

It happens that with many breakthroughs, scientific or otherwise, in the testing phase of ideas and inventions, there are no witnesses; no one to verify or astound. However, this project of Alicia's, in retrospect, seemed destined from the start to be viewed spontaneously by the gestalt.

All effort, of course, had been directed toward the first "guest" to make an appearance inside the SCAN device. Still, expectation is one thing while the immediate reality of success is significantly another. All had been caught off guard that wind swept morning in March 1997, stormy weather had been predicted for the Easter Holidays. As they went about making final preparations in the softly lit laboratory they heard Wednesday's excursion train from Springdale to Van Buren whistle the crossing down on Dixon Street.

Alicia had her back to the silver A frame making herself a cup of camomile tea at the make shift kitchen counter in one corner of the room and listening to her friend, Toni Marceletti, macro physicist. "So, your meditation with the "SCAN" went well this morning?" She said.

Alicia shrugged her shoulders and stirred her tea. "As my mother was fond of saying, "The proof of the pudding..." She let the old saw hang.

Singae, a structural engineer, mumbled something about torque. He remeasured the distance between supports with a laser-like beam, then reached out and, with three fingers, stroked the silver frame as one might do to a seemingly dead fluorescent tube to bring it back to life. Not from any known deficiency in the device was this done, but it seemed more of an intuited gesture, a gesture invited.

Zee stood across the room quietly talking with Raul Fine and Nance Bigalow electrical engineers, as they worked with an electrothermic wand they had also invented, while George Middleton another engineer, directed their efforts with what looked to be a hand held compass. None was a part of the device nor did they come in contact with it.

Dr. Marceletti was saying something animated about a crucial alignment to Alicia when suddenly she shouted, "Stay!"

Alicia turned and saw the shape of a young girl inside the device.

Some sound, like air escaping from a pneumatic valve came from somewhere within the device as if a portal of sorts had opened.

"Stay calm everyone!" Alicia shouted at the startled crew. "Hold on to your hats guys, here we go..."

"Toni," she said, tea forgotten, as they walked quickly forward. "If you will please, give me the measure of heat."

To the girl Alicia said, "Well, hello there. If you will just stand still, stay where you are, everything will be great." The two looked to be the same age but for the dark circles under the eyes of the newcomer. "You gave us a bit of a surprise, didn't you?" Alicia said and nodded in response to Toni's answer, "Heat O, all reflected."

The girl squinted out at them as if through a bright light. She tried to speak, her mouth opened and closed, but, when no sound was emitted, tears spilled down her face and she moved one hand up and covered her mouth. Her round eyes spoke of a distant terror.

"Steady now. Take it easy. Everything is under control. You will be fine. Just relax.... think of why you wanted to come here." Automatically Alicia put a hand out to her.

"No!" Toni reached and grabbed her wrist. "You mustn't." She said simply. "The reduction is a bit off."

"It's alright." Alicia said to the girl. "We have all the time in the world."

Alicia smiled as she took in the tall girl's appearance. Blond curls fell across an even featured face. Light colored eyes appeared as scared as a rabbit's and made a vivid contrast against her clear olive skin. She wore what appeared to be an old fashioned basketball team uniform. Dark blue in color, the long shorts were banded in white around the tight legs. The white wool shirt was V necked and sleeveless with the word COMETS printed in large blue letters across the chest. Her navy sport shoes looked worn and highly favored.

"I think we're all feeling a little out of alignment here." Alicia said softly. "Zee," she said without taking her eyes away from the girl's face, "could you please get the mirror from my bag."

Alicia always went on instinct. She felt the girl needed an immediate grip on reality, at least as far as reality, at this point, could be known. She held the mirror at an angle to eliminate glare and watched the girl's face as her likeness came into the glass. At first glimpse of herself the girl looked stricken as if she had indeed seen her own ghost but quickly recovered as her own familiar face seemed a halcyon to calm.

By the time she was finally able to talk she began haltingly to explain who she was and how lost she felt, everyone in the room had pulled up a chair to listen while the first 'guest' to accept their invitation to appear inside the SCAN "A" device, told her story.

Twenty

Walks Upon The Wind

Juliana DuBois died in February 1924 when she was seventeen years old. Had there been anyone below, it would have seemed she unceremoniously jumped to her death from the school's fourth floor observation deck. She was the only child of Evelyn DuBois.

To say she jumped from the balcony of the Crescent Hotel at five o'clock on an unseasonably warm winter's afternoon would not be entirely accurate.

Buildings have a way of outlasting generations of people. But, from beginning to end, seldom do they remain unchanged.

From 1908 to 1934, September to May it became financially necessary to convert the Crescent Hotel into the Crescent College and Conservatory for Young Women. From June until Labor Day it continued operation as a resort hotel.

A continuation of Maddox Seminary of Little Rock, Arkansas, nonsectarian but strictly Christian, the college became a source of pride from coast to coast as girls and young women came to Eureka Springs from thirty nine states to receive their higher academic education.

Alicia recalled hearing that for many years a hand lettered sign in the hotel lobby made this elaboration:

The Crescent College and Conservatory for Young Women was founded in 1908 to supplement lagging winter hotel business. The most exclusive girls school in the area operated from September to May with a student body of 88. From June until Labor Day it operated as a resort hotel.

This arrangement remained in effect until 1934 when results of the depression ended both the school and the hotel.

The thing that set Juliana apart in the expensive and exclusive, all girls school was that she did not come from money. She had not arrived at the Conservatory as Annalee Benoit or Mary Katherine Gauthier had, from the Garden District of New Orleans where some of the richest, most influential professional men, large plantation owners, oil and ship owners lived. Lived, where, from birth to death, life was uniformly ordered for young girls. Lives studded, as they were with mansions, ponies and thoroughbred horses; lives strung from beginning to end with such accustomed things as silver rattles tied with pink satin bows and spoons and cups with baby's arabesque engraved minutiae'. Silver handled hair brushes were never still long enough to tarnish for they were customarily taken up by Negro nannies who sat by the hour stroking to its shining glory their young mistress' hair while she fidgeted and sipped lemonade and waited for callers on the side veranda where it was shady and the air fragrant with honeysuckle and confederate jasmine. A young lady of high breeding was pale of skin and tended to follow her mother into a languorous, naturally delicate way of life. And if they, perish the thought, were caught out of doors without a parasol and a freckle or two cropped up in evidence of this heedless behavior, nannies would cluck their tongues and rub lemon juice faithfully on the offending spots morning noon and night until they quietly faded.

Debutante balls and coming out parties were thrown and formal ball coronations religiously attended; all observed with the highest regard to protocol, solemnly affirming their historical rites of passage; where the privileges of wealth guaranteed a young lady a life of luxury no matter whom she later chose to marry. A set wealth. A diamond and ruby tiara kind of wealth.

Though Juliana knew all about that kind of lifestyle; hadn't she heard it in her mother Evelyn's envious voice every day of her life?, They did not move in those circles.

Juliana could not recall when she had first heard her mother say things like: "This is the way Annalee likes to wear her hair, why don't we just see how you would look with your hair done up like hers, long, with a nice bow on the side." Or: "Annalee looks so good in pink, why don't we just see about a new pink dress for your birthday."

It was always Annalee said this, or Annalee did that, until for the first five years of her life Juliana felt she was some kind of Annalee doll. She felt she must be some kind of pretend doll her mother held in reserve for off days, to dress up in Annalee's cast offs and preen over.

'Stand up straight', or 'walk this way with your hands turned up like this', her mother would say and play-act with her until she felt as a reflection must feel and Annalee the real little girl in the looking glass.

Evelyn Dubois was born a second generation mulatto from the Quarter and had been in the service of the Maurice Benoit's since her own mother had died and left the beautiful sixteen year old Evelyn alone in the world.

Evelyn's mother's best friend Margarette worked for a rich family 'out yonder aways' and rode the streetcar with the Benoit family maid.

After her mother died Evelyn went to live with Margarette and had been told that Maurice Benoit, a brilliant young lawyer had recently married himself a new genteel wife and she, being a"good catholic girl", was soon expecting their first child. The serene ennui which had served her well as a young debutante had become a constant travail in pregnancy and she desired the services of a personal maid.

Evelyn had caught the streetcar early one morning in late July from the steamy quarter out to what she called "a foreign land". As a child she had ridden the streetcar very few times and only when her mother had no one with whom to leave Evelyn, would she be taken along.

Once when she was eight years old Evelyn remembered her mother had sent her all the way back to the quarter from the house she tended way out Dorgenois Street, to get a pair of work shoes she had left behind. She remembered the time as both terrifying and enlightening.

Evelyn's mother had hung the house key around her neck and given her instructions as to what street names to look for: Canal, Magazine, Dorgenois, how to change streetcars and hurry back. The thing that her mother neglected to tell her was that Dorgenois was a very long street and when Evelyn got off the streetcar on the way back that she would not get off at the same corner where she had boarded. She had not instructed Evelyn to turn right and walk until she came to the house. Everything went like clockwork until she stepped off into a completely foreign looking neighborhood. Nothing fit. Panic immediately set in as she watched the back end of the street car grow smaller, taking with it the only tie to the known world. Her sense of security, however slight, disappeared altogether and she was loath to take steps in any direction except maybe in the direction of the diminished car, swaying and creaking it's heavily lacquered wooden back end dutifully toward it's known destination. She waited until she saw it disappear down the length of the wide, tree lined boulevard; debated whether to stay in one place, like she had been warned many times before if she got lost in crowds or anywhere. "Stay in one place, Evelyn, and sooner or later I'll find you." She felt rooted to the spot. Still, she knew her mother would not welcome the proposition of going off the job and traipsing around looking for the likes of her little lost girl. How Evelyn longed to see her familiar face peer from around an open door. Her heart pounded as she saw another streetcar approaching. Should she catch it? But, to where?

She scanned up and down the street searching frantically for any familiar thing, house, tree, face; anything to give her back a sense of direction. Nothing. Her ears began to buzz and the scene was infused with an eerie quiet as though a thick cotton quilt had been thrown over the alien scene and she thought she might swoon. No living soul, either on the street or on the deep shadowed, unfamiliar porches; none she could tentatively walk up to on her shaking skinny legs and ask directions. Evelyn felt as if her world had been turned upside down and she had been shaken out the other end.

Her heart began to pound and the oatmeal she'd had for breakfast began to threaten the back of her throat and she wanted more than anything to sit down on the curb and cry. But something like the gumption it took to swallow caster oil or take a sulfur tablet took hold of her backbone instead and she began to walk down the sidewalk with a determination equal to that of any becalmed explorer. Had anyone watched it would have appeared as though the young girl knew exactly where she was going and what she expected to find at the other end. It was that tough grit and determination that made the difference when, within only a few minutes, there appeared on her side of the street a group of older boys coming toward her down the sidewalk. Without hesitation, because she had been warned many times"you know how older boys are', she turned on her heels and began walking faster in the opposite direction, but not so fast as to draw attention to herself. She supposed the situation somehow called for an outward composure much like trying to ignore a neighbor's vicious dog with him telling you all the while he won't bite and you know good and well he can sense your fear. Because of this serendipitous turnabout she had not walked off into God only knew where, not into the certainty of the lopsided, heart pounding hell she imagined for herself at the hands of such boys but instead, found herself standing with a confidence belying her years, in front of the appointed door which she waltzed through as easily as if she'd been there everyday of her life.

Much later, an older, more adept and wise Evelyn stepped from another streetcar to enter the mansion where she hoped to find employment. In the quarter, it's tiny houses, buildings, cemeteries, crowded side by side and even sometimes overlapped, threatened to close in on a person until it was hard to know where to stand, which way to face for enough air, especially in the summertime. Here, Evelyn saw the long avenues of manicured lawns and trees, the stretches of green openness divided by the shelter of magnificently scented shade which epitomized the Garden District.

The overpowering fragrance of roses was as much a fixture in the dimness of the great hall as was it's 15 foot ceilings. Reminiscent of her mother's funeral, the cool white scent crowded Evelyn's sense of security and she wondered if someone had recently died here. An old servant frowned her displeasure at her presumptuous behavior, "The very idea comin' up the front walk and right into the white folk's house like that! 'member yo place chile," she said. "You wait righchere, now!" And disappeared down the hall.

Evelyn reached a tentative hand to the corner of a massively carved hall tree and peered into the front parlour without moving her feet to make a sound. Heavy, luxurious draperies covered the windows with flounces of gold brocade and silk wrapped cord. Gilt framed pictures of bridges and pastures she saw as scenes from a truly foreign land lined the walls. A grand piano set between the front windows, radiated a promise of the designed gaiety locked within it's black and white keys. Around the large square room pieces of well placed ornately carved furniture, secretary and chairs gleamed a mahogany patina solely due to years of hand rubbed care. Crystal vases filled with yellow and pink hybrid roses were everywhere and the silver urns flanking the fireplace mantle reflected the window light and it's bent radiance.

Evelyn quickly dropped her hand and straightened as a lovely dark haired Clotilde Benoit emerged from the rear of the house and floated toward her all the while fingering, as if by rote and measure of her devotion, a crystal and silver rosary which she at the last minute slipped into a side pocket. She wore a stylish, soft grey morning coat which matched perfectly the color of her doe shaped eyes but hid not at all her obvious maternity. Around her neck dangled an ornate, silver crucifix which her husband Maurice had placed there after his last trip to Paris.

As Clotilde asked her proprietary questions of Evelyn she watched Clotilde's delicate blue veined hand run the crucifix up and down the chain and was reminded of what her mother, who was not catholic used to say, "Those who wear crosses, have crosses to bear." Evelyn wondered what possible cross the beautiful Clotilde had to bear here in this great house; in this glorious life, but felt just the same, a shiver run over her skin. 'Someone's walking on my grave,' she thought of the old superstition.

For her part, it seemed Clotilde was to the manner born, taking the hiring and firing of servants as a matter of course and so did not really see Evelyn for the young and vibrant beauty she was. To Evelyn, Clotilde had a protracted, melancholy quality about her. She seemed soothed, if not thrilled that Evelyn had come and her questions turned out to be a mere formality. She was hired to look after the mistress of a great house and the infant when it was born.

After only a short month a beautiful girl baby was born into the world of that high quality life but in the process her mother Clotilde, hands folded with entwined silver crucifix on her bosom, was borne out of it. Borne out from the magnificent house and the life which did not now appear to be at all fixed and into the mausoleum where a silent Maurice, much too often, sat and stared at the space reserved for himself beside her.

It was not until Juliana was thirteen that she was taken by her mother to the Benoit mansion. She would never forget that pale dry winter day when they had stepped off the street car. The cold wind sang in the tops of trees and lashed her face and bare legs like fine needles and reminded her of times when she had disobeyed her mother and been whipped with a narrow switch pulled from the peach tree in the picayune back yard. It was times like those she had cried into her pillow and wished for a father.

She had questioned her mother many times about her father and been given the same answer. He was killed in France during the war, Evelyn would say, with about as much compassion proffered as would be expected if he had gone around the corner and never came back. That was what Juliana had at first been told.

A major quivering in the pit of her stomach had begun as they started up the long driveway. They walked between tall hedges interspersed with waxy magnolia trees.

The pristine whiteness of the columned mansion held a closed, secluded expression and might have been so but for the music coming from within.

The haunting piano notes of DeBussy's Claire de Lune could be heard to advance and recede from side windows as they walked around to the back entrance.

"Oh, Mama, that sounds so pretty!" Juliana said, looking dreamily into her mother's eyes. At thirteen she was already as tall as her mother and reed straight.

"That's Miss Annalee playing, Suga." Evelyn said softly; caught up her own daughter's elegant hand, examined the long slender fingers.

As they climbed the steps onto the broad back porch she said absently, "Suga, you really oughta have learned to play the piano." The music majestic, soothing. Just when or by what means she was supposed to have accomplished this feat, Juliana had not the slightest notion.

From the minute Juliana entered the kitchen she knew that wherever she went for the rest of her life she would carry as proof of wealth, the mixed scent of fruit and furniture polish in a house.

The cook Marigold was busy at the table chopping bell peppers for the red beans simmering on the back of the stove. Green stems and white seeds were heaped on top of a mound of cold coffee grounds in the middle of yesterday's Society Page of the Times Picayune; to be joined shortly by peelings of garlic and onion she would chop next for the okra gumbo before taking the whole mess of scraps out back to throw onto the garden to start the cycle over again.

"Mornin', Miz Evelyn." Marigold looked up and paused in mid-chop to take in the sight of Evelyn's child standing before her in the kitchen. Marigold called Evelyn Miss because of the class distinction observed between a cook and the higher position of au pare Evelyn now enjoyed.

"How's yall," she said. Flat. And went on examining Juliana's face.

"Marigold." Evelyn said. Just that, nodding her head in the cook's direction and passed through the swing door into the dining room and out into the great hall, headed in the direction of the music at the front of the house before Juliana caught up to her.

"Mama?" She skipped to catch up. Her shoes made a conspicuous clattering sound on the polished hard wood floor between carpet runners. "Mama?" She said again, "Did you see the way Marigold stared at me, it was like she'd seen a ghost!"

"Umm." Evelyn murmured. The music gained in volume as they entered the front parlor. Before Juliana could take in the warm gold infused room with it's broad windows covered in swirls of brocade, she saw a very large blond dog lying beside his mistress. He raised his regal head and cast a look of superficial interest in her direction, she stood in the middle of the room transfixed by her first sight of Annalee Benoit's face over the top of the grand piano.

A cascade of blond curls swayed across the young girl's set face as she labored intently back and forth at the keys. The music swelled and her hands poised in mid-air as Annalee Benoit's round green eyes raised and her mouth formed a silent O shaped word.

She pushed herself away from the keys and came around the side of the piano and Juliana realized, though there was hardly enough time to take it all in, that Annalee Benoit was in a wheel chair.

They each stared at the other's face and it was like looking in a mirror. Though Annalee was at fourteen somewhat older the girls saw they were all but twins. Quiet surprise played in Juliana's own sage colored eyes. "Annalee...." she breathed as if talking in her sleep and knew with a mixture of awe and regret that she might someday soon now stop being afraid of her own shadow.

Annalee spoke first. "My, my, we are the alike ones, aren't we?" Sarcasm barely disguised.

"Annalee!" A deep voice said from behind them in the doorway. Juliana turned. A handsome tall man, wave of blond hair bouncing above an arched dark eyebrow came into the room and held both hands out to Juliana.

"Annalee," he repeated into Juliana's face in that crooning, sing-song fashion Juliana had sometimes heard men use for babies and their wives. "Be sweet now, precious, won't you? Come over here and say hello to Evelyn's little girl." He pressed Juliana's hands, looked into her confused eyes but still, addressed Annalee. "Politely now?"

The cajoling voice continued, seemed of necessity

to follow a long observed tradition to plead a prescribed course. "Pretty please, with Suga on it?" Her
father never took his eyes away from Juliana's face
until Annalee finally allowed a little smile to flirt at
the corners of her cupid's bow mouth as a narrow
token to bestow upon her father.

"And Juliana." He continued as if the slight had
never happened or been apologized for. "Juliana, I
am Maurice Benoit, dawlin.' He shook both her
hands in his. The same sing song voice addressed
her. "We're very pleased to meet you, at last." There
was a calm, resolute air about him. That and the fragrance of leather and spice.

Evelyn stood to the side with something like
gratitude and awe in her heart as she watched
Juliana look into the eyes of her father for the first
time. Her shoulders involuntarily lifted in relief as
she took in air and realized she'd been holding her
breath. Perhaps for a very long time.

Annalee had, over time, grown more and more
cross and sarcastic. Maurice thought she needed
more attention. Thought she simply needed to be
around girls her own age. Perhaps Juliana could
help to fill the great yawning boredom which seemed
even to drip from Annalee's fingers into the divisions
between piano keys as though to cover the inexact
seams of her life. Maybe that would solve the
problem. He had tried to fill her life from top to
bottom with everything a young lady could wish for.
Tried to make up for the void she must feel without
a mother. Tried and had failed to protect her from
every adversity.

He remembered the afternoon Annalee had been
riding her horse in the side pasture. She was nine
and had proudly saddled Close Quarters all by
herself with the help of a step-stool and taken him

relentlessly through the required paces, while Bremmer, her beloved Irish Wolf hound led with his great black nose at a strict cosmopolitan tilt, his taffy colored tail curled up behind, ran pace for pace and seemed to think he served as some kind of frontispiece for a dressage primer. Maurice watched while both their heads of blond curls bounced in unison as they circled before him in the brilliant July sun.

He had lounged peacefully there on the side porch sipping Bourbon and branch water, when the horse had brought a limp rag of a girl around for the last time. He had taken one look at her ashen face and ran to pull her down; carry her into the house frantically calling for Marigold to draw a cold tub bath. Evelyn had stripped off Annalee's clothes and continued to bath her even though halfway through she began to shake convulsively.

The doctor had said Infantile Paralysis and that Annalee was lucky she did not have to be put into an iron lung for the rest of her life but, instead, would never walk again.

Born into luxury, Annalee had been given every advantage. As if to make up for the mother's absence, the only tragedy before in her short life, Maurice now devoted himself to her complete well being while Evelyn fetched and carried, thought to be her legs. Now, this too seemed to have been a further handicap rather than an advantage for Maurice could not furnish the one thing Annalee lacked.

He could not, for love or money, supply Annalee with a generous, kind soul. She did not seem to miss the mother she had never known. The absence of adversity in her short life had done little to soften an already set character. So, when paralysis left Annalee without the use of her lower limbs, Evelyn tried to supply the legwork. When bit-by-bit sarcasm exacerbated the natural tendency with which she was born, Maurice cajoled and apologized until the once elegant, composed man began to appear clownish in his effort to divert attention away from her lack of grace. In their concerted effort to make Annalee's life glad, they, and not she, had accepted full responsibility for that gladness. This strong responsibility could have caused many reckless words to fly between them but instead it brought them closer.

Maurice had supported Evelyn from the beginning and Juliana when she was born, but, had always maintained a decorous separateness. There was never a question of marriage between them. These kinds of things went on behind back stairs, and in back alleys, but no one was witless enough or imprudent enough to deliver the evidence of their passion onto society's doorstep. Instead, Maurice did what others had done when the show of their indiscretion grew too obvious and vital an issue to ignore. The usual course of action taken by people of power and wealth was to ship one's sons and daughters off to military or private school.

After a few inquiries Maurice learned from a friend and cohort, Jules Gauthier, of a very prestigious and discreet school for young ladies in the Ozark Mountains of Arkansas, The Crescent Conservatory for Young Women, in Eureka Springs. Jules' own daughter Mary Katherine had spent a year there after finishing her primary education in New Orleans. Why not send both girls Maurice told Evelyn after receiving information regarding curriculum and activities. The school was willing to make an exception for the underage girls. Juliana, he said, could look after her invalid half-sister Annalee.

Twenty One

Roses Have Thorns, And Silver Fountains, Mud

From the outset, it became clear that Annalee had planned a different role for herself. She did not envision an invalid in need of assistance. Out from under the ever watchful eye and coddlings of Maurice Benoit she seemed to sense it was now or never for her and so began a surreptitious program to regain the use of her legs.

She had once enjoyed the outdoors. Whether it was organized sports or games with friends, she was driven to win. Moreover, she must best her competitors any way she could. Winning was everything. She had taken up the piano only after her affliction had ruled out running, swimming, riding. She hated having to give up her riding and at first had spent hours watching from the confines of her wheel chair Close Quarters romp and run with the stable of other thoroughbred quarter horses until Maurice could no longer bear to see his small daughter pining after her horse. All of the horses were sold and the stable's closed.

Now in off hours at school she began to visualize herself riding Close Quarters again. She would try to grip and flex the checked muscles of her legs against the horses warm, broad sides and imagine galloping across green swelling meadows, jumping logs and fences. Before she fell asleep each night she put herself through these mental exercises. Month after diligent month of this concentrated effort she thought she felt a warm tingling in her right leg and would grip

harder. In her imagining she urged Close Quarters
ever forward as she talked to her muscles as if they
were alive and stout. Nothing, she thought, stood
between them that they could not hurdle together.

When she could not join in the more active side of
school life, Annalee would wheel herself into the
dinning room which doubled as a ballroom and so
had a grand piano at one end. She soon realized that
when she began to play, suddenly as if by some prearranged signal, girls would gather around, entreat
her to play the more popular songs of the day and
sing along.

As was the custom with such institutions, each
girl, before she arrived on campus, had received a list
of requirements: a bible, hot water bottle, laundry
bag, walking shoes, raincoat, umbrella and rubbers,
a counterpane (coverlet, quilt or bedspread), and
napkin ring. They were to wear a white 'Peter
Thompson' dress for fall and spring and a navy blue
coat-suit with matching 'waist' (blouse) for winter.
Other anticipated cool weather needs were warm
woolen underwear, long sleeved woolen house dresses,
heavy stockings and shoes, and they were not to
make additional purchases in town without the
principal's permission.

Annalee asked again and again to be allowed to
buy sheet music of the latest show tunes and spent
much of her time in the music store downtown where
Juliana and the other girls pushed her wheelchair
down the boardwalk. Music became their common
bond.

As custom dictated the school took its conferred
responsibility of surrogate parenting seriously. The
girls were allowed to correspond only with those
whose names and addresses were on a list their
parents furnished at the beginning of each semester

and any suspicious letters were read and/or forwarded to them. Correspondence with anyone in Eureka Springs was not passively or moderately discouraged, it was forbidden.

However, nature will out. Exceeded only by an instinct for territorial dominance, species survival is more powerful than fear of reprisal or expulsion so, during their free time in the afternoon, it was the girl's habit to stroll gossiping and flirting with the local boys as they helped Juliana guide Annalee's wheel chair down 'Crescent Walk' to the drugstore in town, enjoy ice cream sodas, browse in the music store and meet their "heart throbs". However daunting the rules, like teenagers of every era, they did not suffer well the stuffy and hypocritical dictates of their elders, as relationships developed in spite of or perhaps even because of this restrictive background. These girls, given the recent history of high excitement surrounding Eureka Springs' development, may well have wondered how their parents had gotten, in so short a time, a disinclination for adventure.

Annalee was always one trick ahead of everybody else and even though confined to a wheelchair enjoyed a reputation of daring. She knew how crazy about boys some of the girls were, she herself would dimple and preen in front of the mirror for hours before flirting outrageously with William Winslow, clerk at the Melody Music Shop downtown. "He is so handsome and dashing, Cherie!," She would say to her friends. Such a rare kind of paramour, she thought, with his slick brown hair and eyes as dark as the far side of the moon; William Winslow's eyes were that dark. The tall and most handsome, Mr. William Arnold Winslow. She knew all the ways his name could appear for she spent hours dreaming and scribing with ink the myriad of possibilities on scraps of paper, on notebook covers, on the soft part of her hand: Mr. William A. Winslow, she drew; sometimes adding Esquire on the end or Doctor to the beginning. Yes, that looked nice, she would see and be gratified. It might be Dr. Will Winslow. Dr. and Mrs. William Winslow request the pleasure of your company. Annalee Benoit Winslow, her fancy far reaching, knew no boundaries. There must be a way to get them together, she thought. To that end a plan was hatched.

As the school had a strict lights out policy, Annalee devised an elaborate scheme whereby the boys would come up the hill from town after dark and whistle softly. The girls would lower a large laundry basket by a rope from the second floor balcony and in this manner one by one the fun loving boys would be hoisted into the arms of the waiting girls.

This worked well until a rumor about what was going on reached the ears of the president of the college. A young man himself he could understand and sympathize but he was also concerned about his young charges and so devised a test for their antics. One evening, after the call for lights out, he crept underneath the balcony and gave a low whistle. After a few minutes the basket was lowered, he got in and they began to pull him up. About half way up Juliana saw who he was and signaled to drop the basket, spilling the hapless administrator amongst the tulips and begonias. For a while the poor man limped around on a sprained ankle looking guilty but said nothing about the incident. Fortunately for Juliana he had not seen her face over the railing.

What she did not know was that Annalee had started the rumor about what was going on and planned for Juliana to be blamed.

Twenty Two
Tincture In The Blood

Annalee had always known how to use other people. Turn their frailty to her advantage. She must win in any situation.

To be heedless of another's shortcomings was to have missed a rare opportunity to make herself look good by comparison. Taking other's triumphs and winnings as a personal affront, she was never able to celebrate another's victory, always turning it inward, comparing, measuring, calculating these against her own accomplishments.

Juliana had many personal victories at school but over the years none had so rankled Annalee as her outstanding basketball performance, driving the Crescent Comets from one outstanding win to the next. During basketball season Juliana was the toast of the town and people hailed her on the street. Trophies were presented and newspapers from Little Rock to Kansas City printed thousands of words of praise for the team and Juliana DuBois.

During basketball season Annalee felt all but abandoned. She spent many sleepless nights agonizing over the shouts of admiration and applause she heard accorded Juliana but all of this rancor paled beside the humiliation of watching Juliana fawned over by one William Winslow. By the middle of basketball season 1929 she became physically ill whenever William complimented Juliana in her presense.

"Mon petit, homeless punchinello," she muttered over the sleeping Juliana caustically. "Mon Dieu, you would not be here if not for me!" When William fawned over Juliana, she held hurtful conversations with herself. "Qu'est-ce que c'est?" her heart would ask, what is this? "Pas bon, Annalee, pas bon," her heart was sad to say in response, not good, not good. "Just listen to him go on. And her, so polite. Always so modeste, never taking credit for herself, c'est Mademoiselle Froo Froo. Always talking about THE TEAM. THE TEAM was everything; game was not important. Winning not important. Team Spirit. That was important. She always talked of team spirit and everybody loved her for it!" Annalee told herself if she never heard another word about the precious Crescent Comets it would be too soon.

It seemed at one point Annalee became so desperate for the spotlight she began to chastise and ridicule Juliana publicly while shamelessly courting and fawning over

Juliana's friends, outrageously complimenting them for every small thing. It became painfully obvious that she was trying to take the attention away from Juliana and put the spotlight back onto herself, the very charming, witty, and ever popular debutante Annalee Benoît from New Orlean's high society. She never missed an opportunity to put Juliana in her "place" after all, even though they were step sisters, she was no more than her servant, really. One who was sent to look to her every need.

At these times, which came more and more often, Juliana would simply withdraw, absent herself in disbelief from the venomous cloud of Annalee's lamentable shade. Had Annalee suddenly gone mad she wondered?

On that last fateful day Annalee sat brooding in her room. It had been ironic how the school kept assigning them the same #110 room year after fateful year. Because it was the only dormitory room downstairs and because of her disability, her father had requested it on their behalf.

Annalee sat in her wheelchair until she heard the familiar thud of the elevator as it arrived across the hall on the first floor. She could see Juliana, in her minds eye, with the ever present basketball under her arm, tapping her foot waiting for the elevator to take her upstairs. Waved to some of the girls as they went into the dinning room for supper. Each afternoon, after basketball practice, it was her habit to continue shooting hoops on the fourth floor balcony where the school had set up a goal against the north wall. She knew Juliana chose this time while everyone else was eating, to be alone, to concentrate on her shots. Mon dieu they even saved a plate of food for her now. Pas bon.

Annalee sat waiting for some minutes listening to the whir of elevator cables in the walls. Light from the window drew a firm line down the middle of her face, divided her eyes into pits of fire and ice. Her face was a mask of shadow and light, like a harlequin in makeup; one side tragedy, the other comedy. The lower half of her body was completely covered to the tips of her scuffed shoes by the long uniform skirt. It was supposed she wore her skirts long to cover her withered legs.

Now, as she rose in front of her wheel chair, Annalee stood on strong, sturdy legs. Long hours of visual exercise, imagining she rode and walked and swam, had eventually led to small, tentative steps. At first it seemed hopeless to push herself up, support her entire weight while she stood for seconds with arms trembling, ready to snap back as a trap would crack over the head of a mouse. She had fallen and crawled back to begin over again so often as to put black and blue marks all over her body. Never you mind, she told herself, the uniform covered all scrapes and bruises.

It had taken many long and arduous hours to master even the smallest personal care of herself. She had insisted on bathing herself with a wash cloth from the sink in the bathroom with the door closed. Kept hot compresses on her legs as long as time allowed each night. Juliana always thought she took so long at her toilet because of the apparent difficulty of such a thing and would often try to help, especially when they first came to school.

But, more and more, at home on vacations or at school Annalee wanted no one to see her body. Eventually however Juliana had walked into the room and caught her out of the chair, all the way across the room from it, in fact, and Annalee had begged her not to tell. She wanted it to be a complete surprise to her father she said.

She smiled a little smile now and smoothed her skirt down and very calmly walked out the door. There was no one in the hallway nor did she expect there to be. Everyone was in the dining room at this hour.

The pungent odor of corned beef and cabbage always served on Mondays assailed her nostrils and turned her stomach. She despised this"Yankee" food and promised that soon now, very soon, Crab and Shrimp Gumbo would be waiting for her at home in New Orleans. She hurried to the end of the hall and pushed a small panel door to the secret stairway and heard the din of voices and the sound of clinking silverware before the door closed silently behind her.

As luck would have it, she emerged onto the fourth floor and walked around the corner just as Juliana, her back to the door, teetered awkwardly on the balcony railing in the process of trying with the tips of her fingers to coax loose the basketball that was lodged in the gutter of the gabled roof.

The born grand Annalee, with a will to impose now had only Juliana to impose it upon, quickly looked around and without a moments hesitation silently crossed to the opposite side of the balcony and with both hands yanked Juliana's feet out from under her and with arms made strong by years of exhaustive exercise pushing the wheelchair, flipped her over the side. It was almost too easy.

With the thin repercussion of a scream still hanging in her mind Annalee quickly retrieved the wheelchair from their room and was in the dinning room regaling everyone with a humorous story when halfway through the meal, someone screamed. She too was somewhat surprised and could not at first place the two acts together as relating to herself in any way.

Twenty Three

Where Airy Voices Lead

Alicia straightened and walked toward Juliana and the "A" device. "And everyone assumed you had slipped and fallen to your death while reaching for the basketball?"

The strength of Juliana DuBois began to waver. "Oui," she said. "And for a long time I did not know, je ne comprends pas." She began in fits and starts of English, reverting to French as if it was a comfort used to allay her fears but tried to check herself when she remembered to whom she spoke.

"'What happened?' I asked myself." Pas, bon." She shrugged. "I did not remember falling down. My body was down there, on the ground, oui, but, I am not…, I am up here." She gestured with her hand above her head.

"At first it did not even resemble myself. Qu'est-ce que'est? Then, eh mon dieu, doucement; I recognize those familiar features! My own face! Très bien." She rolled her eyes in apparent disbelief and threw her arms out to the side and let them fall against the blue basketball shorts.

"Then suddenly someone on the porch began to scream and scream, oui and everybody began rushing out from the dining room and I could not seem to get anyone to listen to what had happened. I tried and tried. It was a thick fog or something." She looked stricken and colorless in the fracted light.

"Malade, oui, mon dieu. Douleur, non, non. No pain. Sick, yes, my God. But no pain." She covered her face and sobbed into her hands.

Alicia stood very close to the "A" device and put

both hands up, palms outward. "Juliana," she said. "Let me help."

Not a sound was heard as everyone listened to Alicia. "Don't reach to touch me as there is a matrix screen between us which cannot be breached but, if you will, simply put up your palms toward me and I will send you energy."

Alicia closed her eyes and began to breathe deeply. At each inhale she swirled the life giving force around in the top of her own head and on the exhale directed pure thought the color of violet to that vestigial sensory organ at the base of Juliana's scull. If this force could have been interrupted, excised and studied it would have been found to be spiral in form, infinite in range, and magnetically permeable to ectoplasm.

As Alicia connected with the spirit nature of Juliana, instead of the usual dawning realization and concomitant acceptance, she felt an unbidden presence take shape beside Juliana in the "A" device and knew without question who it was.

The word "Crétin!" was heard to come out of the gathering molecules before the atoms were fully formed. There was a collective sucking in of breath throughout the quiet room at the sight of Annalee Benoît, lips curled and eyes flashed as she stood beside her step-sister.

"Voilà, she arrives! Va-t'en, Annalee!" Juliana slumped in resignation. "Why have you come here?"

"Pas bon. I am sure I could not say." Annalee said, her words coated with sarcasm. She crossed her arms on her chest in defiance and nodded her head toward Alicia. "Why do you not ask her? N'est-il pas?"

Alicia, eyes still closed to sight, felt a spontaneous wave of compassion rush out from her in the direction of the voice and Annalee reacted as if a wake had hit her. She dropped her arms and took a sidelong glance at Juliana.

"Mon Dieu, pardon Juliana, but it was you and not I who spoiled everything. Because of you we were sent off to school. You, who took me away from my Papa. You knew I was in love with William! Non, Non," she shook her head in disbelief. "What else could I do, you left me with nothing." She pouted like a petulant enfant gâté. But, even as she said these groundless, hate filled things the fire and ice she had intended seemed to have quit without plan.

"It was not important to you to be the best at everything. But you were. It was not important to you that everybody thought you were wonderful, so talented and beautiful. So kind and sweet like cane syrup. But, sacrcbleu, it was important to me! I hate you for ruining my life!"

"Excuse me." Alicia opened her eyes and saw the two, except for the clothes, so twin-like before her. "If you want these issues between you resolved, then you, Annalee will have to take complete responsibility for your actions. Killing Juliana did not solve your problems did it? What you did has tormented you and drove you inexorably to your own death." A gasp went up from the onlookers.

"And you Juliana must finally face the real reasons you put yourself in the direct line of her ire."

"You did not just happen to be born within sight of each other; within reach of each other. That's not how the universe works. There are no accidents. We can just as well take one road as the other but when viewed from the perspective of purpose, we must make real choices for our lives according to that agenda. At each opportunity, no matter how small, we must realize that there is one thing and one thing only that will keep us on track. Intent. Intend negative and you will receive negative. Attend to beauty and love and it will attend you. And, one involves the other only at their mutual consent."

At this last, Juliana seemed shocked. "But I did not ask to be pushed over the side of the balcony at school and out of her way forever!"

"No." Alicia said. "But, you were there. In that place, in that instant. You must ask yourself why you would put yourself in that tenable position. In your heart you know. And, finally you must take the responsibility for the answer."

Alicia stopped and wondered how best to say this next. "As to the forever of it, you are surely not rid of each other yet and it's been something short of forever.

"You must reconcile these differences so that you can go on with your separate agenda."

She turned her attention to Annalee. "There is no doubt that you have acquired a serious debt to Juliana. You must feel it. In your heart you know it by now. That you must deal with it in your own time and in your own way before you can get on with your agenda, is beyond question."

"But I've tried and tried, n'est-ce pas, to figure these things out and it will not right itself. It feels like I missed something, somewhere, but no matter how far back I go, it's not there! Part of the equation is left out." Annalee said. "How can you solve a problem when part of the equation is left out?" Her hands made fluttering gestures at her mouth."Je ne comprends pas."

Poised in mid-thought, Annalee brushed aside comprehension as if it were a pesky mosquito swarming about her head. "The Sisters who taught me catechism never mentioned anything about what you say,"debt and agenda." If you sinned, the priest had you say Hail Mary's. Before I died a year later, as a result of complications from an operation on my legs, I must have repeated, 'Hail Mary, full of grace, pray for us sinners now and at the hour of our death, Amen', enough times to fill the vault of heaven. Mon Dieu! but I was so scared of going to purgatory!" Annalee said and hugged her middle as if in physical pain. "I knew I had committed a mortal sin and I was afraid." Her hand raised in front of her and made a sign of the cross.

"Ahhh....", Alicia's head went back and a sigh of empathy was heard and felt at the core of those listening before the two children. "Annalee, we pay dearly when we resist change. We cleave to the traditional, comfortable way of doing, thinking, working. We pull a cloak of arrogance about our shoulders, become complacent, satisfied with our rituals and beliefs. Everything about our religions, our science, warns us not to delve too deeply or ask too many questions for we are told often enough to leave these things to those whose business it is to worry with the why of this and the wherefore of that. They say why be concerned with things we could not, with any hope of clarity, understand anyway. It is, after all, beyond our finite ability to comprehend. Leave it in more capable hands. Leave the judging to those who are beyond judgement. Hand over to someone else the responsibility for your deeds.

"Additionally, as if this disenfranchisement were not enough to sacrifice, we are to be grateful for this takeover. Willingly, even gratefully, we furnish that authority with undying allegiance and give them unlimited, expressed credit for every joyous thing that happens to us. We, in our naivete, must trust with nary a scant regret or so much as a nod to any kind of reason or logic, assign no blame for the injurious, unjust or tragic events that occur in our lives. Conversely, they say you must always be thankful to whomever, outside yourself, for your happiness, strength and wellbeing. While in the same breath they warn that you must never place blame on this same all powerful authority. No. For this negative aspect of life, another agent is invented and accused. Another agent on which to transfer guilt, another upon whom to vent blame. They so badly want you to believe that this is true, they are willing to risk all, even your ultimate withdrawal from authority to keep you uninformed and ignorant. They use the overwhelming threat of heresy and blasphemy like the sword of Damocles and you the ignorant peasant server.

"Look what they did to Galileo Galilei whom they sentenced to life imprisonment because he lacked the temerity to disavow the evidence in support of Copernicus' theory that the earth revolved around the sun. Evidence he had gathered with his strange little astronomical telescope which incontrovertibly proved that the heavenly planets did not in fact behave in the manner taken by the official views of the church. Showed clearly that the earth was not the center of the universe the church needed it to be and was denounced as dangerous to the faith.

"He was shut away from family and the society of friends and cohorts that were his life. Shut away where his voice and opinions could not be heard. The freedom to embrace family and walk among friends was denied him forever. Years came and went as the church insisted on his denouement but he never recanted. The church imprisoned him because his knowledge of natural science threatened their position of authority. He was disallowed the freedom, the opportunity to express his conclusions based on these natural principles. He died there in that tower room looking out over his beloved city of Florence. But, alas, even in death the noble spirit that was Galileo Galilei could not escape their tyranny, for they, as the final insult, placed his mortal body in the Church Of Santa Croce where it has been held prisoner ever since; the final betrayal of an extraordinary genius. There, his mortal body lies within a magnificent Foggini sculpted tomb today as testament to the church's power and might. They thought to own his body would show the people they own his mind. What it shows instead is how little they understand spirit. On the tomb the bust of Galileo is flanked by two female figures, representations of Astronomy and Geometry.

Now I ask you how many people can see the irony in that action. Galileo took the responsibility for his actions. The most difficult and courageous thing you will ever do is to take back the responsibility for your own life.

"As children not many of us know the direction our lives should take. We are susceptible to leadership, so malleable to manipulation. We place trust in our parents and institutions to give us true knowledge. I implore you not to follow another's direction for your life unless they are guided by unconditional love for you and a resolute reverence for truth. Truth. The missing part of the equation, without which, your personal power and energy will be siphoned and replaced with guilt, blame, shame and regret." Alicia held her hands out to show they were empty. "C'est trop cher a jayer mes amis. Very costly business. It will cost you your imaginations and your reason for being."

"Look," Alicia continued. "It isn't so very hard, Annalee. When you involve yourself in competition you involve yourself on a very basic level of living. If you are not very careful It, (the competition) will become everything to you. Can you see that if it had not been Juliana, it would have sooner or later been someone else to best you at your own game? It could have been anyone, in fact, if you are honest with yourself you know it happened many times before. Remember your little cousin Elizabeth Chloetilde in your first piano recital? She was so good you decided you were too ill to play that evening. And, what of Marcus? Remember riding the very best you knew how, then watching Marcus Prejean ride one triumphant round after another until you wanted to kill him?

"Of course you almost had it right. We are by our very nature duty bound to flourish. Nevertheless, soul growth, true growth does not come from carved litany but from knowledge, rightful effort and the stretching, expanding of our natural talent, making the connection to mind. You simply got sidetracked by fast results.

"There is no winning or losing." Alicia talked to both girls now. "There is either progression and regeneration or dormancy. It is never too late to wake up, arouse ourselves, make amends; adjust and begin again. Some call this reincarnation, which is so little understood. Just as the seeds that were found in ancient Egyptian tombs have been germinated; aroused from dormancy, impelled to new growth, there are many examples of this regeneration principle in nature. In Arizona a man named J.G. Allen germinated squash seeds taken from long entombed Aztec ruins. If this life, this surviving creative energy, can lie quiescent in a seed for countless centuries, how likely is it that it would allow the soul of man to perish?"

"There is no "sin" as such. The disgrace is in losing

sight of your agenda. Your reason for being. You, Annalee, became impatient and took the negative path as a shortcut." Alicia looked at Juliana in turn. "Understand your reaction to these events Juliana and you will surely make swift progress. N'est-ce pas?"

The two girls looked at each other with the beginnings of a new insight. "Vraiment? Alicia, est-il possible?"

Alicia said, "To quote your father, 'Mon cher 'tete fes, why don't you just kiss and make up, my sweet bébés, each bien?!"

Their mouths popped open in astonishment. "Maurice always used to say that!" Juliana said.

"Mon Dieu, how we hated it when he did that." Annalee said. "Je ne comprends pas. Qu'est-ce que c'est? How did you know this?"

They stared at Alicia and each other in astonishment. Like a shy school girl for the first time now, Annalee took a deep quivering breath as if the sorrow of decades were inhaled, so long a putrid enemy; breathed out and let the sadness go."Assez, assez," She said finally.

"Oui, assez. It is enough. Au revoir Mademoiselle Alicia."Merci beaucoup, très merci bien." Juliana said and winked. And, then they were gone.

Juliana, instead of her life being taken in that single unpublished act of desperation, had been doomed instead, to recite it endlessly throughout time in countless rooms and miles of corridors, only to repeatedly bring herself to the brink of her misfortune, there to tremble violently against the balcony's cold stone edge before falling into emptiness until she could no longer separate the sequence of events in her mind; sometimes imagining the whole of it had only just began when her living body was dashed against the paving stones below and not the other way around.

The room could have been on Mars instead of in Fayetteville, Arkansas for all the high strangeness each of the researchers felt. How could they realize at that moment just how far reaching these events would extend into their lives, rearrange their former way of thinking, and as with so many endeavors, influence the extent of their success?

"Wow! What just happened here?" It was not important who said it. It was in everyone's mind to ask.

Everyone came forward and began to talk at once. "Not "what", I believe "when" happened here." Someone else said.

They all laughed nervously and another said, "God, that was great! It worked! It really worked! What a kick!"

In front of them the silver "A" frame, twinkled a quick glint the color of bright steel as if suddenly struck by a near rent in the cosmos and sounded a small, A#"ping!" as if the note struck fine crystal.

"Let me say this." Alicia said. "If nothing else is learned here today." She inhaled deeply as a swimmer might before diving. "It doesn't matter what a grand breakthrough you think this is. Do not expect applause or even congratulations. Most people will view this with indifference, some with rage. Few will understand.

"If this work has taught us anything it is that we can no longer afford to think in the old traditional ways. Mind-set is an enslavement. There is no freedom in cast pattern. As to the technology involved, I have had a few times in my life been given an insight into things as they really are." It was as if Alicia had read their thoughts.

"Each time it leaves me with the clear knowledge that, while it might not be an intentional oversight, we do not really see or examine, much less comprehend, whatever we are looking at."

Arms folded, or hands in pockets, they stood, each staring at the "A" device. No one made a move to leave as the day faded into lambent light.

Someone said, "How are we to see, then? As you say,----- really see in order to comprehend?"

Toni cleared her throat. "Ah...," She had not spoken for over an hour. "Alicia, do you mind?"

Alicia stood with her hands folded into one another like two small pink clam shells stacked against her white silk dress front. "If you would, please, Toni." She said and nodded.

"Well, people, as you know, classical physics can be defined as the physics of objects that are not noticeably altered by observation. But, along comes quantum mechanics with it's dictum, 'No phenomena is a phenomena until it is an observed phenomena' and blows that theory out of the water. So I guess you could say that classical physics is, as the popular saying goes, the 'what you see', and what you hope to see of quantum physics is the 'what you get.'"

"I am," Singae said, "how can I say it? Spooked! Spooked, to think I may never have seen what was really there but only what I expected to see! Are you saying, Dr. Toni that I expected to see Juliana and Annalee? Excuse me, but, if this is so, how is it possible? These people were unknown to me until just a few minutes ago."

"Were they, Singae?" Alicia examined his eyes with a penetrating stare as though she read an inchoate knowledge there. "Were they really completely unknown to you? Are we not, on some basic level, all known to each other. It is said that a certain level of knowledge instructs and informs, allows us never to meet a stranger. From that level of consciousness

Singae, did they not seem somehow familiar to you? Think about it.

"We now know with certainty," Toni turned to address the room, "that on the microscopic level everything depends upon the observer and the observer is defined as one who operates an observing device and participates in the making of meaning." She stood with hands deep in the pockets of her white lab coat and stared into the empty space between the "A" device struts.

Alicia said, "Yes Toni, and I am curious...now...as to spatial continuum... humm..."

"Uh, oh!" Zee said suddenly from behind and began walking rapidly toward her but he was not quick enough. Alicia had simply taken one step forward and disappeared into the "A" device.

Twenty Four

Eternity In A Night

Explorers, like philosophers and poets, often succeed by making extravagant leaps of imagination free from reason's shackles.

To move into other realities is to venture into the unknown at a level of personal risk such as has not been attained since man took to the cosmos for answers.

Just as any other explorer, Alicia was willing to risk everything, no matter the height, depth or breadth of her seeking, like the great blue sky navigators of old were often on their knees, importuning God in heaven above to save their frail crafts amid chaos and onerous atmospheric conditions, her gathering need also had something of the flavor of prayer.

The point of prayer, in her view, was not that a known god was listening so much as it was a connection to Self, and if the connection was maintained, how much easier, smoother the travel.

In this regard, the young traveler, explorer, knowing meaningful intelligence exists, may spend years sifting through information before evincing the bright trust which is our legacy to ourselves which is the wholeness, the oneness of the Universe.

Compulsion does not wait to be invited. Creativity cannot be stored away until its use is convenient. Indeed, if it is stuffed often enough back, out of mind so to speak, it will return less and less often until even the most needful conscious beseeching cannot court its reemergence. Imagination is a precious commodity that comes when a person is ready, as a teacher appears when the pupil is ready. One does not stop in the throes of positive creativity to analyze why this or that should be done. Only the 'how' can it be done is considered.

Alicia was no stranger to these creative forces. She was not a passing wanderer in the starry heaven, exercising no control over her destiny, neither was she a mere browser in the cosmic department store, content with an 'as is' philosophy. She, for her part, knowing that there is no thing endowed with life, no creature great or small in all the universe which does not sway it in turn, was ever mindful of the greater good; the intention behind the word, the action.

Alicia had always made continuous adjustments within to align herself with the environment. Aware of a self actualizing nature, each step forward, though it might seem infinitesimal, brought her into a more aligned universe. Compared to that, this step was like moving to the surface out of the great void.

Twenty Five

The Lark at Heaven's Gate Sings

The fire crackled, shot sparks up into the dark sky, changed the brown and grey dead wood into amber colored firefly's of light. 'Alive, the fire is'. The boy thought. 'Warm, the fire is'. He had gathered wood today. Gathered wood and thoughts; it was the custom.

Each day he must make an ever widening circle to find wood. The fire at night, was everything. As the others must find shelter and food, he must mind the fire. His name was Joshua and he was nine years old.

Alicia found herself behind his eyes; saw with his eyes, sensed with his perceptions. Knew instantly, as one knows ones self, to be this gentle, intelligent young boy not quite the desert nomad he seemed to be.

The small group squatted close to the fire. The desert grew cold when the planet's orbit took it's dark turn around the sun. Together they worked and planned. Together they were absorbed by the task at hand and smiled into the whirlwinds of fire; each imagined they watched their future selves dancing as bright sparks from the original cosmic body they represented. While each knew the measure of their sacrifice, they felt no sense of weight from the task before them, instead, held the moment to be light, intrinsically satisfying to carry. They had found and embraced this new planet as if their very lives, and future lives as well, depended upon it. A unit around the fire.

A fresh wind blew into the fire and sidled layers of

orange tinted smoke against the bright expectant faces. Joshua looked at them as if for the first time and saw them wholly. Together they had chosen this extreme effort; together they had accepted the challenge. Strength and intense endurance he saw beneath the sweet mortal aspect of their faces. Faces familiar, dear to him, but deeper, recognized their spirit, felt their energy and he wondered at his good fortune to have found parents so profoundly dedicated to the furtherance of their race; marveled at the ease with which each member of the expedition had connected with the other.

The future of mankind seemed to hang in the balance. Joshua knew it to be a momentous occasion; one life ending, another one beginning. He knew it was impossible to end one without beginning another. The true metamorphosis. Knew too, the importance of the task they had set for themselves and was proud. How long would this group's association last, he wondered, and suddenly felt it vital he remember, record it to a wider knowledge, mark this exact moment.

A final, nebulous stirring began within himself. As firelight swirled it's white mesmerizing brilliance up toward the star lit heavens, an unbidden heat began in the region of his solar plexus and true to it's task of signaling meaningful change in the body, radiated and spread it's vibrating warmth like representative spears of lightning streaking throughout the nervous system. He instinctively knew the quickening signaled one phase ending, another beginning, evolving into what, he did not know, but that it was fast approaching he was certain. Time only to set emotions and ideas into a tangible, retrievable unit much as one would throw essentials from a burning house, Joshua now filled his mind with the only things which can be taken into the next dimension, willed with every fiber of his being, each specific face, every individual contour be burned into memory like a fire brand. All too soon he watched the dear and familiar forms around the circle move rapidly away from him, secure in the knowledge that he had been in the right place at the right time. No, it was she instead; Alicia, who was seized as if fastened to an emotional chevelure of some yet unidentified energy on it's inexorable rounds of a world without end.

He stood alone, this time at the edge of an open air pavilion high on a plateau overlooking the vast desert; one brown hand held an intricately carved willow staff away from his body as he contemplated the scene below.

The sun at it's zenith beat down a shimmering oppressive, oven-like heat. As far into the distance as the eye could see there was only sworn emptiness and the ever shifting white sand. Within the immediate confines below however, the scene was one of incredible industry. The pavilion with it's broad gallery provided the only shade for miles around. From this vantage point he supervised a vast area of construction.

Giant stone blocks were being lifted and placed into row upon row of ascending steps by means of a device which hovered before him in mid-air. The device, which could best be described as resembling a small platform, hummed and vibrated as it attached itself to each block as if magnetically attracted to the stone. The vibration of sound varied constantly as if it were adjusting to some unseen calculation of weight or density within the stone.

The megalithic structure being assembled before him had sloped, pyramidal shaped walls which were meant as protection to the main structure of chambers, tunnels and shafts. The work was going well. Several hundred men and women were there to visually guide the blocks into place. Some knelt on fringed tapestry rugs atop the small flying platform which had no visible means of propulsion, spoke into a phonation exchange device which was held in their right hands and whose cords were connected to a small djed shaped pillar attached to the rear of the platform. With the left arm and hand they made swirling gestures in the air above their heads and swayed their bodies almost as if they were themselves a necessary part of the flying device.

A large bennu bird or phoenix flew overhead and as the overseer lifted his head Alicia watched with his eyes as the bird joined others sunning themselves on the banks of the Nile. The phoenix bird, she knew, shared the cult of the rising or shining sun with Re, inhabiting the benben stone (the primordial mound), or living in the sacred willow tree. The symbol of life after death, "the rising of the phoenix" was seen as a manifestation of Osiris.

"You were Osiris." The voice said.

She heard the familiar voice of her angel plainly and realized for the first time that it sounded distinctly androgynous, expressing at once, femaleness: compassion, empathy. Maleness: powerful, authoritative. "You were Osiris." It had said simply yet embodied all.

Alicia shook herself as though she had been entranced. She thought she remembered the name in connection with Egyptian mythology. She did not remember being particularly impressed at the time. That was all she had known of him. Until now.

Alicia looked down at herself to see a male body clothed in a white floor length robe of a soft

288

cotton-like fabric. A green stone about the size of a quarter hung around his neck and dangled in the middle of his bare chest. She watched it alternatly glow and dim in time with his breathing and felt a sudden realization that the stone was necessary to facilitate his life. Flat brown leather thongs wrapped around his feet and she felt more than knew he was tall. A staff, held in his right hand, was all over carved with cartouche columns of Egyptian hiero-glyphs and several round buttons of smooth colored stones, which he manipulated with his thumb, were lined around the top. As his head bent forward she saw and felt some sort of protuberance coming out the top of her head. Thinking it might be a helmet of some kind, she reached to touch her temple and immediately a series of electrical impulses shot into her brain and continued until her hand ceased it's investigation of the contraption. She removed and replaced her hand several times, with the same quick results. The helmet itself felt almost a part of her, like another appendage.

Suddenly from the left there appeared over the rise, one of the flying platforms, which stopped in mid air before her. The pilot glared non-blinking at her with large, black wraparound eyes. The exceptionally small nose and slim mouth was set into an expressionless, yet strikingly beautiful face. Something about the look said female. A silver colored helmet started where her high forehead stopped, covered her ears and the rest of her rather outsized head. Still, the platform hovered not four feet away as she stared at Alicia.

"What is taking place? Your input has suddenly shifted." Without moving her mouth the pilot's question came into Alicia's head. "Life on this plan-et will be good." She added without waiting for an answer. She swiveled her head around and looked back at the scene below. "The work is progressing according to your plan. It is positive, that which you do." Alicia heard the voice in her head and knew that even as the pilot addressed Osiris she recognized and accepted the "otherness" she now saw there within herself. Alicia managed a simple, "All is well!" and the pilot swirled her left arm over her head and the platform returned to it's former position below.

A sudden realization came upon Alicia as she recognized, acknowledged that they constructed the Great Pyramid of Cheops. The air quickened, a slight breeze was felt to whip the bottom of her robe, brushed a sudden cool gust against the side of her face and with one last, quick glance around, the plateau of Giza and the wholeness which was the beginning of that singular golden civilization faded from sight but not from endorsed mind.

Another past life experience. It explained her complete fascination for anything Egyptian though her life now was about as far removed from Ancient Egypt and it's culture as Helen of Troy would have been from life in Northwest Arkansas. Yet, there were too many similarities, too many coincidences, too many parallels with very little reason to dismiss them. She had trusted the voice before and found no reason to distrust it now.

To paraphrase Molliere: To judge great and lofty matters, she must have such a soul.

Twenty Six

A Budding Morrow In Midnight

Zee looked inquiringly from one to the other of experts around him in the silent room. Their blank, ashen faces offered no answer. There was only one incontrovertible fact. The "A" device remained empty. Alicia had simply vanished into it without a clue, without prior warning or apparent reason for her going.

"On the other hand," he reasoned aloud, "she must have had good cause, must be safe, even if we can't know it. Alicia has always had things under control. We just have to wait and trust her judgement."

It had been seven days, one hour, thirty six minutes, thirty seven seconds since Alicia had stepped through the portal of the "A" device as easily as if she'd done it every day of her life. Vanished as completely into it as if it were part of a routine magician's trick and would no doubt return the same way. They had not been prepared for this contingency; knew of nothing they could do to bring her back. There was only the interim of watching, waiting. No matter how painfully anxious their kinship, they knew her recovery would be strictly up to Alicia.

At first, they were frantic to do something, anything. It was not like Alicia to act so impulsively. Dare they hope she could return on her own, with no harm done?

Toni and Singae alternated with Zee who, but for a quick trip back to the carriage house after the second day to feed Grouch and leave a note for Alicia's cousin up at the house, pick up clean clothes, kept an almost constant vigil over the "A" device.

Zee had told the group about Alicia's and Morris's affinity for each other. All thought it was a good idea to bring him to the warehouse. Morris was accustomed to waiting for Alicia.

On the eighth day a bleary eyed Michael, hair and clothes disheveled, burst through the door of the lab and demanded of Zee. "What's happened? I know something has happened to Alicia!" He was terrified to ask and terrified not to.

"Oh, Michael, you're back! Beth Anne told you where to find us. Am I glad to see you!" Zee took Michael by the shoulder and gently led him aside, explained what had happened. How the "A" device was conceived by Alicia and constructed by the team. Told of it's first highly successful attempt at receiving the spirit energy for which it was built. "And then, the two girls vanished and before anyone knew what was happening, Alicia had just walked in as if she went strolling down the sidewalk after them, and she was gone." He stared between the silver struts as he had done for days as if willing Alicia's bright face to reappear out of that emptiness so complete. One large hand went to his eyes, plied the closed lids back and forth from the lax corners. "We just don't know what has happened to her. How did you know something was wrong?"

"It was so eerie! Zee." Nothing like it has ever happened to me before. But it was just like something she would do!" Michael faced him, wanting to see the sure reaction in his eyes. "I was just sitting there eating a great desert, thinking about her and...well, you know how Alicia loves chocolate." Michael told Zee. "Well, yesterday while having lunch in a small country inn out of Girverny, with a forkful of Chocolat Bouch'ee suspended halfway to my mouth, suddenly, she was there beside me. I almost turned the fork around to her! But she just smiled, said "Michael" and vanished without another word." His shoulders drooped. "She would have said the pudding had a touch too much cinnamon anyway." He tried to convey to Zee the feeling that she was so palpably with him he could have reached out and touched her. He had known instantly that she was somehow in trouble and without hesitation had put down his desert fork, went to the desk and made arrangments with the manager for a few odds and ends of art he had picked up at independent dealers to be shipped home, all other paintings and sculpture had been previously shipped, made plane reservations for immediate departure and called his mother at the gallery in Eureka Springs. Lesley had been entirely sympathic and she and a friend would meet him at the airport in Fayetteville. They had dropped him off at the lab and were having dinner nearby at the Powerhouse Restaurant.

He had flown all the previous night, sleepless for the most part, thinking of her, hummed an old familiar tune while the words, like silver tongues, sang in his head. "You came to me from out of nowhere." He had hummed out of Paris. "You took my heart and found it free. Wonderful dreams, wonderful schemes from nowhere, made every hour sweet as a flower for me--," intoned over Brest and out over the prolonged North Atlantic night.

Zee sounded anxious. "I have all the confidence that Alicia knew what she was doing when she disappeared. The question is not if she will return, only when can we expect her reappearance."

"Oh, My!" Expelled as thought more than breath out of Michael. Yet thoughts of Alicia continued to fill the space inside his heart, fill his empty lungs;

spasms of compassion stirred on each expelled breath. He stooped to scratch Morris' ears.

"Whatdaya know Morris old fella? It's good to see ya." Morris seemed completely content, drowsing at his ease before the "A" SCAN as though warmed by a cozy fire.

"She's all right, isn't she guy? You'd go get her if you could, wouldn't you? I'll bet you could find her. Sure you could."

Toni and the crew came with sandwiches. Introduced themselves to Michael and seemed to be encouraged by his message of Alicia and continued pacing a slick path in the grey concert floor. From dim corners fears were thought and whispered about. Questions, just questions. Exasperating questions flew from one to another which none could possibly answer, none had the experience to answer. The simple sounding "What happened?" could not even be approached. How could they know the answer, no one, to their knowledge, had ever done such a thing as this before. They dared not speak loudly as they strained to hear the slightest nuance of sound from the SCAN.

Then, Morris was discovered to be dead.

Twenty Seven

The Infinite Doors Of Perception

Alicia knew no sense of time. If an account must be exacted she would have volunteered her time away from the laboratory as maybe two hours tops. In truth, she had no concept of 'absence'. Held no want of rest; bore no sign of fatigue or hunger. Felt instead, an all permeating glow of experience and knowledge. A deeper hunger being satisfied.

She found herself in a round, vacant room; doorways without doors, windowless yet cooled and light filled. Empty of cast shadow. The walls, ceiling and floor were seamless walls of an even white light and could have been suspended in akashic splendor for all she knew. The air was sweet with expectancy.

As she watched from this inner advantage, her father Hank, brown eyes twinkling, peeked his head in the doorway at her as he had done every morning of her childhood. Oh! her heart filled with love and gratitude at the sight of his face! Oh! She thought, it's just like him to do that!

Her father in life was hard working, wore a working man's clothes, either khakis or green shirts and pants, an old, sweat soaked felt hat, and scuffed lace-up boots. But when it came to "good" clothes he dressed himself in as fine a material as he could afford. Sometimes, especially in later years, even going beyond the average expense to look good. But now. Just look at him now! Her heart raced with the glad sight of him. No more of this "farmer Brown" look for him now, no sir. He wore a rich, dove colored double breasted suit with brass buttons. White French cuffs showed below the sleeve with a hint of gold links and tack in the center of a pale yellow silk tie. "Oh!" Alicia almost blurted, "Daddy, you are so fine to see!" In the crook of his right arm was cradled a huge bouquet of long stemmed yellow roses, her favorite. As he came toward her she was suddenly seized by all the pent up emotion and longing that his sudden death had left behind in her brave young heart.

"Daddy," she cried and flew into his arms while the scent of crushed roses mingled with the light and could not be separated. Until that moment she had thought she handled his going very well. Now as she sobbed into his collar she felt another pair of arms around her. Another, whose touch was unmistakable. "Mama." She said simply. "Oh, Mama," and Rachel's starched outdoor fragrance was everywhere present.

The three stood wrapped in each other's arms as they often did when one shouted,

"Family hug! Family hug!" and it might have been yesterday, today or tomorrow for all the relevance such a concept bears on reality.

"'Licia, sweetie," Rachel, ever the practical one said finally, "come with us. There is much we must show you." Alicia stood with her arms full of roses while her mother took her by the hand and as she had in the long ago game of 'blind man's bluff" she had played with her father as a kid to find water for the new well, Alicia closed her eyes.

The air about them thickened and swirled a flinty green and brown. Alicia felt her mother's hand suddenly jerk away. Her eyes flew open as she began to move rapidly against a tide of people. She was jostled back and forth by crowds of beleaguered looking people who were fleeing cities which had crumbled in the far distance. People of all ages, creed and color carried heavy loads, dressed in all manner of clothes, pushed or pulled shopping carts, bicycles, anything with wheels, weighted with personal as well as household goods. She saw one man dressed in a three piece Armani suit dragging two golf bags stuffed with groceries.

Crying babies shared stroller space with the odd assortment of blankets and food, their own disposable diapers and she knew that soon, if they were wearing anything at all, it would be their parents torn Tee shirts or discarded mattress covers.

Those walking had, for the most part, abandoned cars and trucks as they ran out of fuel coming from one city or another. Those who still had fuel must creep as far as they could but knew eventually, they too, would have to walk, to where, they knew not.

Abandoned pets ran in packs along the ragged outside edge of what was left of the pavement, hunting for food before they themselves became wild or someone else's nourishment.

No planes flew overhead, the sky looked an ominous pea green. At least the worst of the tremendous earth quakes and floods was over.

Astronomers had long ago been able to predict the approach of the planet they dubbed X. With the launching of the IRAS (Infrared Astronomical Satellite), a heat- sensing satellite, into orbit 560 miles above earth at the end of January 1983 as a joint U.S.-British-Dutch effort, it was able to track many celestial objects. Including an "enigmatic comet like object."

Several newspapers had published the story. The Washington Post went so far as to report a heavenly body, possibly as large as the giant planet Jupiter and possibly so close to Earth that it would be part of this solar system, had been found in the direction of the constellation Orion by the orbiting telescope

IRAS.
Scientists, noticing a regularity in the extinctions of species of Earth (including the dinosaurs), proposed that a "death star" or planet with a highly inclined and immense elliptical orbit periodically stirs up a shower of comets that bring death and havoc to the inner solar system, including earth.

The "comet like object" had traveled at such a high speed that by the time it could be seen it was far too late to do anything about it. The catastrophic influences of the foreign "comet like object" entering into the Milky Way galaxy had exerted such tremendous suction-like forces upon the surface of the earth that it caused the sudden rising and falling of ground levels which formed new mountains and valleys. Earth's poles shifted and it's crust slid on molten lava and, as with pole changes in the past, continents sank and new ones had risen. The globe, as it had been known, charted and mapped, was unrecognizable.

As she moved away from the mutilated cities and highways Alicia found people squatting on river banks, hiding in deep forests, guarding entrances to caves deep in the sides of mountains. These, she knew, were the fortunate few who would probably survive.

These, having prepared themselves for the most grueling race of their lives, had experienced the most divesting earth changes the stars and high energy forces could hurl at them along the way. They had endured hardships the likes of which are seldom demanded and won the super-human battle over the elements. Some felt a set end had been reached, a goal met. Could then see it, claim it as valid experience. Some even reveled in the situation, saw it as a race against time, replayed it as they would a "photo finish" and looked to the future as a bright new beginning.

Alicia knew the point of her witnessing was not to focus on the coming catastrophe. To be forewarned, yes, but instead to concentrate on the birth of the new planet. Exchange the few brief moments of pain for a joyous association with the newly born earth.

With this thought of regeneration, the air shimmered a luminous frosting across the landscape and Alicia stood in a greensward glen beside a stone wall which ended where a shallow brook began. Bubbling softly over time smoothed rocks, it had emerged centuries before out of the mountain called Chorm instead of the box of water colors which it resembled even more. Broad strokes of pale green laid itself along the grass as it climbed out of sight over round knolls and swiped at the tips of tree branches; bright red and magenta flew across the sky on the backs of small birds whose song trilled the air and added harmony to the peaceful scene. She stood expectantly on a white gravel path beside the washing brook and watched as Rachael and Hank walked toward her over a moss speckled stone bridge holding hands like school kids.

"'Licia, darlin' girl." Hank said, "We're sorry to have put you through that ordeal but it was important that you experience it alone. We thought it best for you to know the extent to which you will have to prepare yourself, your clients and your family in the very near future. You must clear your mind, remain calm in the center of the storm of chaos in which you will have to live daily."

"Yes, Daddy, I understand." She said flatly and felt burdened at the prospect of revealing this divesting information to the people who put their faith and trust in her. "It will be a hard, challenging time for everyone. Can you pinpoint the time of this crisis?"

"Can't tell exactly Alicia. From where we are it looks like the comet path will come closest to earth in November or December of 2012." Rachael said and brightened, "Still, nothing is absolute Alicia. People have been working for decades on changing the objects course. If enough positive kinetic energy is concentrated on redirecting it,------well, who knows?" As she said this last, her manner changed. "Hello, what's this?" Furrows knitted her brow as she focused on something over Alicia's left shoulder.

As Alicia turned, the air in front of her wavered, thickened. An animal like groan, once, from it's center. Twice. Clearer. Where had she heard that sound before? The image formed. There! "Oh, it's Sister Dolly!" Alicia exclaimed.

A disheveled, confused looking Sister Dolly Garvin stood bleeding from a large ugly gash on her forehead, her hair matted with blood, twigs, small pebbles, torn clothes dripping wet, weaved back and forth, labored to focus her eyes on Alicia as though trying to decide who was part of what nightmare. From the nightmare, "Crash?" She managed weakly. Her eyelids dropped shut and trembled.

"Sister Dolly!" Hank stepped forward. "You must go back. You are not supposed to be here!"

"Want..." She managed. "Oh! The light. Stay inside... the light..."

"Oh, Sister Dolly, please, you can't stay." Alicia said in a small voice. "You must understand. My father is trying to tell you that it isn't your time to die. You must go back. As I must. There is so much to do."

Sister Dolly summoned all her wits, "You....? Don't.... send me." She stopped, faltered. "Can't do...oh, help me...." Sister Dolly took hold of her sleeve, pleaded to Alicia.

Before Rachel could reach her; put her hand on Alicia's arm to keep her from going, Alicia had followed the soul reaching out, followed Sister Dolly back through her miasmic cloud of pain.

As the couple in a white Jeep passed Thorncrown Chapel, rounded a switch-back curve on the mountain west of Eureka Springs, their headlights spotted a girl frantically waving to them from the right side of the road.

"Please call 911, a car went over the side, crashed into the ravine there." Alicia pointed with one hand at the broken guardrail while the rest of her faded and disappeared.

"Did you see that Margaret?!" The driver's pinched voice was frantic to his silent wife beside him. His face was white and his hand trembled at the dial on his cellular car phone.

She waited with her eyes open, her body peacefully bent at the bottom of the ravine where her face was submerged up to her ears in the shallow river water. The few air bubbles representing her life had long since ceased to swim to the surface and when she could think of nothing more to do, Sister Dolly Garvin died.

She left her body, she could see it there like so much discarded rubbish back on the river bank. She felt she was in a small boat floating over the dark water. In a sudden move the boat shot into a fast moving stream and light began to play over the dark water as she arrived beneath a glowing cross suspended in midair. The light was so bright and beautiful it was indescribable. It began to pulsate and form around her. Engulfed by the light she was filled with such love and peace; happiness the likes of which she had never known until silent tears overflowed her eyes and their perfect glow brandished her cheeks.

The light was luminous like a glowing cloud. From inside it she heard a voice. "Sister Dolly!" It said. Was that God? Who...? Alicia Townsend? Could that possibly be Alicia Townsend there? And those others around, all telling her she would have to go, leave the beautiful light. Leave this enormous feeling of absolute love, this unconditional love? It would be like tearing her heart out. No one ever before had loved her like that. Inconceivable! Never-the-less she knew, no, felt, the full value of going back. She was needed wherever "back" was. Not to teach, she suddenly realized that no one can teach another, you are your own teacher she would tell them, yet felt she could guide instead, show them in a more empathic, loving way. "Back" there she would bring the forgiving messages. Messages that with sudden knowledge had in an instant flooded her brain. She would give with all her heart to them the true message of love and kindness which she had been given. And, Oh! She thought, Mama! Mama in Chicago, and Damion, oh God! what of dear Damion, the brother she had turned her back on, cast him cruelly away because he was a homosexual. She had seen only that which she wanted to see. Saw now with such clarity that they were not the cause of the rift between them. She had been the problem. Her closed mind had been the problem. Her own selfish fear and stubborn will had for years kept them apart. For years she had cast them away telling herself it was the Lord's will and that they must repent before she would have anything more to do with them. Oh, the waste, all those years, she grieved. The burning shame. Could they ever forgive her? In hopes that it wasn't too late she made a solemn vow to try. With that her body was pulled from the water.

As the rescue team carried the stretcher with a fully resuscitated and comprehending Sister Dolly up and out of the ravine they thought they saw a small ball of light ahead, lift and float like a luminous bubble from a child's pipe. No one spoke as their climb back up the mountain was made easier. No one spoke. They had seen stranger things in their line of work.

Above the dark rounded mountains the back lighted thunderclouds were perfectly illustrated in the open bible that had remained just beyond her reach on the rocks. A slight breeze riffled it's thin pages to reveal a hastily written note she had placed there: Michael arriving Fayetteville Airport Tuesday 9:05 p.m.

She had been browsing in Michael's EAGLES RISE GALLERY on Monday when she overheard his mother speaking to him on the telephone with the urgent message of his untimely return to this country. Sister Dolly had all but ran out past Leslie, who would not have known her from Adam's goat anyway, in her surreptitious haste and excitement to leave without being detected. Michael was coming home. She must make plans. She must meet his plane, even if she could not drive him home, follow him to the ends of the earth. Oh, yes. Follow Closely. Almost as good, she thought. Almost as good. Her mind flitted over minor details of preparation as she drove to Muldrew's gas station on the corner. The brakes on her car had been sticking but Buzzy the mechanic was out sick with the flu and it couldn't be all that important anyway, she'd let it slide for now. She had no time to tend to trivialities. Michael was coming home.

Had it been a quirk of fate which put her on the

road that rain soaked night? Was it a coincidence that the note was placed in the Bible where she had with red ink encircled these verses in the First Book of Kings:

But the Lord was not in the wind: and after the wind an earthquake: but the Lord was not in the earthquake;

And after the earthquake a fire: but the Lord was not in the fire: and after the fire a still small voice.

In the margin beside the verse she had written: "What does this mean?"

Time had no meaning.

Rachel's manner had changed from frank solemnity regarding the drastic earth changes and their encounter with Sister Dolly, to sparkling enthusiasm as Alicia reappeared beside the little brook. She reached out and took both Alicia's forearms. "You were right in helping Sister Dolly. She is by no means free of guilt and regret, still, she is on the correct path now and will have a more fulfilling life. However, that is not the only reason we brought you here." She said, and turned her toward the bridge. "Just so you will know the future is not all bleak, doom and gloom stuff, we would like you to meet someone."

As Alicia turned, a man's head began to appear coming from the opposite side of the bridge. The glistening red hair on Great Michael's head and the mischievous twinkle in his green eyes could not be mistaken for anyone else as he walked toward them, the wide grin on his face threatened to invade his ears as he became taller and taller over the bridge until, as she watched, another, smaller fiery head and equally mischievous twinkle emerged to walk by his side.

"Oh, my!" She managed, with a sudden knowledge, a mixture of fear and elation flooded the back of her brain and she held a hand up as if to shield a pounding heart and breathed, "Oh, Michael!" more than spoke it. She could not bear to look away from the wee boy's perfect face; could not, at the moment, bear her runaway thoughts.

Alicia felt her Mother's light touch at her elbow as Great Michael stopped in front of her on the path and it wasn't until then, she really knew he was there.

Great Michael beamed from ear to ear as he lifted the boy's wee hand and placed it in Alicia's not much larger one. "Alicia, darlin'," he said, the green of his eyes became pools of clear untethered bright emotion. "I'd like you to make the acquaintance of me great, great, grandson." Great Michael paused, looked down at his charge. "He'll make ye a fine boy and man, won't ye lad! He will. He's your son, lass, your's and Michael's and, what else,----- he answers to the name o' Michael. Michael Cross McKinney he is and ever will be!"

Alicia could scarcely breathe, nor could she speak, enchantment flooded her being as she held the hand of her son. She, independent of thought, kneeled to take his other small hand and there passed between them a thousand conspiracies, enraptured and intense thoughts, sweeping all else aside until they each saw within the other such an inviting look of mischief and merriment, they began as if on cue to giggle, to laugh, with heads back and mouths open they laughed sweet secrets into being. With that first twinkling Alicia was committed heart and soul, captivated beyond affection, and every bright promise was made, read there and called by name; a bond forever inseparable.

Great Michael dained to interupt the touching scene. His mission was twofold. "Alicia, wha hae wi' to do? It's me gold cross tha hae me gang round in circles," Great Michael laughed at his own good humor. He took the cross from around his neck and handed it to Alicia."I'm dun wi' warldly possessions... Lassie kin', tak it to Michael... return it round his dear neck. He will in his time place it round his own son's neck for he truly has a heart aboon them a'."

The wind swayed the green trees, nodded the leaves into shades of light and dark as if they, in answer, agreed that in all likelihood, the wee boy would indeed live up to his openly declared future.

"Shall I go alang wi' her now Great Michael?" Wee Michael said up at his chaperone.

At that instant Alicia felt a warm familiar snaking around her ankle. "Morris!" She cried, turned and lifted him. "Such a fine fellow! Did you think I had forgotten about you?" She spoke into his eyes and realized that he had made his own peaceful transition.

When she looked up Rachael and Hank were gone. There, in the place where Great Michael and the boy had stood, lay a small nosegay of violets and white baby's breath. As she picked up the bouquet the very air began to breathe, vibrate in a rosy orange glow.

Alicia turned toward the light source and saw a stage in the middle of the park-like setting. On the platform stood an enormous screen. Musical notes, everywhere present, splashed a miasma of color or was itself that vibrant color splashed onto the screen. Each color swirled and dipped as if projected from the four corners of the earth until it could not be contained by any stage or platform. Notes of brilliant yellow, pearlescent blue, surged to bright blue as D, E, F#, A# sounded, vibrated the air---; as these notes, C# and G#, strewn in cosseted splendor, streaked silver, violet and purple across the open sky.

Rudolph Stiener once wrote: You have your eyes, you have your ears: look with your eyes on the things of Nature, hear with your ears what goes on in Nature; the spiritual reveals itself through color and through tone, and as you look and listen, you cannot help feeling how it reveals itself in these. "In it's precise clarity F# heralded the advent of bright blue again, followed by the silver trumpet sound of A# and D# and then Alicia heard singing.

"You came to me...from out of no....where, you took my heart...and found it free..." The words and music written so long ago by Edward Heyman and Johnny Green sang in her head. It's fox trot rhythm beat in her heart.

"Wonderful dreams, wonderful schemes, from no....where... made every hour, sweet as a flower for me... If you should go...back to your no....where, leaving me with... a memory..."

"Michael."

"I'll always wait for your return out of nowhere,... hoping you'll bring your love to me."

"Oh, Michael."

Afterword

Wolfgang Pauli and psychologist Carl Jung jointly proposed a theory of synchronicity or an acausal connecting principle to account for phenomena which do not yield to classical science.

Jung often told the following story which exceeded all rational explanation. As he was counciling, listening to a woman patient describing to him her dream of a giant golden beetle, they were interrupted by an insistent tapping at the window. When he opened the window, a large golden scarab beetle flew into the room. Jung's response to such phenomena was to say that some experiences are not merely irrational, they are beyond reason and may only be grasped intuitively. He proposed a theory of synchronicity that connected nature with some mysterious non-rational protocol inaccessible to our rational minds, but accessible to our unconscious.

English physicist Michael Faraday said that nothing is too wonderful to be true if it be consistent with the laws of nature.

And nothing is too wonderful to be true if you listen to your inner voice.

In this case I almost missed it.

Names come easily to me. While Linger By My Side is primarily a work of fiction it is firmly based on historical fact. The singular name Michael; William "Coin" Harvey; Norman Baker were actual names of corporeal people whose lives make up the warp and woof of the Crescent Hotel and are, on balance, equally as vital to its history as the wood and limestone must be to its inarguable substance. The rest of the characters flung wide the door to their own catharsis, gave expression to the intermidable pain which had begun in legend so long ago and remain, to me, no less real. Beginning with Alicia. Alicia came into my head before her character was fully formed in my mind.

At some point during the six years of research and writing Linger By My Side, I was looking at a State of Arkansas map and noticed there was a small town in the Northeast named Alicia close to Evening Shade, the location of the popular television show of the same name. As I had never heard of Alicia, apart from my main character, it did somewhat pique my already crowded interest. I thought it a small coincidence and forgot about it.

Also, during the writing, I sometimes came across a gap in my information so I would turn off my computer and travel to various places to do more research. I would go in search of some illusive, undefined something, following a hunch, an intuitive nudge, in hopes of uncovering the obscure fact.

This is the way I write. It works for me. At the end, examining all loose ends; ends I sometimes found left dangling in the malapropos breeze, in this case the coincidental name of Alicia, Arkansas not only lingered but flapped and taunted like a loose window screen in the middle of the night.

So, one sunny day not so long ago, my husband Bob and I set out across the top of Arkansas, East to Hardy and South to Hoxie and Powhaten. The Powhaten Court House State Park is the site of Lawrence County's quaint old restored County Court House and Museum.

Did anyone there know how the town of Alicia had gotten it's name? I inquired. As no one had asked the question before, it took the curator several trips to the well guarded files and a phone call or two to produce a thin document that might contain the desired information.

As Bob toured the rest of the Museum, perusing the area's history, I read the document which stated that a superintendent by the name of Swift, while building the railroad through the area, named the small town of Alicia after his wife as a romantic gesture.

We continued South on Highway 67 to Alicia, and as predicted, we were disappointed. "You'll not find anything of interest to you there." One of the curators at the museum had assured us.

Alicia is a small village, few houses, fire station which doubles as City Hall, that sort of thing, scattered on either side of the railroad tracks. We drove every street, looking at street signs, craned our necks to see around back in churchyards looking for tombstones, out into the countryside in the other direction; searching for what I was not certain. In fact, I had said as much to Bob even before we began the trip which, to an Engineer's pragmatic mind, is very hard to understand. They want something concrete to wrestle.

I asked a man where was the town's cemetery. He stopped digging in the trunk of his car long enough to tell me he "was not from here, but I think I remember my wife saying there was one a long time ago on the other side of the tracks, over there," he pointed. I supposed no one in recent memory had died there.

We drove along the tracks in that direction but found no clue, no remnant of a cemetery. It seemed then, we had come all that way and sure enough, we had found nothing of interest to us in Alicia. Still, there was that ignoble flapping.

Back at the highway we sat for some minutes at a

stop sign debating whether to turn South or back North in the direction we'd come. We did not create a traffic jam. Except for one very slow moving white pick-up truck on a back street, traffic was non-exisistant. On impulse, I chose South.

In ten or so miles we passed a road sign: SWIFTON. Well, well, we brightened,

Alicia Swift's husband must have named this town after himself. Almost immediately we saw a large community cemetery sprawled over several acres on the right-hand side of the highway. This, we thought, might be worth looking into.

Yet, it must be said, even if we found a dozen Swift's and even an Alicia or two buried there, what would it prove? What would it signify?

Actually, it would be expected. You would naturally assume that in a town called Swifton there would of necessity be at least a couple of Swifts buried in the local cemetery. However, that distinct possibility did not excite me. The expected was definitely not what I was looking for. And even I, while holding out such lavish hope, had to admit that the probability of finding anything at all to connect my fictional Alicia to that very real cemetery, connecting her in any way to any of those real people, living or dead, in Northeast Arkansas was indeed remote. So remote, in fact, the odds of a meteor squashing us flat at that moment was a far greater possibility.

There was no one around as we pulled into a narrow lane in the back and parked. The day was overcast, threatening rain as we set off in different directions, Bob on the right, me on the left. Reading names and epitaphs we continued in a more or less orderly fashion along the many rows of large and small head stones. Surprisingly, we found no Alicia, no Swift.

I soon joined Bob on his circuitous trek in the front of the cemetery and we worked our way slowly back, heads constantly turning left and right like reading titles in a library, down the remaining neat rows we walked, pausing every now and then to read an especially poignant inscription; searching, ever searching for that uncommon nebulous something I knew in my bones had to be there.

We walked a little faster toward the car as the grey clouds began to sprinkle the granite stones around us and my own high spirits began to dampen. "Oh well," I said as I do when I've tried everything I know to try. I waved my yellow legal pad as if to the universe above and covered my head with it. "It is what it is." I said, to whomever listened.

In the last row, next to the road there stood a substantial, waist high black marble stone I had not noticed before. On it's gleaming black surface, engraved next to the deceased's name, a single engine airplane was dipicted climbing toward the sky. What a fitting tribute, I thought. No doubt, to a man who loved flying.

Aircraft of any kind has always fascinated me and I love to fly, but beyond that, it was highly unusual to find that kind of elegant remembrance in a country graveyard. And something else began in the pit of my stomach. Something about it, placed there among the commonplace, the usual; set my heart to beat a little faster.

I stepped around to view the back of the monument and could not believe my eyes.

In order for the reader to feel and fully appreciate the incredulous impact the incised words had on me, perhaps a bit of background into why I chose to make Alicia Townsend an integral part of the Springdale High School Symphonic Winds.

Under the superb leadership and inordinate guidence of the real Ellie Patterson, Pat Ellison, they have continued year after incredible year to gain National and even International attention. Consistently bringing home honors and awards. It is not simply because they are excellent muscians and performers that this is so, as well, they are beautiful, Self-respecting human beings.

This article was written by me and published in THE MORNING NEWS of Northwest Arkansas in May 1993:

Before the last note of "Sailors and Whales" (five scenes from Melville), one of the most intricate pieces of music this writer has ever heard, had echoed in the woman's gym, it brought down the house. The Springdale High School Instrumental Music Depart. had done it again.

If they were not reciting Cherokee for the emotionally charged "Trail of Tears", they were performing the equally moving "Precious Lord, Take My Hand," "A Jubilant Overture" and "Handel in the Strand"--- grand, eloquent stuff speaking volumes for their instrumental talent; but who could have expected then to be regaled by a chorus of beautifully matched voices in the third scene from Melville. A truly unexpected treat.

The attitude of these players was as amazing as their music

was professional. Each group, whether it was Varsity, Concert or Symphonic Winds, as they waited seemed to be as profoundly interested in how and what the other was performing. In a hot, almost airless gymnasium, a group of teen-agers in dress uniform, buttoned, tied and zipped; some were in high heels, some were in flat, but all of their shoes were shined and all of them black; those waiting to perform or already performed acted as attentive and pleased as if they were watching younger brothers and sisters, listening and perhaps even learning together they sat quietly respectful and gracious, neither talking nor milling about as do so many of their disruptive peers. It was obvious these students, when offered the chance of renouncing a present competency, chose a higher more difficult one. Commitment to their music is truly a promise toward their personal growth, their own life's enhancement.

There to lend enthusiastic support were parents, townspeople, boosters, and hard as the benches were (no backs , no cushions), hearts were soft and supportive. In an age when more and more children are suing their parents for neglect and abuse (in the words of one such child, he simply "wanted a place to be"), Springdale Band parents, boosters and the entire staff of the Instrumental Music Department not only provide a safe place for their children to "be", they have consistently invested their time and effort in creating a place where their children can excel. Beyond this, every citizen of Springdale who, like an extended family, voted for the milage increase to fund the Springdale High Shool Center for the Performing Arts, science wing, library, etc. Springdale should be shirt-bustin' proud they chose to show the nation and the world that which they deem the most valuable; show just what they think of their children and their town. Springdale really cares and it shows.

Much has been said and written in praise of the excellent instruction and direction the Springdale players receive and surely those talented, dedicated educators are important, deserving of every accorded praise; however, the ultimate commitment to making good music must come from the players themselves. The kind of commitment it takes to be consistently invited to perform in the National

Cathedral and the Kennedy Center in Washinton, D.C. The kind of proud commitment it takes to be chosen one of four bands out of 150 applicants, including those high schools from Europe and Japan, selected to perform at the 47th Annual Midwest International Band and Orchestra Clinic to be held at the Chicago Hilton, Dec. 14-18, where Springdale High School's instrumental music director, Pat Ellison, will be teaching performances played from five different grade levels.

When the last of the applause, standing ovations and cheers faded and the crowd walked out into the night, there could be seen across the way an outline, high and firm against the dark sky. A light shone out from the rafters in the upper reaches of the long-hoped-for auditorium while a large paint spattered tarpaulin blew slowly back and forth, beckoning like a curtain above the stage from which the sweet, sweet sound of our children making music could already be heard.

Later, in the new Performimg Arts Auditorium, I was stunned by the power and excellence of their performance of John Curnow's, Where Never Lark or Even Eagle Flew, based on the poem by John

Gillespie Magee, Jr.

We stood in the Swifton, Arkansas cemetery, aghast at the words we saw incised before us. The clouds had sped, the sun shone down it's full brightness on that black slab of granite, highlighting the very words I had long since committed to the pages of Linger By My Side.

"Oh, I have slipped the surly bonds of earth
and danced the skies on laughter-silvered wings.
Up the long delirious blue
I've topped the windswept heights with easy grace,
where never lark or even eagle flew;
and while with silent, lifting wind
I've trod the high untrespassed sanctity of space,
put out my hand, and touched the face of God.

There, real in every way, the synchronous words carved in granite for all the world to see, stand a testimony to the unseen forces at work in the Universe and our lives. I would not have been made aware of the exalted work of John Carnow had he not been inspired by the heartfelt words of John Gillispie Magee, Jr. without the music performed by Springdale High School Symphonic Winds, and they would not have performed Where Never Lark or Even Eagle Flew without the conscious selection of Ms. Patt Ellison... Every Thing is connected to Every Thing connected... and the beat goes on... In that place, in that country graveyard representing death, I thought of life. I thought of life and dancing the skies on laughter-silvered wings.

Nothing is too wonderful to be true if it be consistent with the laws of nature.

JoAnn DuCote Smith
Eagles Rise

Readers Note

There is a renewed energy in the Crescent Hotel. Elise and Marty Roenigk came from East Hampton, Connecticut to see what all the excitement was about. They found, despite her neglected and forlorn appearance, a compelling vitality in the 112 year old structure. Found an alive, incomparable spirit within her tattered walls. They felt an immediate kinship and decided on her purchase with definite plans for her future. To that end they hired Jack Moyer as General Manager, Tracy Pierce as Publicist, Jill Hodge, Concierge and installed Ken Sawyer, a renowned Chef, in the Crystal Dining Room where Presidents and their ladies once dined and danced. They began a renovation of 35 rooms. The biggest change they have thus far effected however, is in the once dark and dank basement. The basement has been completely revamped into a light and airy New Moon Spa. In the process they tore out Great Michael's bar. Cat Berstein, who manages the Spa has already seen a miasma of ectoplasm, real enough to touch. Is Great Michael trying to tell us something? Perhaps it's Norman Baker or his nurse Cassie's presence she felt. Can anyone hear the thin remnants of Juliana's scream as Annalee dumps her over the side of the balcony? Do Chuck, Boyd or Barbara at the front desk see Morris sitting on the fireplace hearth in the lobby waiting for Alicia or have they seen Coin Harvey watching out the front windows? Who knows, perhaps the whole cycle will begin again.

The Legend Continues.